PRACTICAL GUIDE TO LITIGATION
TRAVERS SMITH BRAITHWAITE

SECOND EDITION

PRACTICAL GUIDES

Other titles in this series are:

Arbitration
by Michael Reynolds

Chartering Documents
by Harvey Williams

Costs in Arbitration Proceedings
2nd edition
by Michael O'Reilly

Insurance Solvency Analysis
2nd edition
by Jim Bannister

International Shipping
by Bruce Farthing

Introduction to Insurance
by D S Hansell

Introduction to P&I
2nd edition
by Chris Hill,
Bill Robertson
and Steven Hazelwood

How to Manage Risk
2nd edition
by Jim Bannister

Marine Claims
2nd edition
by Christof Lüddeke

Maritime Law
4th edition
by Chris Hill

The Nuts and Bolts of Reinsurance
by Keith Riley

Professional Negligence and Insurance Law
by Neil F Jones & Co, Solicitors

Reinsurance: London Market Practice
by Carol Boland

PRACTICAL GUIDE TO LITIGATION

TRAVERS SMITH BRAITHWAITE

BY

JONATHAN LESLIE
and
JOHN KINGSTON

SECOND EDITION

Routledge
Taylor & Francis Group
LONDON AND NEW YORK

informa law
from Routledge

First published 1996 by LLP Reference Publishing

Published 2022 by Routledge
4 Park Square, Milton Park, Abingdon, Oxon OX14 4RN
605 Third Avenue, New York, NY 10017

Routledge is an imprint of the Taylor & Francis Group, an informa business

Publisher's Note

The publisher has gone to great lengths to ensure the quality of this reprint but points out that some imperfections in the original copies may be apparent.

British Library Cataloguing in Publication Data

A catalogue record
for this book is available
from the British Library

ISBN 978-1-859-78170-8 (hbk)

Text set in Plantin by
Selwood Systems,
Midsomer Norton

PREFACE

This is the second edition of the *Travers Smith Braithwaite Practical Guide to Litigation*. The first was privately published in June 1996. Its publication was marked by a reception held at the Draper's Hall in the City of London, at which we were honoured that Lord Bingham of Cornhill, the Lord Chief Justice, agreed to be our guest speaker. Following the success of the first edition we were delighted that LLP Limited should have asked us to prepare a second edition for publication by them. One obvious question that we posed was whether a new edition should await the introduction of the Woolf reforms. We agreed with LLP that it would be preferable to prepare a second edition now, for three reasons. First, it was necessary anyway completely to revise the chapter on Arbitration, which had become out of date following the coming into force of the new legislation in 1997, and to make other amendments to reflect changes occurring since the first publication. Secondly, although it is reasonably apparent that at least a modified version of the Woolf proposals will be implemented, it cannot be known when exactly they will be introduced, or to what extent the draft rules in their present form will be finally adopted. Thirdly, whilst the procedural rules may change, in many cases (for example, in claims for injunctions or judicial review), the underlying principles are likely to remain the same.

We intend at the appropriate time to write a comprehensive new edition of this Guide, which will deal with all the new philosophies and procedures when it is known in more detail what will be the final form of those new rules.

This Guide is not intended to be for use by specialist professional practitioners in England. It is deliberately written in a style and format that we hope will make it accessible and interesting to those who, whilst not being English litigation specialists, become involved in the process either as parties or as professional participants such as company executives, or as lawyers in other jurisdictions. They may wish to follow the procedures and understand the relevance of what is being done at any time, without necessarily having day-to-day responsibility for a case.

This Guide is not in any sense definitive but we very much hope that it may make your lives easier when involved in litigation, and make the process, if not actually an enjoyable one, then at least more intelligible and, by enabling you to participate effectively, lead to successful results.

The format followed in this Guide is intended to distinguish points of different degrees of importance. Thus, the mark "—" indicates a point of specific or detailed significance, and italicised paragraphs mark an area in which special care needs to be taken. Wherever possible, practical examples are given to illustrate particular issues. We have tried to avoid using technical language, and have deliberately not cited authorities in support of statements of law or practice, so as to avoid distracting from the text.

Finally, a word of caution: this Guide is not intended to be, and should not be, relied upon in any particular case and it is not a substitute for advice on any specific problem where the need for it arises. It is purely a general introduction and we would urge you to take fully considered and expert advice on particular problems as and when the need may arise.

This Guide has been contributed to by the Partners and members of the Travers Smith Braithwaite Litigation, Employment and Insolvency Departments, for all of whose very considerable and expert help we are extremely grateful.

JONATHAN LESLIE
JOHN KINGSTON

Travers Smith Braithwaite
10 Snow Hill
London EC1A 2AL

December 1997

CONTENTS

TABLE OF CHARTS AND FORMS

CHAPTER 1

INTRODUCTION

In recent years there has been a proliferation of litigation in England that has followed similar trends in other countries, especially the United States of America. Many disputes that might before have been settled amicably nowadays tend inexorably to lead to lengthy contested battles, as the amounts of money in issue increase, the legal and factual issues multiply and the parties themselves show a greater willingness to employ litigation as a tool of corporate policy. This trend has been matched by the development of litigation practices in law firms.

Lately, this tendency has itself been arrested as disputants, concerned by the difficulty and expense of resolving disputes, have embraced methods of assisted settlement.

This Guide is intended to describe the important movements towards alternative processes for dispute resolution; to offer an introduction to the process of civil litigation[1] and arbitration in England for the use of those who sometimes, or even frequently, become involved in commercial disputes; and to explain the recent initiatives taken by the judiciary to improve and streamline the current system.

THE CURRENT SYSTEM OF LITIGATION AND ARBITRATION IN ENGLAND

Before describing the system of litigation and arbitration, we begin by drawing attention to the extremely important initiatives that have recently been adopted by clients and lawyers alike to promote the early settlement of legal disputes by a flexible process that encompasses a number of similar methods that are together known as "alternative dispute resolution", or "ADR". ADR aims to avoid the distractions and costs of legal battles by promoting early settlements, often through a neutral mediator. Settlements of this type are becoming a deservedly more popular and effective means of resolving disputes before the formal legal process begins. A detailed account of this process is set out in Chapter 2.

1. We do not deal with the quite separate system of criminal procedure.

Consideration should almost always be given to the possibility of an early settlement. Indeed, the courts have recently espoused the principle of ADR and may ask the parties to consider such forms of settlement; but, if it is not possible to achieve that objective, it is necessary to consider what other means exist for the lawful determination of a dispute.

The two principal ways in which legal disputes in England[2] are resolved in the absence of settlement are by *litigation* and *arbitration*. They are, in a sense, rival systems, and each has its supporters and detractors. Neither may be said to be "better" than the other, although they may each have advantages and disadvantages that make them more or less appropriate in any given case. "Litigation" is the name given to the process of the compulsory determination of legal disputes through the courts. "Arbitration" is the voluntary determination of such disputes by a procedure agreed to by the parties without initial recourse to the courts. The two systems, although different in a number of important respects, have in England become alike in many ways, but both have significant differences from the legal processes adopted by those countries with a codified system of civil law, such as apply in Continental Europe. This Guide concentrates on civil litigation, which is still probably the most common method of dispute resolution in England in the majority of cases.

These two systems have dominated the procedural landscape for generations. Their efficiency has come under increasing scrutiny. We describe below the main faults in the system of litigation, and the current movement towards reform. Other methods of resolving disputes have now become an important part of the litigator's repertory. Those methods are all fully explained later in this Guide.

English civil procedure is distinguished from the procedures of some other systems by a number of important features. First, it is *adversarial*: that is, it involves the court sitting impartially to determine disputes among a number of hostile participants, each of whom has a case to assert or to defend and where the court plays little part in the process of identifying the facts and the legal issues to be tried. This is different from those Continental systems that adopt an *inquisitorial* role, in which the courts dominate the procedure and place more emphasis on ascertaining for themselves the relevant facts.

Secondly, these participants, to a large extent, formulate the issues for the court to decide, dictate the pace of the case and the general way in which it is conducted and decide on the evidence to be adduced. Despite some recent judicial exhortations to the contrary, the judge currently plays a less *interventionist* role than in some other countries and will not normally interfere of his own volition with the way any case is put in law; with the way in which it is presented; nor with the lengthy pre-trial preparations. It is for the parties, and not for the courts, to ensure that all necessary evidence is made available.

2. Generally, throughout this Guide, when we refer to the procedures of English litigation and arbitration, these should be taken to include Wales. Scotland, Northern Ireland, the Channel Islands and the Isle of Man have their own separate laws and procedures. We comment on the relationship between the English courts and the European Court of Justice in Chapter 39.

Further, there are often much more onerous obligations than in some other countries to disclose documents to an opponent, even though they may be damaging to the discloser's case.

Lastly, in England, cases are ultimately decided in public in open court after oral argument and the examination of witnesses. Although recent innovations have placed rather greater emphasis upon written submissions than before, this tradition of *orality* still lies at the heart of the English process.

These features often seem strange to many litigants, particularly those from overseas. We hope that advance warning of the idiosyncrasies of the English system may avoid some unwelcome surprises, both for those overseas, and indeed, in the United Kingdom.

Litigation in this country is conducted under procedural rules that are derived from a mixture of statutes (that is, Acts of Parliament), common law (that is, law created by the judges in the course of deciding cases) and what is called "the inherent jurisdiction of the court", which is the power of the courts to regulate their own procedures, subject to statute and to common law precedent. The rules are frequently updated to reflect changes in the substantive law. "Substantive law" is the term for the general system of law that creates rights and liabilities—for example, the law of contract, trusts and torts. "Procedural law" governs the system by which those rights and liabilities are adjudicated in the courts, and is equally important, for without it there are no means of giving effect to the substantive law. The two systems are interdependent: a sound knowledge of what may perhaps seem to be a dry subject is essential for the proper conduct of a claim. Without a grasp of procedure, a good claim cannot be pressed home; and a poor defence can often be advantageously deployed by a superior knowledge of the process involved.

Often, the rules of procedure cannot and must not be circumvented, but the litigator's skills are to improvise and to explore ways around procedural obstacles. For both reasons, a mastery of the rules can often enable a party to achieve results better than the legal merits of the case might seem to justify.

A consequence of the adversarial system is the extent to which the results of litigation often reflect the comparative skills and strengths of the lawyers involved and, just as importantly, the dedication of the client in pursuing or defending his claim.

One of the points that we hope will emerge from this Guide is the extent to which litigation can only successfully be pursued by a team effort that involves the lawyers and the clients working closely in full co-operation. Justice will not be done to a case in which the lawyers merely accept the role of supine agents "following instructions" or slavishly go through the motions set by the books' procedures. Equally, to do their job properly, lawyers need the purposeful and knowledgeable support of their clients. As litigation generally takes far longer to conclude than do commercial transactions, the client's involvement and enthusiasm must be sustained over an unusually long period during which it is possible to lose sight of where you are and where you should be going.

We are often concerned that clients may not fully understand the litigation process, however large or sophisticated their organisation may be. In almost all other branches of commercial law, a client will be experienced in the type of transaction in which he is taking legal advice; but in the case of litigation, the client's knowledge and experience, his sense of direction, of "what's coming next" and how to think ahead of the game, is seldom as extensive.

The purpose of this Guide is to give an overview of the litigation process, so as to create a sense of direction through this maze of procedure; to know roughly what should be done when, by whom, to what purpose and with what effect.

Before you approach the parts of this Guide that deal with the details of civil litigation practice and procedure, it might be helpful to give a brief summary of the whole process. A more comprehensive overview of the litigation process appears in Chapter 5, and the succeeding chapters go on to set out in more detail the individual stages that are commonly encountered.

Litigation[3] begins with the issue and service of a writ.[4] Unless the matter is settled, it ends with a trial in open court involving oral argument, the analysis of documentary evidence and the examination of witnesses, after which judgment is given by the court. Subject to any appeals, that judgment can be enforced against the defendant personally or against his assets.

There is usually a choice between starting an action in the county court or in the High Court. Although the historical limitations on the powers of the county courts have now to a large extent been removed, in practice the more important cases, and especially those involving a degree of specialist knowledge, will be started and tried in the High Court. This is in turn divided into the Queen's Bench, Chancery and Family Divisions, each of which caters for different types of case. At this level there are some specialist courts such as the Commercial Court,[5] the Companies Court, which deals with questions of the constitutions and liquidation of companies, and the Official Referees' Court, which deals mainly with construction industry matters. Each has a very strong tradition in dealing with complex claims. Above the High Court is the Court of Appeal[6]; and, higher still, the Judicial Committee of the House of Lords,[7] which (excluding the European courts) is the last appellate court of England, Wales, Scotland and Northern Ireland.

All civil trials are heard by judges,[8] usually after hearing oral evidence. Most preliminary matters are dealt with by less senior judicial officers (known as

3. In this Guide, we concentrate on litigation in the High Court, which is the forum in which most commercial litigation takes place. The system in the county courts is similar, but where it is significantly different, we draw attention to the areas of difference. A summary of county court litigation is contained in Chapter 28.

4. Or an Originating Summons: see Chapter 26. In the county court, the equivalent process is called a "Summons".

5. See Chapter 27.

6. See Chapter 25.

7. See Chapter 25.

8. In the case of defamation actions, the judge can sit with a jury. Although it is technically possible for civil cases involving allegations of fraud to come before a jury, this hardly ever happens in practice, and in all other cases the judge sits alone.

masters in the High Court and district judges in the county courts) on the basis of evidence given by affidavit—that is, written statements made on oath. Judges have wide powers but their decisions are frequently appealed from. In specialist courts such as the Commercial Court, the judges alone deal with preliminary matters.

The average time that elapses between the issue of a writ and judgment is about two years. It may be more or less depending on the complexity of the issues, the amounts at stake, or the urgency of the case. It is the trial which usually absorbs the extensive costs most frequently associated with litigation, although in cases involving significant volumes of documents or a large number of witnesses, the stages of discovery and the preparation of witness statements can also involve significant expenditure.

Between the issue of the writ and the trial, there is a prolonged pre-trial period during which "interlocutory" steps (that is, steps before trial) are taken, when the issues are identified and preparations for trial are made. This period can be frustrating because it may seem that nothing serious is going on; but it is in fact when the foundations of the case are being laid and tactical positions taken that will influence the outcome of the trial or, as is usually hoped, lead to a favourable settlement. It is, therefore, a crucial period of tactical development.

The conduct of court cases in adversarial litigation is often likened to a game, in which tactics enable the participants to take advantage of the weaknesses of their opponent. Thus, a plaintiff's lawyers will usually try to use every rule to force the defendant to face trial as quickly as possible, whilst the defence team will often strive to create tactical delays in the hope that the claim will lose impetus or the plaintiff will run out of money or interest. To a very large extent, the courts permit the parties to fight as they will, and seldom intervene to assist someone whose lawyers or resources put him at a disadvantage to a better organised or more powerful opponent. It is a system in which the parties must look after themselves and, within the procedural rules, "no holds are barred".

Thus, a defendant may take advantage of delays in the system to avoid or defer his liabilities. A plaintiff may exploit the rules that permit pre-emptive strikes and generally win him the procedural initiative. But only up to a point: the rules of procedure, the most important of which are described in this Guide, may be seen as the courts' way of regulating the sometimes liberal environment in which the tactical battle takes place.

In addition to the rules themselves, it is possible to discern various principles and objectives underlying the English litigation process. (These principles and objectives have in the past seldom been spelt out. This contrasts noticeably with the methodology of the Arbitration Act 1996 and the proposals contained in the Woolf report entitled *Access to Justice*, both of which adopt the novel approach of expressing their overriding objectives and principles.) For example, the rules are designed to ensure that all parties may know before trial the nature and extent of the case against them. There must be no "trial by ambush". Proper notice must be given of all points on which you or your adversary will rely, and of all steps to be taken in the case, and where time does not permit this, stringent penalties apply to any abuse of the court's discretion. Subject to various privileges[9] all relevant documentary evidence, however harmful, must be disclosed before trial, as must statements of factual and expert witnesses. Sham or shadowy claims or defences will not be allowed to proceed. The settlement of disputes is encouraged.

But often with the adversarial system these principles and rules are only invoked at the instance of the party aggrieved. The courts will not generally intervene, of their own volition, to see if an abuse is being practised behind the scenes, nor volunteer a remedy. It is for the parties and their lawyers to take steps to protect themselves. They may even, and frequently do, agree to waive procedural requirements if it is sensible to do so, and the courts will not usually object. Although the courts will not police the day-to-day conduct of the parties, they will, when confronted with procedural defaults, impose penalties that, in extreme cases, can be as severe as to strike out a claim or a defence. You cannot, therefore, afford to play "fast and loose" with the rules, and your lawyer must exercise his judgement responsibly.

In order to help you make sense of the current system, we have organised this Guide conceptually, whilst generally following the chronological order of "typical" litigation, although, in fact, there is no such thing as "typical" litigation: there are many situations that do not arise in every case and you may neither wish nor need to follow every procedure or apply every rule to achieve what you want in any given situation.

This Guide covers the following subjects:

Alternative dispute resolution (usually known as "ADR")

We begin with a chapter[10] that describes the important developments towards non-contentious methods of resolving disputes, as alternatives to litigation and arbitration, or as complements to those processes. As many clients wish to avoid contentious claims, the possibility of settlement should be considered at the outset.

The roles of solicitors and counsel

In this chapter,[11] the different roles of the two branches of the legal profession are explained.

9. See Chapter 18.
10. See Chapter 2.
11. See Chapter 3.

Preliminary safeguards

It is important to bear in mind the steps that need to be taken before litigation or arbitration begins. This chapter[12] sets out the most typical protective measures that should be taken at the outset of any dispute, so that no advantage is unnecessarily lost.

A general summary of the litigation process

Before we embark on our detailed review of the whole process of litigation, we set out in this chapter[13] a summary of the most important steps encountered in any lawsuit.

Matters involving the jurisdiction of the courts

A party to litigation will often have to decide whether to begin his claim in the courts of England, or in those of another country. This is a threshold issue which involves the following questions: Which country is the correct forum for the dispute? What happens if an action is begun in England, or abroad, and it is necessary to contest the jurisdiction of the courts? What happens if two similar sets of proceedings involving the same parties are begun in different countries? What happens if the defendant is not based within the jurisdiction of the English courts? This chapter[14] contains the answers to these and other questions.

Instructing lawyers

This chapter[15] deals with the considerations that should be borne in mind when instructing lawyers in litigation, so as to help obtain the most favourable results.

Starting proceedings through to the close of pleadings

Here are explained[16] the most important steps that must be taken to launch an action.

Third party and related proceedings

A defendant may want to join others into an action begun against him. This chapter[17] explains what is involved in the process and what steps he may take to protect his position.

12. See Chapter 4.
13. See Chapter 5.
14. See Chapter 6.
15. See Chapter 7.
16. See Chapter 8.
17. See Chapter 9.

Pre-emptive strikes: Injunctions: Preservation of property before trial

Litigation is subject to well-known delays that may defeat the purpose of the action. The English courts help to avoid this by enabling a plaintiff to obtain immediate remedies that preserve the status quo until the trial takes place. Two chapters[18] explain how these remedies may be obtained, and what they involve.

Avoiding trial in clear cases: Summary judgment

The courts will enable a plaintiff to obtain swift justice in cases where he can demonstrate that he has an unanswerable claim and should not have to go through the whole process to trial to obtain a remedy. This chapter[19] describes how a plaintiff may achieve this result.

Preventing abuses of the process: Striking out bad claims: Remedies for delay

Equally, the courts will assist a party whose opponent refuses to follow the correct procedures, and will allow a defendant who is unfairly subject to unmeritorious proceedings to apply to strike them out, rather than have to defend himself up to trial. These chapters[20] explain what is involved, and what conditions have to be satisfied by the defendant to enable him to obtain this remedy, and what penalties the courts may impose when faced with a party who will not comply with orders and rules.

Pre-trial protection: Interim payments: Security for costs

During the course of litigation, a party may apply to the court for relief to prevent hardship whilst awaiting trial. These chapters[21] set out the chief remedies available to parties who may be prejudiced by being denied damages whilst awaiting trial, or by being faced with proceedings brought by a plaintiff who may not be able to meet the costs of the action if he fails.

18. See Chapters 10 and 11.
19. See Chapter 12.
20. See Chapters 13 and 14.
21. See Chapters 15 and 16.

Preparations for trial

A number of chapters[22] set out the rules involved in the following areas:

Evidence generally.
Documentary evidence (or "Discovery").
Witnesses of fact.
Expert witnesses.

Settlements, payments into court and discontinuance

The English courts favour the private resolution of disputes. This chapter[23] explains how the rules of the courts facilitate this objective, and assist a party who wants to settle when his opponent may not.

Trial

This chapter[24] describes what is involved in the preparations for trial, the attendances at court, and the course of the trial.

Remedies and judgments

Here we explain[25] the main remedies that the courts will award at trial, including interest on damages, and non-monetary relief such as declarations and orders for specific performance of a contract.

Costs

This chapter[26] describes the rules relating to the award of costs in English litigation.

Appeals

This chapter[27] explains the system whereby the decisions of one court may be challenged in another court by way of appeal.

Originating Summons procedure

Most of what is described in this Guide relates to actions that are begun by writ. But there is a separate and often equally important

22. See Chapters 17, 18, 19 and 20.
23. See Chapter 21.
24. See Chapter 22.
25. See Chapter 23.
26. See Chapter 24.
27. See Chapter 25.

procedure used in certain types of action that are begun by Originating Summons, and this is outlined in this chapter.[28]

The Commercial Court

The Commercial Court has played an extremely important role in the development of commercial litigation, especially litigation involving an international element. Its main features are described in this chapter.[29]

Enforcement

There are numerous ways in which orders made by the courts may be enforced against an opponent who cannot or will not comply with them. These are explained in this chapter,[30] which deals with the enforcement of both English and foreign judgments and arbitral awards.

We also look at some specialist areas of litigation involving *representative and group actions,*[31] *landlord and tenant disputes,*[32] *insolvency,*[33] *employment litigation*[34] and *judicial review.*[35] The procedures described in this Guide are primarily those of the High Court. A separate chapter[36] outlines the procedure of the *county court.*

In Chapter 31 we give an account of the system of *arbitration*, considered from both a domestic and an international perspective.

Whilst this Guide is not intended to deal with specialist fields of litigation, we address in two chapters[37] some specific problems associated with *banking* and *insurance* litigation. We have not, however, dealt with other specialist topics (for example, shipping, or intellectual property) which do not properly belong in what is essentially an introduction to general litigation and arbitration procedures.

The important subject of *contempt of court* is dealt with in Chapter 38.

We deal in Chapter 39 with references to the *European Court of Justice.*

A Glossary of essential terms that are used in this Guide is contained in the last section.

28. See Chapter 26.
29. See Chapter 27.
30. See Chapter 29.
31. See Chapter 30.
32. See Chapter 32.
33. See Chapter 33.
34. See Chapter 34.
35. See Chapter 35.
36. See Chapter 28.
37. See Chapters 36 and 37.

THE FUTURE OF LITIGATION AND ARBITRATION IN ENGLAND

The current system of determining disputes in court that is summarised in this Guide has existed in England for over a century. During that time it has been reformed periodically and piecemeal but has become clogged up with ancient procedures and practices. The result has been a system the fundamental merits of which have been buried beneath a cumbersome superstructure of procedures that have sometimes prevented justice being done economically, quickly and intelligibly.

The main criticisms levelled at the system of litigation are that it:

— Costs too much: only the rich can afford to go to law.
— Favours those who can afford to bring cases by permitting them to grind down their poorer opponents with wasteful tactics.
— Allows disputes between parties of equal financial might to become clashes between gladiators, occupying precious court time with endless tactical applications.
— Gives too much power to the lawyers to dictate the pace of the case and the way in which it is conducted, to the cost of their clients.

Many of these criticisms were also directed at the system of arbitration, which often mirrored litigation in its practices and procedures.

As a result of the increasing public discontent, which has been shared by many practising lawyers, in 1994 the Lord Chancellor's Department instigated a review of all the procedures of civil litigation, with a view to reform. This review was conducted in two stages by a team headed by Lord Woolf, now Master of the Rolls. The first stage was consultative and led to the presentation in June 1995 of his interim report *Access to Justice*. There followed a further period of public and professional consultation which led to the publication in July 1996 of his final report which was accompanied by a draft of the general rules that are intended to form the core of a new and comprehensive code of rules which will apply to all litigation, irrespective of the court in which it has begun.

The Lord Chancellor, Lord Irvine of Lairg Q.C., subsequently instigated an independent review of the recommendations of *Access to Justice* and it is likely that at least some of the proposals will be introduced, possibly by 1999. We devote a concluding chapter[38] to a description of the main proposals that lie at the heart of the Woolf report, and offer some preliminary predictions of how effective they might be in practice.

We also at this point draw attention to the recent reform of the process of arbitration in England. This is dealt with in detail in Chapter 31. Over many years there had been criticism of the shortcomings of the arbitral process in England. As a result, legislation was enacted in 1996 and brought into force

38. See Chapter 40.

in 1997 that fundamentally revised, clarified, strengthened and improved the procedure of English arbitration. In many ways, the reforms of arbitration spring from the same concerns as were voiced in the Woolf report, and the overriding objectives of the Arbitration Act 1996 are very similar to those of the Woolf report.

CHAPTER 2

ALTERNATIVE DISPUTE RESOLUTION

Most disputes are ultimately resolved by a settlement negotiated between the parties. Such settlements are often, however, not achieved until a relatively late stage in a lawsuit. Recently, a movement has developed towards the promotion of early settlements, before the positions of parties have become entrenched. This chapter describes in outline the main features of what is now generally known as "alternative dispute resolution" (or "ADR"), which can be used to assist the parties in reaching a settlement before or soon after a dispute becomes litigious.

A. INTRODUCTION

ADR has only relatively recently emerged and been recognised in England as a useful technique for resolving disputes outside traditional litigation or arbitration. It has, however, been widely used, in one form or another, in other countries (particularly the United States of America) and it is fast gaining ground in England as lawyers and their clients have embraced it as a means of achieving a cost-effective solution that promotes the clients' real commercial objectives.

ADR bears no real comparison to litigation or arbitration: its function is not to *impose* a resolution of a dispute on the parties, but rather to *assist* them to agree a resolution between themselves.

B. ESSENTIAL CHARACTERISTICS OF ADR

The overriding purpose of ADR is to help parties who have been unable to settle their dispute by traditional negotiation to find an amicable solution without the need for intervention or further intervention by the court. It may be seen either as alternative to litigation and arbitration, in the sense that it may precede the commencement of proceedings; or as complementary to those processes, by assisting the resolution of disputes once they have developed into legal actions.

This purpose is achieved by a variety of somewhat different but flexible means, the most typical of which is a structured meeting or series of meetings between the parties and a neutral mediator or adviser, whose job it is to help each party conduct a realistic assessment of his or his opponent's case; to facilitate commonsense dialogue; to assist in solving problems or breaking deadlocks; and to encourage a settlement that is agreed, as opposed to a resolution that is ultimately imposed by the court or arbitrator.

ADR is a wholly consensual process. Thus:

- The parties cannot be forced into ADR; they must all agree that it should be used.[1]
- The precise procedure to be adopted and the identity of the neutral mediator or adviser must also be agreed.
- A solution or decision cannot be imposed on the parties; the dispute will only be resolved if everyone agrees terms of settlement.

The courts are increasingly taking steps to encourage the consideration and use of ADR. In the Commercial Court lawyers are required to consider both with their clients and with the other parties the possibility of attempting to resolve the dispute or particular issues by mediation, conciliation or otherwise, and in all High Court actions lawyers are required to file a checklist answering questions which include whether they have discussed ADR with their clients and opponents and whether ADR might assist in resolving or narrowing the issues. Lawyers and clients who ignore ADR altogether run the risk of criticism by the court and, in extreme cases, the possibility of a penalty in costs.

ADR is generally conducted on a "without prejudice"[2] and confidential basis.

- Documents produced for and statements or admissions made at ADR meetings are therefore *without prejudice* and so cannot be used as evidence in litigation should a settlement not be achieved.
- Everything that is said at ADR meetings is confidential to the parties and the neutral mediator, and everything that is said in private meetings between each party and the mediator is also confidential, unless the mediator is specifically authorised to disclose it to another party.

C. TYPES OF ADR

Because of the flexibility of ADR procedures and the development of a number of hybrids in the United States of America, ADR terminology can be somewhat

1. Sometimes, the agreement to consider or use ADR is contained in a clause in the contract under which the dispute has arisen. It is a moot question, however, whether such clauses are enforceable.
2. See Chapter 4, section F for an explanation of this term.

confusing. In England, almost all ADR procedures can loosely be described either as "mediation" or as "mini-trials".

Mediation

Mediation is a process whereby a neutral individual is engaged to mediate in settlement negotiations between the parties. He acts as an independent go-between in the conduct of negotiations and attempts to facilitate an agreed resolution of the dispute. Mediation is by far the most common form of ADR in use in England. A typical mediation procedure is described below.

Mini-trials

Mini-trials are more formalised settlement conferences, involving the abbreviated presentation of evidence by representatives of the parties to a panel usually consisting of one neutral member and one senior executive of each disputant who, ideally, has no detailed knowledge of the dispute. Mini-trials may be more appropriate than mediation in large commercial cases involving particularly difficult questions of law or fact.

D. TYPICAL MEDIATION PROCEDURE

The initial stage of any mediation involves the taking of various preparatory steps for the mediation meeting.

- It is usually sensible to sign a short-form agreement setting out the basic ground rules for the mediation.
- One of the most important decisions is the identity of the mediator. A key factor in the choice of mediator is his experience in the underlying subject matter of the dispute. In certain cases, it may be appropriate to agree that an experienced mediator who practises in one discipline (for example, a lawyer) should be assisted by another mediator with expertise in the area of business or other activity giving rise to the dispute (for example, a banker).
- Brief "position papers" should be prepared by all parties and exchanged and copied to the mediator, along with any key documents on which the parties wish to rely, in advance of the mediation meeting.

A number of independent ADR organisations exist to assist the parties in these preparatory phases. They are usually able to suggest a range of suitably experienced and qualified mediators and, indeed, to facilitate the agreement to mediate in circumstances where there may be considerable hostility between the parties.

Once the preparatory steps have been taken, the mediation meeting itself can go ahead. The mediator usually determines the precise format of the meeting, but it will generally be structured as follows:

— The opening session is attended by all parties and the mediator, at which each party has an opportunity to make a brief presentation of his case to the mediator and to the other parties. This presentation will usually be relatively short and should concentrate on the key legal, factual and commercial issues.
— The opening joint session usually concludes with a short general discussion at which the parties and the mediator have the opportunity to ask each other questions and request clarification of certain points.
— The meeting then adjourns to a series of private meetings between the mediator and each party at which the mediator probes and clarifies each party's position on a confidential basis and attempts to facilitate a settlement by "shuttle diplomacy". This is probably the most important phase of the mediation. The mediator attempts to bring the parties' positions closer and closer together with the aim ultimately of concluding a settlement.

It is essential that the mediation is attended by representatives of each party who have full authority to settle the dispute.

— At the end of the sessions of "shuttle diplomacy", the joint meeting is reconvened either to agree the detailed terms of a settlement which has been reached in principle and to record those terms in a written agreement or, if no settlement has been reached, to conclude the mediation.

Although a settlement cannot be imposed on the parties, if they reach agreement they will be bound, as in any contract, by its terms. If no agreement is possible, no harm is suffered, because of the *without prejudice* nature of the process, and the parties are free to carry on with their dispute by whatever means available.

E. WHEN TO USE ADR

ADR is not a substitute for traditional settlement negotiations between the parties. It supplements the ordinary negotiating process by providing neutral assistance when traditional negotiations have broken down or have reached deadlock.

Nor is ADR a substitute for conventional litigation. Because of its consensual nature, if either party is intransigent and is determined to take its case to law rather than to settle, ADR will fulfil no useful purpose.

ADR should always at least be considered in any dispute where negotiations have broken down and the only other alternative is litigation. It should be remembered that most cases in which court or arbitration proceedings are commenced do eventually settle, but often only after the commitment of a great deal of management time and expense which might have been avoided if the services of a neutral mediator had been called upon to facilitate an early settlement.

There is definitely no "right time" to use ADR during the currency of a dispute. ADR methods are sufficiently flexible to allow them to be used at almost any stage. Logically, however, the most obvious time to consider and use a mediation or other ADR process is before or shortly after commencement of proceedings.

F. THE ADVANTAGES AND DISADVANTAGES OF ADR METHODS

Advantages

ADR provides the following benefits not usually available with other means of resolving disputes:

- *Cost*: the costs of ADR are significantly less than litigation or arbitration. Statistics show that, although some ADRs fail, some succeed. Because of this, in many cases a cost/benefit analysis will clearly favour attempting ADR, at least where none of the disadvantages listed below apply.
- *Speed*: ADR generally provides a much faster resolution of disputes than either arbitration or litigation.
- *Control*: the process of resolution is totally in the hands of the parties.
- *Flexibility*: the procedure of any settlement option (including business solutions as opposed to merely monetary awards) is completely flexible.
- *Continuity of business relationships*: ADR enables the parties to preserve and, possibly, enhance their business relationships by defusing and possibly avoiding altogether the hostility which can develop in hotly-contested litigation.
- *Confidentiality*: the procedure involves none of the publicity sometimes associated with litigation.

Disadvantages

ADR will not generally be appropriate in the following circumstances:

- When one party has no genuine interest in settlement.
- When a legal ruling or precedent from the courts is required.
- When one party needs a protective court order, for example, an injunction or specific performance of a contract.

- When one party thinks it needs to start or continue legal action to bring the other side to the negotiating table. In such cases, however, ADR may still play a complementary role at a later stage.
- When one party wants to have his dispute aired in a public forum so as to use resultant adverse publicity to apply commercial pressure for a more favourable settlement.

It is sometimes said that ADR involves an unfortunate show of "weakness", and denotes a lack of resolve to fight if necessary, combined with the need prematurely to show one's hand. This may be true, up to a point; but if settlement can be achieved nevertheless, no harm has been done; and if not, images can be restored soon enough. Further, as will be shown later, litigation itself is conducted on the basis of full disclosure, and so what is revealed in ADR processes will usually have to be disclosed in court proceedings in any event.

G. THE ROLE OF LAWYERS IN ADR

Lawyers should advise if and when to use mediation and, wherever necessary, assist in the process itself.

Some companies now insist on ADR clauses in their commercial contracts.[1] This sets the scene for an attempt to resolve any dispute in this way before becoming entrenched in a dispute contest. Lawyers should be skilled in drafting such clauses.

Lawyers may be involved in drafting the summary of the case, putting forward the initial presentation to the mediator and, if necessary, drafting the settlement terms.

H. ADR ORGANISATIONS

The ADR movement in this country is growing. There are a great many bodies which provide ADR services of various types. Prominent among these are the Centre for Dispute Resolution, popularly known as "CEDR", and the City Disputes Panel.

CHAPTER 3

SOLICITORS AND COUNSEL

The majority of lawsuits that are conducted in England, whether by litigation or arbitration, in practice involve both solicitors and counsel. Although they have largely different roles, often they will work together on the same case. Clients may wonder why this should be necessary and why additional costs are being incurred. This chapter explains the part played by solicitors and when and why it is necessary or prudent to employ counsel.

A. INTRODUCTION

In England the legal profession comprises solicitors and barristers. They are subject to different governing and disciplinary bodies, the Law Society and the Bar Council respectively; have somewhat different training although they are subject to the same educational qualifications; and perform broadly different functions.

"Counsel" is a word commonly used for barristers, whether individually or as a group,[1] whose profession is known generally as "the Bar". There are two ranks of barrister: a "junior" is any barrister who, regardless of age or length of qualification, is not a Queen's Counsel; and Queen's Counsel, sometimes known as a "silk" or "leading counsel" or, more frequently, a "QC", is a barrister who has been recognised by the Lord Chancellor's Department as particularly skilled in his or her field.

Solicitors in private practice generally operate as firms comprising partners, assistant solicitors and auxiliary staff. It is they who have the initial and most regular contact with clients and others such as accountants, bankers and brokers, and factual and expert witnesses in litigation.[2] A client's contract is with the firm of solicitors as a whole even though he may regard the individual with whom he deals most regularly as "his" solicitor.

Counsel are sole practitioners but are invariably grouped together in sets of chambers in or around the Inns of Court. Those chambers typically offer

1. Note that in England "counsel" is a term reserved for barristers rather than for lawyers generally.

2. Counsel may take instructions direct from certain professional clients, but this is not regularly followed in practice for contentious work (as opposed to advisory matters).

advice in most fields of law, but some will tend to deal only in civil law and some in criminal law. Some barristers devote most of their time to advising clients in chambers on non-contentious matters such as tax law; but the majority divide their time between advising in chambers either on non-contentious issues or on matters arising in litigation that has not yet reached court, and court appearances. Counsel are assisted by clerks who organise their time and negotiate their fees.

It is a common misapprehension that counsel are specialists and solicitors are general practitioners. In fact, increasingly nowadays, and especially in the larger law firms, solicitors are recognised as having a high level of specialisation in complex areas of law and commercial practice.

Whilst in most non-contentious areas of practice counsel do not tend to be instructed frequently as a part of the legal team, in contentious litigation counsel are necessarily involved on a greater scale. This is because counsel generally exercise greater rights of audience in the higher courts than do solicitors. Furthermore, as counsel will almost inevitably be briefed for trial it is often wise to involve them during the course of pre-trial preparations.

The skill of the solicitor is to devise the strategy and tactics of the case and to steer it from inception through to trial and usually to negotiate the settlement when the time is right. Counsel's particular skill is to present the case in court. But although these two skills are fundamentally different and, indeed, difficult to combine in terms of time and practice as well as of training, they should properly be seen as complementary: a solicitor, however able, cannot win his case if let down by counsel; and counsel, however eloquent, can only ever be as good as his brief. Successful litigation is a product of effective teamwork in which all the lawyers know what is happening at all stages of the case; what each other is thinking; what they each know and do not know; and, which is every bit as important, what their client is expecting to achieve from the action they are taking on his behalf. This harmony and mutual understanding can only be achieved by regular meetings and contact, and it is a false economy to adopt any other approach.

B. SOLICITORS

A client's first contact with his legal team will almost always be with his solicitor, who will attend the first meetings, examine the initial papers, take the preliminary witness statements and consider all the precautionary matters that are described elsewhere.[3] From this position he will form an initial view of the case and identify the client's objectives and legal and commercial priorities. He will assess the tactics that should be deployed to achieve those objectives: for example, whether it is sensible to consider early settlement, or

3. See in particular Chapter 4.

alternative dispute resolution, or whether some pre-emptive court application for an injunction is necessary.

Thereafter, he will deal on a regular basis with the conduct of the case, keeping his client informed at every stage. It will be the solicitor who takes responsibility for the correspondence with the other party's representatives; for the identification and location of witnesses and the taking of their proofs of evidence; for discovery and inspection of documents; for the briefing of expert witnesses and the commissioning of their reports; for advising the client on how developments affect the prospects of success and of the need for, or desirability of, settlement or for the making of a payment into court; and for all the preparations for trial. He is responsible for the choice of counsel; for instructing and briefing counsel before and during trial; and for being present in court throughout the trial to deal with all the problems that can arise during that time: for example, the attendance of witnesses, the late production of documents, tactical surprises created by the opposite party, and so on. It is a vital role, and one that cannot properly be fulfilled at the same time as preparing oral submissions in court. That is principally the role of counsel.

C. COUNSEL

Counsel perform two separate but linked roles in the conduct of litigation. They advise in conference[4] or in writing on matters of law and practice that arise during the preparatory stages of the case; and they appear in court to make the oral submissions of fact and law. Junior counsel may also draft the pleadings[5] in the action, based on the instructions they receive from their solicitor. Counsel do not get involved in collecting evidence, but may assist in the way it is prepared for trial. It used to be against the rules of professional conduct for a barrister to meet a witness before trial, or to take part in drafting a witness statement. This rule has now been relaxed,[6] but a barrister must exercise his discretion when interviewing a witness and do so only when appropriate and when it is in his client's best interests. He must be careful not to appear to coax a witness or to influence his testimony. He may question a witness to enable him to present the evidence fairly, but may not, for example, take part in mock-trials or cross-examinations. Counsel may draft a witness statement but should not, except in exceptional circumstances, take a witness statement in a case in which he will appear as counsel at trial. Generally, leading counsel may appear in court alone, but most prefer to be assisted by junior counsel. In less complex cases, junior counsel will act alone.

It is vital that counsel be fully briefed for trial. Unless they are, they cannot be expected to present the case properly in court. As stated before, this involves

4. A meeting with leading counsel is usually called a "consultation".
5. See Chapter 8.
6. These rules are now approved by the Professional Standards Committee of the General Council of the Bar, with effect from April 1997.

a considerable degree of liaison throughout the whole preparation of the case, not only to ensure that counsel know what is happening, but so they may have the opportunity to advise on the matters in issue and to ensure that what is being done will not have unforeseen consequences. Decisions on these tactical matters are often largely subjective, and it is very important that individual judgements are given full and careful consideration before conclusions are reached. It often happens that the course of a trial can be seriously influenced by tactical steps taken beforehand, so it is of the greatest importance that all members of the legal team, counsel as well as solicitors, are involved in this crucial tactical period. In addition, during this time it may become clear that the case should be settled, and discussions with counsel as to the nature of any offer or counter-offer are extremely important.

Counsel can be sued for professional negligence in respect of work of a purely advisory nature, but not in relation to the conduct of a case in court.

D. COUNSEL'S FEES

Technically, counsel's fees are "honorariums" that are the responsibility in honour of the solicitor who instructs or briefs the barrister. The fees cannot technically be enforced as a debt, but in practice it is not possible to avoid payment except in cases of genuine dispute. If the solicitor fails to pay the counsel's fees he may be liable to professional disciplinary measures. Usually, a solicitor will expect a payment on account from his client for counsel's fees and in any event will require reimbursement.

Each counsel has a clerk who is responsible not only for running counsel's diary and other administrative matters, but also for negotiating counsel's fees and securing their payment. The fees are decided on an individual basis, but generally follow a pattern set by the market and reflect the seniority of counsel, the importance of the case, the urgency of the matter and the time devoted to the work. There are two types of fee. First, fees for work done outside court: for example, written opinions, advice in conference and the drafting of pleadings. Secondly, fees for court appearances, which are known as "brief fees" and "refreshers". The brief fee itself is for the work undertaken in preparing the case for trial and is in addition to any earlier fees incurred on a case in the pre-trial period. Refreshers are paid for each day in court after the first day of trial.

In the case of a brief fee, it is important to remember that it becomes payable when the brief is delivered to counsel and remains so even if the case settles between the date of the delivery of the brief and the trial. A practice arose in the past whereby solicitors who expected that a case would settle at a very late stage would withhold the delivery of the brief until the last minute.[7] This made it very difficult for counsel to master the case in the short time available, and

7. For a discussion of the relation between brief fees and settlement, see Chapter 22, section D.

also meant that if he had declined other work to allow time to be in court he would lose substantial fees. This practice still continues in some cases, but it is not regarded as correct, especially in very major actions that are expected to last a long time, where the current custom is to agree a series of stage payments before the trial begins. The effect of this is that the series of payments begins earlier than usual with the result that only the payments actually made are lost to the client if the case settles before trial: those payments that have not fallen due are cancelled.

CHAPTER 4

PRELIMINARY SAFEGUARDS

This chapter explains some useful precautions that may be taken before litigation begins.

A. INTRODUCTION

A legal dispute is, broadly, a difference that concerns rights and liabilities at law and which is capable of being resolved by the judicial process. Often, the dispute has to be determined by legal process, but once a dispute arises, the parties' objective is frequently to reach a compromise before litigation ensues. This will not always be possible to achieve. If it is not, each party will need to safeguard his position to prevent problems arising later on. Sometimes immediate legal advice will be necessary: for example, where an injunction is sought.[1] In any event, during this early stage there are a number of traps for the unwary which, if not avoided, could affect the outcome of the dispute.

B. IDENTIFYING THE DISPUTE

The ability to identify and analyse the elements of a dispute can give an immediate tactical advantage. For example, an admission may be extracted on a point which might otherwise be in issue, or the imprudent disclosure of documents may be achieved.

It is only when the dispute has been identified that the basic precautions outlined below can be taken so as to ensure that nothing is done before lawyers are instructed which may make their job more difficult or prejudice the prospects of success in any ensuing litigation.

1. See Chapter 10.

C. TIME LIMITS

The time within which a claim may be made is usually limited by contract or by statute. This is especially important where contracts of carriage are involved, or where a contract requires litigation or arbitration to be started within a certain (often short) time from the accrual of a cause of action or the arising of a dispute. Sometimes, it is not clear that a dispute has arisen and the other party may not voice his tacit objections, hoping that time limits for claiming will pass unnoticed.

Statutory limitation periods usually start to run in contract cases on the date the contract is breached and, in the case of most other wrongful acts, on the date that loss or damage is suffered. In most cases, the relevant period is six years from the applicable starting date, but it may be longer or shorter depending on the circumstances and the precise nature of the claim.

> *If a time limit provided by contract has expired it could prevent a claim being made. If a limitation period under statute has expired it may give a complete defence.*[2] *It is important, therefore, to seek to confirm as early as possible any relevant time limits. If in doubt you should consult a lawyer immediately.*

In some cases, the severity of the rules relating to the time limits within which an action must be brought is relaxed. These cases are primarily those concerning personal injuries or fatalities, fraud or concealment, or negligence, although other types of claim can also be affected. The time limits can be extended where, for example, the damage is latent and the plaintiff did not know of the matters that give rise to a claim until after the expiry of the usual time limits.

If the *remedy* sought is the recovery of a debt or damages, the only timing issue will be the statutory or contractual date beyond which no claim may be brought. If, however, you wish to apply for certain remedies such as an injunction or specific performance of a contract, proceedings should be brought as soon as possible after you become aware of your claim. This is because, if the court finds that you have unreasonably delayed the issue of proceedings and that your opponent has been prejudiced as a result, these remedies may be refused solely on the basis of the delay.[3]

D. DELEGATE EFFECTIVELY

Where there are a number of points of contact between the parties, consideration should be given to who ought to handle the case and who ought to conduct the negotiations.

2. See further, Chapter 8, section H, and Chapter 14.
3. See Chapters 10 and 23.

It is generally wise to delegate the handling of the dispute to one person, who (subject to reporting to whomever is appropriate) is in charge of the matter and can co-ordinate the efforts of everyone involved. This will help to avoid confusion and mistakes.

It is a matter of judgement whether the individual most closely associated with the dispute or with the closest relationships with the opponent's personnel should be responsible for negotiating a settlement.

Those who are the most obvious individuals to negotiate a settlement will often be the best choices, but it may be that they are so closely connected with the transaction and the people involved that it would be difficult for them to negotiate effectively, or that ongoing relationships between existing contacts may be damaged.

The negotiations may be more effective if the appointed negotiators do not have authority to settle the dispute. The tactical ability to refer to a "higher authority"—the chairman, chief executive or managing director of a company—often gives the initiative in discussions, and can avoid the negotiator being "pinned-down" on the spot.[4]

E. INVOLVING LAWYERS

If the dispute is limited to fact, or the chosen negotiator is experienced, instructing lawyers may be delayed. However, it may be considered expedient before negotiations begin to instruct lawyers if legal issues are involved or if the opponent has instructed lawyers.

A basic understanding of the legal position is an essential weapon in the negotiator's armoury, and a preliminary opinion on the legal issues can often be obtained quickly and cheaply. It may be a false economy to delay going to lawyers if this means being unprepared later or making crucial tactical errors at the outset.

Sometimes, you may find that your claim is governed by a *foreign law*, where different time limits apply from those to which you are accustomed. Your lawyer can advise on how to cope with such a situation.

As soon as proceedings are served, lawyers should be involved who will be able to deal with immediate problems, such as acknowledging service so as to prevent a judgment by default.[5]

F. ADMISSIONS AND THE "WITHOUT PREJUDICE" RULE

When a dispute arises you should ensure that during negotiations no admis-

4. This procedure may be inappropriate in assisted settlements—see Chapter 2.
5. See Chapter 8.

sions are made which the opponent might later use. Any admissions on a point of fact or law could be damaging.

To overcome this problem, and to encourage parties to settle disputes, a general rule has been developed that admissions made at meetings or in letters the purpose of which is to try to achieve a settlement of a dispute cannot be used in evidence. This is called the "without prejudice" rule.[6]

> *The mere use of the words "without prejudice" at a meeting or in correspondence will not automatically prevent admissions from being deployed in court. The rule will only apply to a communication the genuine purpose of which is to advance a settlement of a dispute. The expression is frequently misused, usually in an effort to avoid the consequences of making inadvertent admissions, and it will not protect such statements unless made in the context of genuine settlement talks.*
>
> *Conversely, a communication will not necessarily lose the protection of the rule if it is not expressly stated to be "without prejudice", but it may do. It is very unwise to initiate settlement talks or correspondence without specifying them to be "without prejudice".*

If in doubt it is probably sensible to use the words "without prejudice", but beware of using the term loosely on any document that may be feared to have a legal effect. A rent review notice labelled "without prejudice" may have no effect at all; and you may later have difficulty in relying on a "without prejudice" communication if you should later wish to do so—for example, because you need to prove that your opponent knew of what was said in that communication.

G. DOCUMENTS AND "DISCOVERY"[7]

Litigation in this country is increasingly document-oriented, and cases can be won or lost by documents that evidence material facts. It is therefore sensible to be wary about what is put in writing at this (or, indeed, at any) stage of the process.

An essential safeguard is, therefore, to avoid the creation of documents that may need to be shown to your opponent if proceedings are commenced and which may be damaging. Parties to litigation eventually have to provide to their opponent all original and copy documents which are relevant to the

6. There is another way in which this expression is used and which has slightly different effects. Someone can say or do things on the basis that they are "without prejudice" to his rights or "without prejudice" to what he will argue in court. In such situations, the court may hear about what has been said or done, but the person making the statement will maintain his ability credibly to argue that he had not been under any obligation to speak or to act as he did or to resile from what he has said or done.

7. See Chapter 18.

dispute other than documents falling within certain defined exemptions. This process is called "discovery".

The discovery obligation extends to internal documents such as memoranda, computer disks and documents generated by computers, reports to the board of a company, board minutes and the like, and all copies of them that are distributed amongst board members or staff. Special rules apply to documents that are covered by legal professional and litigation privilege[7] and these may mean that such documents need not be produced to an opponent.

Care should also be taken with manuscript notes made on documents, whether originals or copies. For example, if you write on a letter received from your opponent a comment such as "He's right about that", this would have to be disclosed and may materially damage your case and prejudice a possible settlement.

Equally, do not destroy or lose any documents that may be required in litigation. Keep track of where documents are stored, and of who has got what papers. They may all be needed later.

It is nevertheless wise to make notes of any meetings you have had with your adversary, for the purposes of proving factually what was said and done. Distinguish this from internal notes that evidence your own thinking, where the rule outlined above applies.

Be especially careful about circulating documents concerning or recording legal advice, as this may involve the waiver or loss of privilege in that advice.

H. INSURANCE

You should check at an early stage if any claims made are covered by insurance. If so, immediate consideration should be given to the claims procedure in the insurance policy, as failure to comply with that procedure may enable the insurers to avoid their obligations.

I. THE SOLVENCY OF YOUR OPPONENT

Checks should be made to ensure that your opponent is able to pay you the damages that you seek to recover in any litigation. It is plainly a waste of time and money to engage in litigation against a man of straw. Enquiry agents or commercial investigators can often provide valuable information about an opponent's financial strength, or assets that may be held overseas.

CHAPTER 5

FROM THE COMMENCEMENT OF PROCEEDINGS TO TRIAL: AN OVERVIEW

Here are described the main stages in litigation before a case reaches trial. A chart showing the steps that are most commonly taken in litigation appears on page 35.

A. INTRODUCTION

The litigation process is split into two chief phases:

— *Pre-trial*

This is often described, interchangeably, as the *interim* or *interlocutory* period.

— *Trial* and *post-trial*

Towards the end of the pre-trial phase, one of the parties will issue a Summons for Directions, in which the court considers the state of preparedness of the case, and makes all necessary orders for the future.[1]

The process described below is based on a straightforward High Court case. County court cases follow a broadly similar course, but the terminology is often different.

B. THE PRE-TRIAL PERIOD

During this time, the most appropriate jurisdiction for the action is chosen, the proceedings are issued and the case is prepared for trial.

In the Introduction, the importance of the pre-trial (or "interlocutory") period of a court case was emphasised. It is a crucial period of preparation and tactical exchanges in which the outcome of the whole case can be determined.

1. In practice, this step is somewhat perfunctory, and may well be radically reformed as a result of Lord Woolf's initiatives, referred to in Chapters 1 and 40.

Most clients hope that their case does not reach trial: they want it to settle first. That is why the period before trial is so important, as your ability to achieve a good settlement is often directly related to the work that is done in this period.

This phase is characterised by a series of time limits, set by the rules of the court, for taking various preparatory steps: for example, the service of the writ, acknowledging service, serving a Defence, giving discovery and exchanging your witness statements and experts' reports.

— These time limits are in practice frequently extended by the lawyers—not from indolence, but because the time limits, which are usually periods of 14 days, do not give enough time for work to be done properly, or allow for instructions to be taken from busy clients, especially in difficult cases.

During this period, applications may be made to strike out a claim or parts of a Defence, to obtain summary judgment or security for costs or to obtain injunctions to restrain activity or protect assets pending trial.[2]

The lawyers must use their initiative to carry on with their preparations. These will involve meetings with their clients, contact with witnesses, and correspondence with their opponents in which papers are exchanged and the preparations developed. But if progress cannot be achieved—if the other side is intransigent, or if the court is required to help on any points in issue—an application to court must be made.

Such applications are made by *summons* to the master or judge. The summons must usually be supported by an *affidavit* verifying the facts and asserting the claim to relief.

In some cases, the summons will be listed for hearing at a later time, usually within one or two months, and could last for 10 minutes on a simple point, or days on a complex matter. The court will hear argument[3] from the lawyers and make a ruling that the parties must obey.

Example
D wants disclosure of documents from P, who has already been ordered to give it. P refuses. D can take matters no further by himself, and must now issue a summons for the court to decide whether P can or should comply.

There is a variety of orders that the court may make on such an application:

— That D (or P) should do what P (or D) wishes within a set time: no penalty is attached.[4]

2. See Chapters 13, 12, 16, 10 and 11 respectively.
3. In most such applications, the hearing is made on an *inter partes* basis, with both sides present. In some urgent cases, the hearing will be *ex parte*, when only the applicant appears.
4. However, the party in default will usually be ordered to pay the other's costs of the application: see Chapter 24.

— That D (or P) should comply by a final date (a "final order"): a stricter order, but still no penalty is imposed.[4]
— That unless D (or P) complies by a set date, he will be debarred from defending (or proceeding) (an "unless order"). This is the most severe order that the court will impose in these circumstances.

Example
P claims that D is in default of an order, and that P is prejudiced in his preparations for trial. D ignores him. P may issue a summons for an order that D should be debarred from defending by reason of his delay. The court may grant that order or, more typically, put D under a final order to comply.

Another type of summons that is frequently issued is a summons for judgment, when the plaintiff contends that the defendant has no arguable defence.[5]

Example
When D has served his Defence, P considers that it is unarguable and wishes to avoid the expense of trial. He therefore issues a summons for judgment. The court may give judgment, or grant conditional or unconditional leave to defend.

Interlocutory orders are usually made by masters or judges, but it is possible to appeal to the Court of Appeal, or—in a very important case—to the House of Lords. In this way, the process of getting to trial may be long-drawn-out and costly, and you should only go to court for orders of this sort where it is absolutely necessary and you have a real prospect of success.

The period of pre-trial preparation is crucial: if you should appear to have lost interest, for example, by not maintaining the pressure on your opponent by correspondence, requests, applications to court by summons; or if you fail to comply with obligations to do or serve things, you will lose credibility and, with it, the tactical initiative. Conversely, if you do all that is required, on time, and maintain the pressure by a watchful and assertive policy, you will be much better-placed to dictate a good settlement or, if that fails, be ready to fight the case at trial.

In major cases, the practice has recently grown up whereby a judge is appointed at an early stage to be the trial judge, and he deals with all preliminary matters, usually at a series of pre-trial reviews in which the parties convene to inform the court of the progress in their preparations and problems that they are encountering. This can lead to very efficient and cost-effective results.

C. THE TRIAL AND THE POST-TRIAL PERIOD

Once the preparations are complete, the time comes for your "day in court". What is involved is described in Chapter 22.

5. See Chapter 12 for a full account of this procedure.

You should think very carefully as the case proceeds to this phase. Litigation is not a science, and it is as much subject to uncertainty and mishap as any other walk of life involving people and impressions. The costs of the trial can often exceed those of the preparations for trial.

As a general rule, you should only go to trial where it has been impossible to settle first, or where there are genuine and inescapable issues of principle that override the economic and practical problems that will inevitably arise.

Once you have the judgment of the court, you must set about its enforcement. In order to make this as effective as possible, your lawyers may have taken earlier steps, for example, to preserve the defendant's assets pending judgment. These processes, and enforcement of the judgment itself both in this country and abroad, are dealt with in Chapters 11 and 29.

THE PRINCIPAL STEPS IN A LEGAL CASE

The chart below describes the steps that are most routinely taken in any litigation.

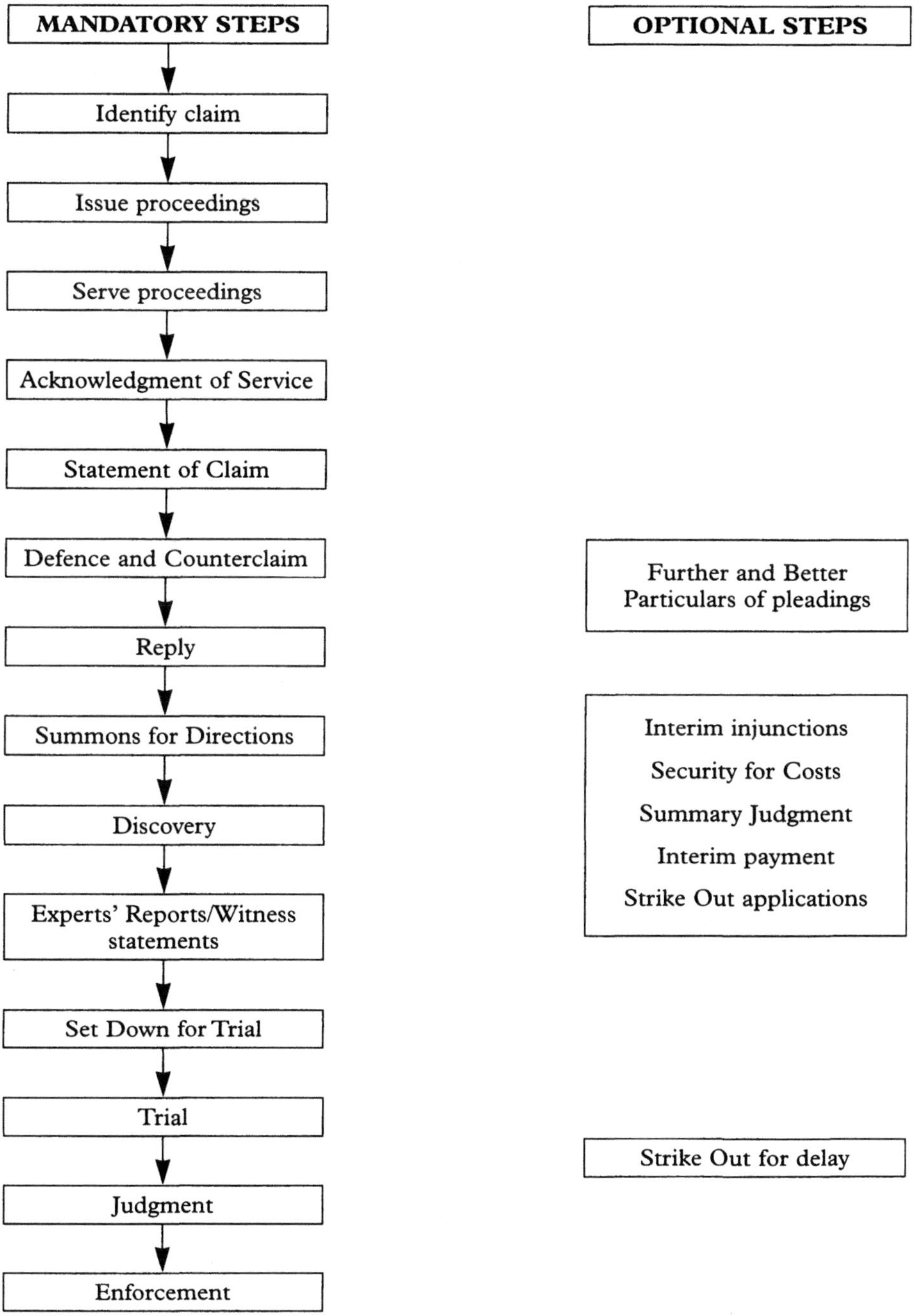

CHAPTER 6

JURISDICTION AND FOREIGN ASPECTS OF LITIGATION

This chapter describes the fundamental rules that determine when cases can be begun in the English courts and when it is necessary to start an action abroad. It then outlines other important aspects of litigation involving a foreign element.

A. INTRODUCTION

Whenever litigation involves a party based outside England, it is necessary to assess whether the English courts have the right to hear and rule on a dispute: that is, whether the English courts have *jurisdiction*. Even if the English courts do have jurisdiction, it is also possible that the courts of other countries will as well, and consideration must be given to the most appropriate forum in which to begin the proceedings.

The question of jurisdiction can be of great practical importance. It may be a substantial disincentive to starting or defending proceedings if a party has to incur the inconvenience and added expense of doing so in a foreign country.

It is important to distinguish between jurisdiction and what is called "the applicable law" of the relationship between the parties, that is, the law to which the dispute is subject. The former determines the country whose courts can hear a case; the latter deals with the question of which country's laws govern the subject matter of the dispute itself. The fact that the subject matter (for instance, a contract) is governed by English law does not necessarily mean that the English courts have jurisdiction to decide the dispute, although this may often be the case. It is also possible for an English court to determine a dispute by applying the law of a different country.[1] Equally, a foreign court may have jurisdiction to determine a dispute that involves the application of English law. Further, the English courts will only apply the substantive law of a foreign country: it will always apply its own *procedural* law.

There is a variety of rules that are used to determine whether the English courts have jurisdiction to hear the case. These relate, broadly, to the *defendant's*

1. It does so by hearing expert evidence, usually from practising foreign lawyers, or academics: see Chapter 20.

location or domicile. The plaintiff's residence or domicile is not normally important, although a non-resident plaintiff may sometimes be required to give to the defendant security for his costs in the action as a condition of continuing with his claim.[2] In very broad terms, there are two sets of rules:

— *"Convention"*[3] rules: Scotland and Northern Ireland,[4] members of the European Union, and Iceland, Norway and Switzerland are parties to one or both Conventions.
— *"Non-Convention"* rules: these apply, in the absence of any applicable convention, to all other countries (including the Isle of Man and the Channel Islands).

B. CONVENTION RULES

The starting point is that a defendant should be sued in the country in which he is based (or "domiciled").

Example
P is an English company. It wishes to commence proceedings against D which is a company registered in France that carries on all its business in France. Under this rule, P would have to sue in France and would not be able to start proceedings in England.

The strict effect of this rule is subject to a number of exceptions. These include:

— Where the courts of a Convention country are given "exclusive" jurisdiction, because of the subject matter of the dispute and regardless of the domicile of the defendant.
— Where a contract specifically provides that the courts of a particular country shall be entitled to deal with a dispute arising under that contract. In such a case, the proceedings may be brought in that country: see section D, below.
— Where the action relates to non-performance of a contract. The proceedings can be brought in the country where the contractual obligation in question was due to be performed, as well as in the country of the defendant's domicile.
— Where the action relates to the non-payment of money due under a contract. In such a case it will be necessary to determine where the payment obligation is due to be performed. Under English law, unless the parties agree a different place of payment, the place of payment is usually the country where the creditor is situated.

2. See Chapter 16.
3. The Brussels and Lugano Conventions on Jurisdiction and the Enforcement of Judgments in Civil and Commercial Matters of 1968 and 1988 respectively.
4. Civil Jurisdiction and Judgments Act 1982.

Example
P is an English company. D is a German company that has failed to pay in England a sum due to be paid there under a contract. In normal circumstances, P will be entitled to commence proceedings in England, because that is where payment should have been made to P.

- Where the action relates to an insurance or consumer claim, where special rules apply to protect whom the Conventions regard as the weaker party.
- Where an action relates to an employment contract. The proceedings may be brought in the country where the employee habitually carries out his work.
- Where an action relates to the operation of a branch office. The proceedings may be brought in the country where the branch is situated.

Unlike in non-Convention cases, in Convention cases it is not necessary to obtain the court's permission to serve proceedings abroad on a foreign defendant.

The exceptions to the rules (other than those relating to *exclusive* jurisdiction in Convention cases) potentially allow for more than one country to have jurisdiction in relation to a dispute. The Conventions therefore provide that where proceedings relating to the same dispute are commenced in two countries, the general rule is that the court of the country where proceedings were *first* commenced will deal with the dispute and that the court of the other country must decline to determine the case.

C. NON-CONVENTION RULES

The general rule is that the English courts have jurisdiction to hear claims against those defendants who are domiciled in non-Convention countries if the defendant is *present* within the jurisdiction of the English courts, even if temporarily, when the proceedings are served. Where a defendant is not present, the English courts have no jurisdiction. (This is the position in the High Court. In the county court, a slightly different rule applies.)

As an exception to this general rule, the English courts may *assume* jurisdiction if they regard the case as a proper one for the service of proceedings outside the jurisdiction of the English courts, *and* the dispute falls within one of a number of categories which include:

- Where a contract specifically provides that the English courts shall have jurisdiction.
- Where a contract is governed by English law.
- Where the breach of a contract has taken place in England.
- Where the claim is for negligence and the negligent act took place in England or the damage was sustained in England.

— Where the action also involves a defendant properly served within the jurisdiction of the English courts, and the foreign defendant is a necessary and proper party to that action.

In order to be able to bring proceedings against a party who is abroad, it is necessary to apply to the court for permission to issue and serve[5] those proceedings abroad. In order to obtain permission, it has to be shown that there is a serious issue to be tried *and* that there is a good arguable case that the claim falls within one of the relevant categories stated above *and* that the case is generally a proper one for service outside the jurisdiction.

On such an application, the court has to conduct a balancing exercise and attempts to assess which court will best serve the interests of all the parties and the ends of justice. The court can take account of a wide variety of factors including:

— The country of the defendant's residence: for example, whether it is his real home or merely a tax haven.
— What language the witnesses speak.
— The country in which the witnesses are located.
— Any choice of law clause in an agreement sued upon.

D. JURISDICTION AGREEMENTS

It is possible to avoid some of the complexities of both Convention and non-Convention rules by specifically agreeing what country should have jurisdiction to deal with a dispute. Clauses of this nature should be included in contracts as a matter of course—even if it appears that there is little chance that a dispute arising from the contract will involve an international element.

Jurisdiction agreements are often expressed to be either "exclusive" or "non-exclusive". Essentially, an exclusive clause means that the parties *must* submit disputes to the courts of the country specified in the clause; a non-exclusive clause means that they *may* do so. It is also possible to have a hybrid clause which is exclusive for one party but non-exclusive for another.

— Where courts of a Convention country are given *exclusive* jurisdiction by the Conventions to determine a dispute, a jurisdiction agreement will be of no effect.

5. Note that it is possible for a writ to be *issued* against a foreign defendant, but it cannot be *served* outside the jurisdiction without leave. If necessary, a concurrent writ must be issued once leave to serve out of the jurisdiction has been obtained. The issue of the first writ may help if the plaintiff is facing limitation periods and does not have time to seek leave to serve it outside the jurisdiction.

E. SUBMISSION TO THE JURISDICTION

Both in Convention and non-Convention cases (except in those cases involving *exclusive* jurisdiction in the Convention cases referred to above), a defendant may *submit* to the jurisdiction of the English courts. This he may do in a number of ways: either by entering an Acknowledgment of Service[6] (or a Defence in the county court); or by some other conduct that shows that he intends to be bound by the rulings of the English courts.

F. CHALLENGING JURISDICTION

If a foreign defendant contends that the English courts do not have jurisdiction over a dispute, he can apply to the court for an order that the English proceedings be *set aside*. This must be done before the time limit for the service of the Defence expires. If a party, after acknowledging service, takes any step in the action without applying to set aside the writ, he will almost certainly be treated as having accepted the jurisdiction of the court and he will be barred from challenging the position. It is important, therefore, that the question of jurisdiction is addressed before any further steps are taken. If the challenge succeeds, the claim will go no further in England. If it fails, the defendant will not be prejudiced by having made the application (provided it was properly made), but he should seriously consider whether to take any further steps in the action, as to do so may have critical effects on the enforceability in another country of any judgment made against him in England.

In non-Convention cases[7] it is also possible for a defendant to argue that, even though the English courts have jurisdiction to hear the claim, nevertheless the courts of another country should hear the case and that the English proceedings should be *stayed*. This argument involves a consideration by the court as to which country's courts are most appropriate to determine the dispute. This requires a decision on which court is the "*forum conveniens*" of the dispute. When English courts consider such applications, they have regard, among other things, to the necessity of showing that the courts of another country have jurisdiction and the need to do justice between the parties. Whether the foreign proceedings would deprive the plaintiff of a legitimate legal advantage available to him in England is a matter to be taken into account, but it is not decisive. Often, a plaintiff may select the courts of a country in which he considers that his chances of succeeding are better than in others, or where he hopes that, for example, an award of damages may be greater than elsewhere. This practice of so-called "forum-shopping" is generally

6. Note, however, that where a defendant makes an application to contest the jurisdiction of the courts in the manner described in section F below, his Acknowledgment of Service will not constitute a submission to the jurisdiction.

7. In Convention cases, this rule will almost never apply, except where the contest is between the English courts and those of a non-Convention country.

deprecated, and the courts, when determining a challenge to the jurisdiction of this sort, will not be concerned with the convenience or preference of the plaintiff (and, to this extent, the expression "*forum conveniens*" is a misnomer) but with the interests of all the parties, whether there is an alternative jurisdiction, and the general need to do justice in the case.

In some cases, where proceedings are begun in England, the defendant objects on the ground that there are similar or identical proceedings between the same parties pending in another country. Where the foreign proceedings are in a Convention country, the rule is that if those were begun first they shall prevail, and the English courts will grant a stay of the English action. In non-Convention cases, the courts in England will apply considerations similar to those set out above in deciding whether to stay the English action.

In some cases, the English courts will grant an *injunction*[8] to restrain the commencement or continuation abroad of proceedings that it considers ought properly to be brought in England. In such cases, it is necessary to show that the foreign proceedings are "vexatious and oppressive" or in breach of a party's legal or equitable rights.

G. SERVICE OF PROCEEDINGS ABROAD

There are a number of international conventions which regulate the *service* in one country of proceedings commenced in another. In some cases, more than one convention may apply to a particular situation. The most commonly applicable convention is the Convention on the Service Abroad of Judicial and Extrajudicial Documents in Civil or Commercial Matters 1965 ("the 1965 Hague Convention") which covers some 37 sovereign states, including the United Kingdom, most of western Europe and the United States of America.

Each of the parties to the 1965 Hague Convention has designated a Central Authority through which foreign proceedings can be served in that country. In England, the Foreign Office and the High Court can act as the Central Authority.

Administrative delays can be experienced if the Central Authority is used to serve documents and it is worth considering whether a different method of service is available. For instance, there is no bar in English[9] law to foreign proceedings being served by post in England and it may be possible to serve proceedings through an English solicitor. It is possible, however, that the law of the country where the proceedings are issued may prohibit service in this manner.

There is a variety of methods by which English proceedings can be served abroad. These include:

8. See Chapter 10.

9. But bear in mind the courts in which the foreign proceedings have been issued may not themselves recognise service by post. It is prudent to take legal advice as to the ways in which any given foreign proceedings should be served.

— Service by a method which is in accordance with the law of the country where service is to take place.
— Service through the relevant Central Authority in accordance with the 1965 Hague Convention.
— Service through the British consular authorities (although this is not possible in independent Commonwealth countries).
— Personal service on the defendant.

It is important to be aware of some of the restrictions that can apply to the service abroad of English proceedings:

— Service may not be effected in a manner which is contrary to the law of the country where service is to take place.
— Service by post may not be permissible under a relevant foreign law.

H. OBTAINING EVIDENCE IN ENGLAND FOR FOREIGN COURTS

English law does not prohibit a witness from voluntarily giving evidence in England, either orally or by producing documents, or both, for use in a foreign court.

Where the witness is not willing to assist, the position is different. The United Kingdom is a party to the Convention on the Taking of Evidence Abroad in Civil or Commercial Matters 1970 ("the 1970 Hague Convention"). In order to introduce into English law the provisions of the 1970 Hague Convention, the Evidence (Proceedings in Other Jurisdictions) Act 1975 ("the Act") was enacted by Parliament. It is the Act that governs all applications to the English courts for orders to obtain evidence in England for foreign courts.

The Act, and Rules of Court, provide a comprehensive, self-contained code for obtaining such evidence.

Furthermore, the Act is not limited to countries that are parties to the 1970 Hague Convention. It governs requests for assistance by a foreign court made under any other bilateral convention, and, indeed, requests by the courts of countries with which there is no convention. The Act does not confine itself to courts of law but extends to tribunals as well.

Under the Act the court has discretion to order:

— Examination of witnesses.
— Production of documents.
— Inspection of property.
— Medical examination of any person.

The orders referred to above will only be granted if the court in which the foreign proceedings are taking place issues a formal *Letter of Request* to the English courts. The Letter of Request must specify in detail the evidence which is required, as the English courts will not grant an order requiring a party to give general disclosure of documents.

This procedure may only be used for the purposes of obtaining evidence for use at a trial in respect of proceedings that have already been issued. It may not be used to obtain evidence to enable someone to discover if he has a claim.

The order is initially obtained without the respondent having the opportunity to contest it. There is, however, a right to challenge the order subsequently.

This procedure is also available in many countries for the purposes of taking evidence abroad for use in proceedings pending in England.

I. JUDGMENT IN A FOREIGN CURRENCY[10]

Provided that the relevant procedural rules are followed, the English courts will, in appropriate cases, give judgment in a foreign currency. The judgment will be for payment of the foreign currency amount "or the sterling equivalent at the time of payment". Conversion takes effect as close as possible to the date of payment.[11]

J. ENFORCEMENT[12]

There is a variety of regimes allowing the registration and enforcement of foreign judgments in England. In broad terms, this is possible in relation to judgments from the following countries:

- Scotland and Northern Ireland.
- Members of the European Union.
- Members of the European Free Trade Association.
- Most members of the Commonwealth.

English judgments are registrable in these countries on a reciprocal basis.

The registration of a judgment can only be challenged on limited grounds, which include:

- If the court which granted the original judgment did not have jurisdiction to determine the dispute.
- If the original judgment was obtained by fraud.
- If the defendant did not receive notice of the proceedings in sufficient time to enable him to defend them.

10. See Chapter 23.
11. See Chapter 23, section B.
12. See further, Chapter 29.

Once a judgment has been registered in accordance with the appropriate rules, it may be enforced in England in the same manner as can an English judgment. The methods of enforcement are dealt with in more detail in Chapter 29.

Where there is no reciprocal arrangement for the enforcement of judgments given in a particular country, it is necessary to commence new proceedings in England based on the foreign judgment. It is often possible to obtain summary judgment in such proceedings, on the basis that there is no arguable defence.[13]

K. FOREIGN ASSETS

In certain situations, the English courts will make orders affecting those who are not parties to the action and who are based abroad, and assets that are based abroad. Such orders are heavily qualified, and typically arise in the case of *Mareva* injunctions and *Anton Piller* orders, which are dealt with in Chapter 11.

L. INJUNCTIONS IN SUPPORT OF FOREIGN PROCEEDINGS

An English court has a discretionary power to grant an interim injunction in support of proceedings in a foreign country. In the past, if a plaintiff began proceedings in a foreign country he could not obtain ancillary relief in England to restrain, for example, the disposition of assets held in England by the defendant. He could only obtain such relief if there existed a cause of action over which the English courts had jurisdiction and where the substantive proceedings were themselves brought in England. In such circumstances, it was not possible to obtain leave to serve the proceedings outside the jurisdiction of the English courts.

The rule did not apply, however, to cases in which the plaintiff sought from the English courts interim relief ancillary to a claim proceeding in a country that was a signatory to the Brussels and Lugano Conventions.

With effect from April 1997, the power has now been extended to all cases, wherever they are proceeding. As a result, interim relief (including Mareva injunctions) may now be given in support of an action begun anywhere abroad.

The power is discretionary and may be exercised only where it can be shown that the plaintiff has a good claim to interim relief. It can be exercised over assets held outside England, and enables the English courts to grant worldwide *Mareva* injunctions in those cases where it is appropriate and just and convenient to do so. This marks an important extension of the powers of the English courts. (See also Chapter 11 for a discussion of the application of this rule to *Mareva* injunctions.)

13. See Chapter 12.

M. NEGATIVE DECLARATIONS

It has been seen that the civil jurisdiction of the English courts in respect of claims with foreign parties involves a broad distinction between Convention and non-Convention rules. An interesting and important difference in the approach of each system exists in the case of *negative declarations*.

A negative declaration is a ruling by the court that the plaintiff is under no liability to the defendant. Applications for such relief may be inoffensive in cases where the plaintiff understandably needs to know what, if any, liability he has to a defendant who cannot or will not put the issue before the court. But English judges have long regarded applications for negative declarations as susceptible to abuse by plaintiffs, as they may be used as a device for seising the English courts with jurisdiction in a case which ought properly to be brought elsewhere, thereby preventing the defendant from starting an action abroad with consequences possibly adverse to the plaintiff in what he suspects is a more hostile forum.

Such attempts at *forum-shopping* are generally deprecated by the English courts, which, in cases where the old statutory rules (i.e. the non-Convention rules) apply, have often exercised their discretion against the plaintiff by refusing leave to issue and serve out of the jurisdiction a writ that seeks that remedy. Equally, they have been reluctant to decline jurisdiction merely because a defendant has in a foreign court already begun proceedings for a negative declaration. In Convention cases, however, the English courts have recently confirmed that stricter rules apply, in that they have no discretion to refuse relief to a plaintiff seeking a negative declaration, except in the very exceptional cases where the plaintiff's conduct is frivolous or vexatious.

Whether a foreign court in a non-Convention country is the *forum conveniens* of a dispute involves considerations of policy and judgement different from those involved in the Convention test of whether a course of conduct is frivolous or vexatious. Under the Convention rules, unless a claim for a negative declaration has no arguable grounding in the Convention at all it may proceed even though a foreign court may on one view be the more appropriate forum for the dispute.

The English courts have often in non-Convention cases appeared to come close to the view that a finding of *forum-shopping* of itself is sufficient to lead to the rejection of a claim for a negative declaration. At the moment, a plaintiff in a Convention case would appear to stand a better prospect of bringing a pre-emptive action for a negative declaration in England than he would in a non-Convention case.

CHAPTER 7

FROM INSTRUCTING LAWYERS TO THE COMMENCEMENT OF PROCEEDINGS

This chapter describes the steps which may need to be taken before issuing proceedings.

A. INTRODUCTION[1]

There is generally a large amount of work to be done between the instruction of lawyers and the commencement of proceedings to ensure that when your writ is issued you and your lawyers have as good a knowledge as possible of the facts and issues that will be relevant at trial. This groundwork may also put you in a position to negotiate an early settlement.

Remember that a corporation cannot take any step in High Court litigation, nor make representations in court, through its officers or staff: only solicitors can be "on the record" for a corporation. There is no corresponding rule, however, in the county court.

B. INSTRUCTING LAWYERS

The division of the English legal profession between solicitors and barristers (or "counsel") and their respective roles are explained in Chapter 3. Your initial contact (and all direct contact throughout the case) will usually be with your solicitor, who will involve counsel when appropriate.

Usually the most efficient way of instructing solicitors is to attend an initial meeting. The person within your organisation with the most factual knowledge of the dispute should attend together with anyone to whom authority to deal with the dispute has been delegated and anyone else who may have an in-depth understanding of your or your opponent's position.

It will often be helpful to send copies of the key documents to your solicitor

1. This chapter, and this Guide in general, deal mainly with High Court actions, but draw attention to the main differences between the two procedures. See Chapter 28 for a brief, separate description of county court procedures.

in advance of the initial meeting. Wherever possible, you should bring all of your files of papers to the meeting so that further papers can be made available should your solicitor ask for them. If the volume of paperwork makes this impracticable, your solicitor will give you guidance as to what other documents or categories of document he will need you to provide to enable him properly to consider and prepare your claim.

Your position may be damaged if important documents do not come to light until later in the litigation.

At this stage, your lawyers will be able to analyse at least on a preliminary basis the most relevant causes of action and defences available to you, the most appropriate remedies and the strength of your position. In some circumstances it may be sensible to take counsel's advice at the outset.

While the most usual remedy is an award of money to compensate the plaintiff for loss suffered as a result of the defendant's action, in some circumstances there may be another available remedy (such as an injunction,[2] an order for specific performance or a declaration as to the rights of the parties[3]) which may better suit the plaintiff's commercial objectives.

Thought should also be given prior to the issue of proceedings to the identity and standing of the defendant. In particular, the following investigations should be considered:

— Searches may be carried out at court and at Companies House (where the public records of companies are held) to ensure that the proposed defendant is not bankrupt or subject to liquidation proceedings. There is little point in issuing proceedings against parties who will be unable to meet judgments against them.
— Consideration needs to be given as to how service will be effected on the defendant. If the proposed defendant is not resident in England it may be necessary to seek the leave of the court to effect service of proceedings in another country.[4] Full details of the defendant's address are required and, in the case of corporate defendants, the registered office will need to be checked and verified.

As litigation, if it ensues, may last for some two or more years, during which time memories will fade and witnesses may die or be dismissed from employment, it can be very helpful to take at least preliminary statements at an early stage from each of the key potential witnesses. What the witnesses say at trial is often just as important as the contents of documents (which rarely

2. See Chapter 10.
3. See Chapter 23 for a discussion of the remedies generally available.
4. See Chapter 6.

give the whole picture), which is why your solicitors will wish to talk to them as part of the preparation for the issue of proceedings.

It is often impossible to give a reliable indication at the outset of the eventual cost of the litigation (because of the difficulty of predicting how the case will develop), but your lawyers will be able to provide you with rough estimates which should enable you to assess the commercial and financial risks of embarking on court proceedings and will explain the financial implications to you and consider whether there is any way to bring the case to a speedy and cost-effective conclusion (such as by an application for summary judgment[5]).

C. LETTER BEFORE ACTION

Although not "compulsory", by convention (and so as to avoid any unnecessary costs exposure) the first procedural step in litigation is usually the sending of a formal letter by the plaintiff's solicitors to the defendant or his solicitors setting out the factual and legal bases of the claim and the remedies sought. It will go on to ask that the remedy be provided within a short period, typically seven or 14 days from the date of the letter. Because this letter will form the basis of the action and may be referred to at trial, it is very important that it is factually accurate and carefully considered.

In circumstances where it would have been open to the plaintiff to write a letter before action but he chooses not to do so and simply issues proceedings without prior warning, it is possible that he will later be penalised in costs.[6]

D. INVOLVING COUNSEL

In some cases, your solicitor may himself draft the formal statement of your claim which will be included in the writ or served later on the defendant, without involving counsel. In many cases, however, counsel will be instructed to draft these formal legal documents and, where the facts or law involved are particularly complicated, you may be asked to attend a meeting with him and your solicitor to answer any questions which they may have and to take advice on the merits of your claim.

E. PRELIMINARY APPLICATIONS

In some circumstances it is necessary or sensible to seek the leave of the court before proceedings are issued. As mentioned above, it may be necessary to seek

5. See Chapter 12.
6. See Chapter 24.

leave before issuing proceedings against a foreign defendant. More detailed consideration of this topic will be found in Chapter 6. Other examples are proceedings against a company that is in administration or that has been put into liquidation by the court, which may not be commenced without leave, or actions on behalf of trustees who may want the sanction of the court for the expenditure of trust assets.

CHAPTER 8

FROM THE COMMENCEMENT OF PROCEEDINGS TO THE CLOSE OF PLEADINGS AND THE GIVING OF DIRECTIONS FOR TRIAL

This chapter explains the steps to be taken to launch proceedings in the relevant court and explains the initial procedures involved. Two charts showing the main steps in High Court and county court proceedings appear on pages 60 and 61.

A. INTRODUCTION

For most commercial disputes, there is a choice of two courts in which proceedings can be commenced: the High Court and the county court.[1] The High Court is based in London and also has a number of regional centres. The county court has a large number of local centres and, whilst having wide jurisdiction, tends to deal with smaller cases.

Although there is a choice of where to start proceedings, the courts have the power to transfer a case begun in the High Court to the county court, and vice versa. As a general rule of practice, the High Court deals with disputes involving in excess of £50,000 and the county court deals with disputes involving less than that sum, unless the case is one of unusual complexity. There is, however, provision for the Central London County Court to determine disputes worth up to £200,000.

Generally, the High Court offers greater freedom to the parties to control the procedure than they have in county court actions. In the High Court it is usually possible to make applications in person to the court's administrative departments and this gives much greater flexibility when, for example, obtaining a hearing date, or entering judgment in default (see section B, below). In the county court, much administrative business is done by post, and there is often a slow response to correspondence or applications.

Whilst nowadays the jurisdiction of the High Court and the county courts is often co-extensive, there are certain cases that must be brought in the county court. These mainly relate to personal injury claims where the sum in issue is

1. See Chapter 6 for a discussion of the question of when the English courts have jurisdiction to hear claims involving a foreign defendant.

less than £50,000. Conversely, some cases (for example judicial review and defamation cases) must be begun in the High Court.

Even if it is likely that a case will eventually be judged in the county court, it can be advantageous to begin proceedings in the High Court. For example, the administrative procedures of the High Court tend to be more efficient and High Court proceedings tend to be taken more seriously by defendants than do county court proceedings.

> *In many cases for simple debts, the action may be begun in the High Court even though it would inevitably be tried in the county court. This is because of the greater opportunities for obtaining a default judgment in the High Court.*

The procedure for the High Court and the county courts is similar but not identical and the more important differences that are referred to below should be borne in mind.

B. ISSUE OF PROCEEDINGS

High Court

Proceedings are usually begun in the High Court by the issue of a writ.[2] A writ is drafted by the plaintiff's solicitors or counsel and to be valid must be issued by the court. This involves the payment of a court fee and the writ being stamped and entered in the court's records. It is important to remember that it is the date of the issue of the writ that determines whether the claim has been brought in time for the purposes of any relevant statutory or contractual time limits.

In most cases, a writ is only valid for four months from the date of issue and must be served within this period, although in limited circumstances its validity may be extended by order of the court.

The writ must either be "generally indorsed" with a brief description of the plaintiff's claim sufficient for the defendant to know what is alleged, or be indorsed with a detailed *Statement of Claim*.[3] (If the writ is not indorsed a detailed Statement of Claim, the plaintiff must serve one within 14 days of the defendant acknowledging service of the writ, the procedure for which is dealt with in section D.)

2. Most commercial actions are begun by writ, but there is an alternative procedure applicable to matters such as trust and probate claims, in which the proceedings are begun by an Originating Summons. The procedure in these cases is different from that in writ actions, and a short description of their main features is set out in Chapter 26.

3. Bear in mind that the court file on which the writ is placed is subject to public inspection. Some litigants take tactical advantage by pleading facts and matters that they hope will embarrass their opponent when the Press gives them publicity.

County court

Proceedings are commenced in most cases in the county court by the issue of a Summons (or an Originating Application—see Chapter 28). As with a writ issued in the High Court, the Summons is drafted by the plaintiff's solicitors or counsel and needs to be entered formally into the court's records to be valid. The Summons has to contain a reasonably detailed statement of the plaintiff's claim.

There are two main types of action in the county court: the *default* and the *fixed date* action. The former is used in money claims; the latter for cases involving, for example, a claim for possession of property.

— A default action can be begun in any county court, usually the one which is nearest or most convenient to the plaintiff, but cases involving claims for a *liquidated*[4] sum are automatically transferred to the court in which the defendant resides, if a Defence is filed. Claims for *unliquidated* damages are not automatically transferred, but may be so on application by the defendant.

— Fixed date summonses must be issued in the county court where the defendant resides or where the cause of action arose.

C. SERVICE

Service of proceedings is the process by which the writ or Summons is formally delivered to the defendant.

There are various rules setting out which methods of service are acceptable[5].

— It is very common for service to be effected by delivering the writ or Summons to the defendant's solicitors provided they have agreed in advance that they will accept service.

— If service is not effected through solicitors, an English company ought to be served by delivering the writ or Summons to its registered office. It is not sufficient merely to deliver the writ or Summons to any place of business of the company.

— An individual can be served either personally, or by posting or delivering the writ or Summons to his usual or last known address.

If a non-English corporation has a place of business in England, it is required to register with the Registrar of Companies the name and address of the person

4. A claim is for liquidated damages if the amount in issue is defined by or is capable of calculation by reference to a formula agreed by the parties before the dispute arose: for example, claims for rent where the rent is agreed as a fixed sum per week or month. Unliquidated damages are assessed by the court.

5. See Chapter 6, section G for an explanation of the procedures involved in the service of proceedings overseas.

on whom proceedings can be served. Where a corporation has failed to do this, service can be effected by leaving the writ at an established place of business of the corporation in Great Britain.

— A writ may not be served by fax.

Generally, the date of service is the date on which the relevant court documents are received by the defendant (or his solicitors). Where, as is usually the case, a plaintiff cannot prove the exact date of receipt, the court will assume that the writ was served on a particular date that is calculated in accordance with set rules. These include the following:

— Where the writ or Summons is posted by first-class post to an English company, service is assumed to take place on the second working day after the date of posting.
— Where the writ or Summons is served on an individual by posting by first-class post or by inserting it through the individual's letter box, service is assumed to take place seven days after the date of posting or insertion.

Some county courts will include with the Summons a note stating the date on which service is presumed to take place. Other county courts will include a note stating that the date of service is to be calculated by reference to the date of the postmark on the envelope enclosing the Summons. It may, therefore, be important to retain the envelope as well as the documents enclosed in it.

In the High Court, service is usually carried out by the plaintiff's solicitors; the court itself will not effect service. In the county court, service can be carried out by the plaintiff's solicitors but, unless the court is notified that this is intended, service will be carried out automatically by the court.

D. ACKNOWLEDGMENT OF SERVICE

In High Court proceedings, the defendant must within 14 days of the service of the writ enter at court an *Acknowledgment of Service*. By doing so he will register his acceptance of the jurisdiction of the court to hear his case,[6] and indicate whether he intends to defend the action.

6. When he does not accept the jurisdiction of the court over him, he ought still to serve an Acknowledgment of Service, but thereafter he should issue a Summons by which he contests the jurisdiction. If he follows this procedure, his Acknowledgment of Service will not constitute a submission to the jurisdiction. He ought not to serve a Defence or take any other step in the proceedings inconsistent with his contest to the jurisdiction. See Chapter 6, section F for a fuller discussion of this topic.

The time limit is extended where the writ has been served in a country other than England or Wales.

If the defendant fails to file an Acknowledgment of Service within the prescribed time, he may do so later but runs the risk that the plaintiff may first enter *judgment by default*. He may do this by swearing and presenting to the court an affidavit of service and a request for judgment. Depending on the nature of his claim, the plaintiff may obtain judgment for a specified sum, or for damages to be assessed by the court at a later date.[7]

If the defendant does serve an Acknowledgment of Service within the time prescribed or before the plaintiff enters judgment, he must then serve a Defence in the manner described in section E, below.

— Note that in the county court there is no equivalent to an Acknowledgment of Service. The possibility of obtaining a judgment in default of Defence in the county court is described in the next section.

E. DEFENCE

High Court

A detailed written *Defence* must be served either within 28 days of service of the writ or within 14 days of service of the Statement of Claim, whichever is later. It is possible to extend this time limit by agreement between the parties' solicitors. If agreement cannot be reached, an application to court can be made on one day's notice to seek an extension. The normal practice is for the initial time limit to be extended at least once by agreement.

As is the case with failure to acknowledge service of proceedings, failure to serve a Defence within the time specified enables the plaintiff to obtain from the court judgment by default. Although such judgments may be set aside, this is only on application by the defendant, and such an order will not be made unless the court is satisfied either that the judgment was irregular, for example, that the writ was not properly served, or that, if the judgment was regular, the defendant has shown on affidavit that he has a proper defence: the court will not set aside judgment unless there is some real point in doing so and will not do so where, for example, the plaintiff could apply successfully for summary judgment under Order 14.[8] *It is therefore vital that these time limits are observed.*

If the defendant also has a claim against the plaintiff (which is referred to as a "counterclaim"), the Defence should preferably be served together with a pleaded Counterclaim. As is shown in Chapter 9, such a pleading is, in effect,

7. See section E for a description of the procedure for applying to set aside a judgment by default.
8. See Chapter 12.

a claim in its own right and puts the plaintiff in the action under similar obligations in respect of the Counterclaim as the defendant is under in respect of the claim.[9]

County court

In the county court, whilst there is no separate requirement to acknowledge service of a Summons, the defendant must serve a Defence within 14 days. If, in a *default* action, or certain fixed date actions, he fails to do so, the plaintiff may enter judgment for a fixed sum, or for damages to be assessed, or for such other relief as may be appropriate. In *fixed date* actions (including those relating to recovery of land or delivery of goods) there is no default procedure, and the plaintiff must still prove his case before obtaining judgment.

> *The problems associated with obtaining judgment by default in the county court (which are exacerbated by administrative delays caused by the requirement to make such applications by post) represent one of the chief drawbacks to county court litigation, and explain why many actions that ought to be begun in the county court by reason of the amounts in issue are started in the High Court.*

The time limit for service of the Defence can be extended by agreement. In the absence of agreement, it is possible to apply to the court for an extension. However, the procedure for making such an application may differ from one county court to another. In some courts, procedural difficulties will make a court application an unattractive option.

F. REPLY AND DEFENCE TO COUNTERCLAIM

High Court

The plaintiff is entitled to serve a written Reply to the Defence. This will only be necessary where the Defence raises factual matters not covered in the writ and Statement of Claim. However, if the Defence includes a Counterclaim, it is essential for the plaintiff to serve a Defence to Counterclaim. If he does not, the defendant may obtain judgment on the Counterclaim by default, in the same way as may the plaintiff in the original action.

The time limit for service of the Reply and Defence to Counterclaim is 14 days from the service of the Defence, although, once again, this time limit can be extended by agreement or court order.

Provision is made for the service of further pleadings, but this is seldom followed.

9. There is no requirement, however, for an Acknowledgment of Service.

County court

The rules of court do not require the service of a Reply, but it is permissible to serve one. It is, however, usual to serve a Defence to Counterclaim.

G. FURTHER AND BETTER PARTICULARS

The Statement of Claim, Defence and Reply and Defence to Counterclaim are together called "the pleadings". Any party to proceedings may seek additional details of the other side's pleadings. These are known as "Further and Better Particulars". Further and Better Particulars can be very useful in clarifying the other party's position where it is not clearly set out in his pleadings. They may also be a useful tactical weapon where it will be a time-consuming and costly exercise for an opponent to collate all the relevant information. If the other party does not provide the particulars voluntarily, then an application can be made for a court order forcing him to provide them. The court will require a party to provide such particulars which it thinks are necessary to explain the nature of his case. However, it will wish to ensure that an application is not being used to exert pressure on the party rather than to provide necessary clarification of uncertain matters.

H. AMENDMENT OF THE WRIT AND PLEADINGS

The rules of court generally allow a party to make at any stage (even during the trial) *amendments* to the writ or pleadings. Often, these will be agreed to by the other parties but, if that is not possible, an application must be made to court for an order permitting the amendments. This is usually granted on terms that require the party amending to bear the costs of any consequential amendments made by his opponent.

> *Note that it is not possible to amend to introduce claims that are time-barred: there is no rule whereby the issue of proceedings extends time for any later amendments.*[10]

I. JOINDER OF OTHER PARTIES

A party, usually the defendant, may join into the action other parties not originally sued. For example, a defendant may by Counterclaim bring an action not only against the plaintiff but also against a new party; or he may bring *third party* or *contribution* proceedings against those who he claims are

10. In order to amend to introduce a claim that is time-barred, it is necessary to come within one of the rules referred to in Chapter 4, section C.

equally or to some degree responsible for the plaintiff's losses. Such steps may be taken at any stage in the action, but the leave of the court is required unless they are taken within the time prescribed for the service of the Defence.[11]

J. DIRECTIONS FOR TRIAL

After the parties have served their pleadings, the next stage is for the court to give directions setting a timetable for the preparation of the case for trial. The exact directions required will vary depending on the nature of the case. They will tend to deal with such matters as discovery, witness statements and experts' reports (all of which are dealt with in more detail in later chapters).

High Court

In the High Court (except in personal injury claims), the plaintiff is required to make a specific application to the court for directions. There can often be a delay of several weeks before that application is heard, by which time it is common for many if not all of the directions to have been agreed by the parties' solicitors.

Although historically the Summons for Directions was intended to be an important stage at which the court would take stock of the case, in practice the court usually accepts whatever the parties have agreed, and does not interfere with that agreement. An opportunity for the court to influence the direction of a case is therefore often lost.

Recently, the judges in the High Court have developed a closer involvement in cases, especially by the encouragement of the system of "Pre-Trial Reviews". This is different from the Summons for Directions and involves the judge (appointed in major cases to deal with pre-trial matters) imposing a greater discipline on the conduct of the case by, for example, curtailing discovery and, generally, ensuring that the pre-trial preparations are as cost-effective and purposeful as possible.

County court

In the county court, it is not usually necessary to make an application for directions because its rules often provide for specific directions to apply automatically. These require most of the preparations for trial to have been completed within 12 to 14 weeks of service of the Defence. In some cases, there will be a Pre-Trial Review, which is similar to a Summons for Directions.

11. The nature of these and other similar proceedings is explained in Chapter 9.

K. SUBSEQUENT PROCEDURES

The initial stages of the action are now completed. There is a "joinder of issue" between the parties, who must now attend to the detailed preparations for trial. These are explained in the following chapters.

COMMENCEMENT OF PROCEEDINGS

HIGH COURT GUIDE

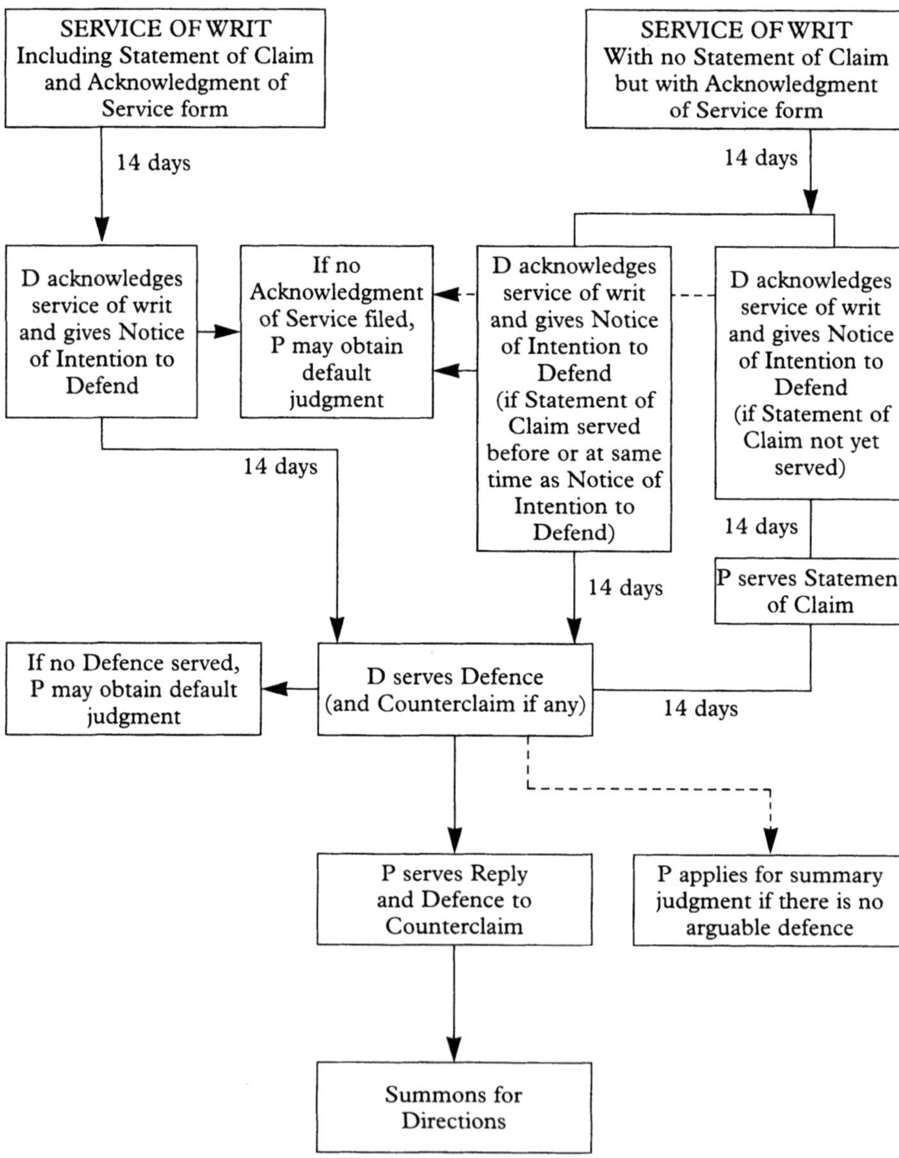

NOTE: the time limits stated above for service of Statement of Claim, Defence and Reply are commonly extended by agreement or by court order.

COMMENCEMENT OF PROCEEDINGS

COUNTY COURT GUIDE

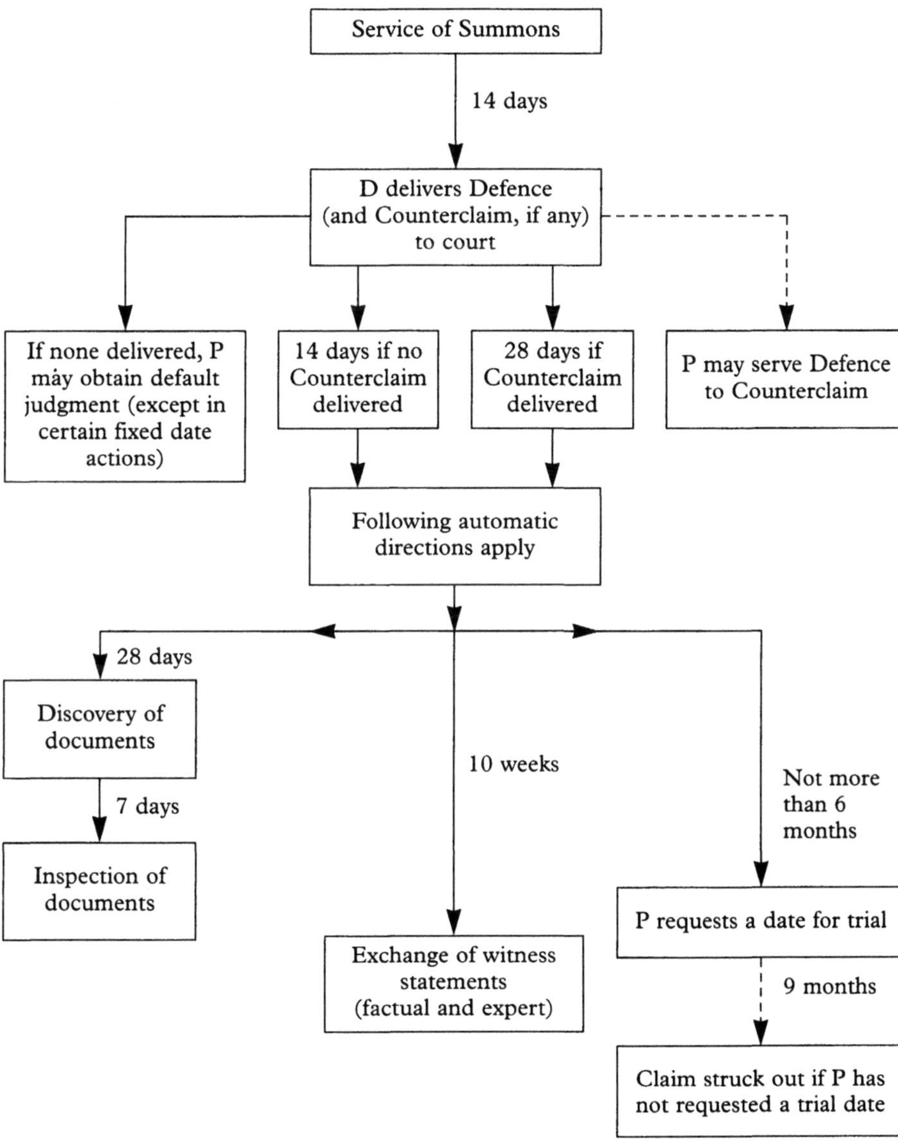

NOTE: This chart does not deal with actions commenced by Originating Application or by Petition.

CHAPTER 9

SET-OFF, COUNTERCLAIM, CONTRIBUTORY NEGLIGENCE, THIRD PARTY AND CONTRIBUTION PROCEEDINGS

This chapter describes the rules relating to various types of cross-claim and similar proceedings.

A. INTRODUCTION

A defendant has a number of alternative lines of defence and/or attack in addition to advancing a straightforward defence to the plaintiff's claim.

- He can raise a *cross-claim* against the plaintiff, which is known as a *counterclaim*, and which, depending on the circumstances, may itself represent a defence (known as a *set-off*) to the plaintiff's claim.
- In some circumstances, the defendant can claim a reduction in the amount for which he would otherwise be liable, on the ground that the plaintiff's own fault *contributed* to the damage which he suffered.
- The defendant can attack a person other than the plaintiff, whether or not that person is already a party to the proceedings, by seeking from that person a *contribution* or *indemnity* or other appropriate relief. Such claims give rise to what are known as *third party* or *contribution* proceedings.

B. SET-OFF AND COUNTERCLAIM

If the defendant has a cross-claim against the plaintiff, he should, if it is a quite separate cause of action from the plaintiff's claim against him, plead it as a counterclaim in the plaintiff's action. However, in some cases, for example where the facts giving rise to the cross-claim are closely related to those on which the plaintiff's claim is based or where the cross-claim is for a simple debt, the cross-claim may also be relied on as a set-off, which provides a defence to all or part of the plaintiff's claim. Normally, in such a case, the claim will be pleaded both as a set-off and a counterclaim.

Examples

P sues D for £10,000, being the value of unpaid invoices in respect of goods sold by P to D. D admits that the invoices are correct, but says that the goods are defective and that he has sustained a loss of £15,000 as a result. D may rely on his cross-claim, both as a defence of *set-off* to P's claim (because of the close relation between that claim and the cross-claim) and as an additional *counterclaim* against P. If D's cross-claim succeeds, P's claim against D, although admitted by D, will not result in any payment to P (because of the set-off) and D will obtain judgment against P for £5,000 (the difference between P's claim and D's cross-claim). If, on the other hand, D can only establish a loss of, say, £5,000, P will recover £5,000 and D will recover nothing.

P sues D for damages of £100,000, alleging a failure by D to perform a contract for the supply of goods which P had sub-sold at a profit. D defends on the basis that no such contract was ever concluded with P. In addition, D says that he has a cross-claim against P for damages of £150,000 arising from a breach by P of a separate and unrelated contract. D's cross-claim does *not* create a set-off which can be pleaded as a defence (because the claim and cross-claim are unrelated), but it can nevertheless be relied upon as a *counterclaim* in the proceedings issued by P. P's claim and D's cross-claim, although unrelated, are then dealt with under the umbrella of the proceedings issued by P.

The distinction between cross-claims which give rise to a defence and those which give rise only to a counterclaim is particularly important in the context of summary judgment,[1] because it is necessary to show an arguable defence to a claim in such circumstances and a counterclaim will be of little avail.

Note also that the question of whether a cross-claim is a set-off or a counterclaim is relevant to the issue of the payment of legal costs in the action. A successful plea of set-off will cause the plaintiff's claim to fail, with the consequent obligation upon him to pay the costs of the action. If the point is only pleaded as a counterclaim, the plaintiff may still win his action and be entitled to his costs of bringing the claim, even if the defendant wins his counterclaim and is also entitled to the costs of the counterclaim. Pleas of set-off are often mis-characterised as counterclaims and vice versa, and care should be taken to avoid this error.

C. CONTRIBUTORY NEGLIGENCE

Where a defendant admits or is held liable for negligence or another actionable wrong, he can ask the court to find that the loss claimed by the plaintiff arose partly from the plaintiff's own fault and that the damages payable by the defendant should be reduced accordingly.

Example

P sues D, a motorist, for damages for personal injury suffered in a road traffic accident. D admits that he was driving too fast, but says that the principal cause of the accident was P's own careless driving. D will cite P's negligence as a defence to P's claim. The court will then apportion responsibility for the accident between P and D and reduce the damages payable by D accordingly.

The court can only apportion liability between P and D on the basis of P's contributory negligence if P's claim against D is or is capable of being made in negligence or otherwise in tort (that is, a civil wrong, other than a breach of

1. See Chapter 12.

contract, for which damages may be awarded). If P's claim can only be made for breach of contract, D cannot ask the court to reduce the damages awarded against him on the basis of P's contributory negligence, although a similar result may sometimes be obtained in contract cases by different means (for example, on the basis of causation of loss).

D. THIRD PARTY AND CONTRIBUTION PROCEEDINGS

The previous section covers the position of the defendant as against the plaintiff, and shows how various defences and cross-claims can be argued. There are, however, situations in which the defendant, in addition to resisting the plaintiff's claim, wishes to pass on to or share with others, who may or may not yet be parties to the action, the losses which the plaintiff seeks to recover, or to make claims of his own against such parties.

The following situations are those that most frequently arise:

— Where the defendant asserts against another party not joined in the action a claim that is based upon a breach of a duty owed by that other party to the *defendant*. In this case, it is not alleged that the other party ever owed any duty to the plaintiff. The defendant defends the plaintiff's claim against him, but brings his own claim against the other. In this situation, the defendant must bring *third party proceedings* against the other person.

Examples

P sues D, a company, for damages for breach of contract in respect of events which occurred before D sold its business and assets to T, a third party. Under an acquisition agreement between D and T, T is obliged to indemnify D for any liabilities incurred by D in relation to the business whether before or after the date of the acquisition agreement. This will not alter whatever liability D may owe to P but D may issue third party proceedings against T seeking an indemnity for any damages D may be ordered to pay to P.

P purchases the shares in a company from D, the shareholder, and brings an action on warranties as to the accounts of the company. D defends, but seeks redress from the company's auditors on the basis of some duty allegedly owed by the auditors to him or to the company but not to the purchaser, the breach of which he alleges caused him to incur his putative liability to P.

— Where the defendant resists the plaintiff's claim, but asserts that if, contrary to his denial of liability, the court should find him liable to the plaintiff, another person as well may be liable to the *plaintiff* and should also have been sued. In this case, the defendant claims not that the others were ever liable to him, but rather that they were liable to the plaintiff, and should meet all or part of whatever is due to the plaintiff. In this case, the defendant can bring *contribution proceedings* if the person to be sued is already joined in the action by the plaintiff;

but if that person has for any reason not been joined, the defendant must bring *third party proceedings* to make the claims.[2]

Example
P purchases the shares in a company from D1, who warrants the accuracy of the company's accounts. Before buying the company, D2, P's accountants, produce an independent report on the company's accounts. P alleges that the accounts were materially inaccurate and sues D1 for breach of warranty and D2 for negligence, claiming that they are both liable for the same damage. D1 and D2 both deny liability to P, but each wishes to claim that, if he is found to be liable to P, the other is also liable in respect of P's loss and should contribute to it. D1 and D2 may issue contribution proceedings against each other. Note that in this situation, neither D1 nor D2 is alleged to have owed any liability to each other independently of P's claim against them: the only issue between them is for how much of any co-existing liability to P they are respectively responsible.

— Note also that particular problems may arise in cases where a plaintiff has entered into complex arrangements with a series of advisers. Thus, a plaintiff may have agreed with a firm of accountants to limit the liability that the accountants may owe to the plaintiff in the event of a breach of duty. That limit will generally bind other advisers to the plaintiff who may not have so limited their liability or even have been aware of the arrangement between the plaintiff and the accountants, and who may therefore be unable to obtain a complete contribution or indemnity from the accountants in respect of liabilities that they, the other advisers, may have incurred to the plaintiff jointly (or individually) with the accountants. This situation poses a potentially very serious problem, which may probably only be catered for by the terms of engagement agreed to before the litigation arises.

E. CHARACTERISTICS OF, AND PROCEDURES IN, THIRD PARTY AND CONTRIBUTION PROCEEDINGS

Third party proceedings must, and contribution proceedings may, be commenced by service of a formal Notice on the third party or co-defendant against whom the claim is made setting out the basis of the claim. The court's permission for the issue of such a Notice is normally required where the person against whom the claim is made is not already a party to the proceedings. No such permission is needed where the person to whom the Notice is directed is already a party to the proceedings.

Where a Third Party or Contribution Notice is served, the recipient must acknowledge service and indicate whether he wishes to defend the claim set out in the Notice.

Thereafter, the third party or contribution claim will usually be treated as a separate action in which the defendant in the main action stands in the position

2. Note that the defendant can, if he wishes, do nothing and await the outcome of the trial before instituting his own proceedings against the other party; but in this case, he runs the risks involving time limits that are explained in section F.

of the plaintiff and the third party is regarded as a defendant. The future conduct of the third party or contribution action will then be decided by the court on an application for directions. Those directions will usually deal with matters such as pleadings, discovery and expert and factual witnesses in the third party or contribution action. The directions will also cover the issue of when the third party or contribution action is to be tried, which will usually be immediately or shortly after the trial of the main action.

In "straightforward" contribution proceedings between joint defendants based upon an alleged co-extensive liability to the plaintiff, no formal procedural steps are necessary to initiate the claim. All that is required is a letter informing the relevant co-defendant that a contribution will be sought from him at trial. In more complicated contribution cases, however, it is probably advisable to commence formal contribution proceedings in order to obtain any directions which may be necessary regarding discovery and evidence to ensure that the contribution claim can properly be dealt with at trial.

F. TACTICAL CONSIDERATIONS: TIMING AND COSTS

Where the defendant thinks that the claim made against him by the plaintiff is strong and that he has a claim for a contribution or indemnity from a third party which he wishes to pursue, it will almost always lead to a costs saving to issue third party proceedings. This is because the main action and the third party action, although separate, will be dealt with largely in tandem, and overlapping issues of fact and law will generally need to be dealt with only once. It may also be advantageous to have involved the third party in the litigation so that he may contribute towards any settlement that may take place.

If, on the other hand, the defendant thinks that the plaintiff's claim against him is weak, it may be better (providing there are no concerns as to time limits, as to which see the following paragraph) to await the outcome of the plaintiff's claim and then to sue the third party only if the plaintiff's claim succeeds. Costs incurred on the third party claim will have been wasted if the main claim from which the third party claim arises fails.

> *It is vital that early consideration be given to whether there are any time limits for bringing third party or contributions proceedings. If what is sought from the third party or co-defendant is a contribution based on co-extensive liability to the* plaintiff *for the same debt or damage, the defendant will usually have two years from the date when the plaintiff obtains judgment or from when the defendant otherwise pays or settles with the plaintiff. In all other cases, however, the time limits depend solely on the circumstances of the third party claim viewed in isolation in its own right and unaffected by anything in the main action. That is, the defendant's claim must be brought within the time limits that would apply if he were suing the other party without himself having first been sued.*

CHAPTER 10

INJUNCTIONS

This chapter explains the law and procedures relating to injunctions. The main steps involved are shown in the chart that appears on page 79.

A. INTRODUCTION

The court's main remedy is an award of money, but sometimes that may not be appropriate or sufficient, and an *injunction* is needed.

B. DEFINITIONS

An injunction is a court order preventing someone from acting wrongfully (a "prohibitory" injunction), or ordering him to put right a wrong he has already committed (a "mandatory" injunction).

Example
P manufactures a range of clothing using his company logo. D launches a competing range, copying P's logo. D may be restrained by injunction from doing so.

In the above example, D may also be forced to "deliver up" to P the infringing goods.

There are two main stages at which an injunction is granted: at trial (a "final" injunction), and when or immediately before the action begins (an "interim" or "interlocutory" injunction). Which is more appropriate depends mainly on the urgency of the claim.

A final injunction is a permanent injunction granted at the end of a full trial, sometimes alone but, more usually, combined with damages or other remedies.

Example
P sues D for damages for breach of contract, and for an injunction to restrain further breaches. The case is not urgent. P claims only a final injunction at trial.

Often, however, in an urgent case the court is asked immediately to grant an interim or interlocutory injunction to cover the period between the issue of proceedings and the trial of the action so as to prevent irreparable damage.

Example
D intends to launch a new product that infringes P's copyright. If he does, P's own business will suffer immediate, irreparable harm. P cannot wait until full trial and will need an interlocutory injunction before any damage is done.[1]

But note that generally the courts will not grant an injunction to restrain the publication of a libel *unless the plaintiff can show that the defendant cannot possibly argue that what he is about to print is true. The courts regard it as an infringement of the right of free speech to prohibit a publisher from printing material which he proposes to justify. If at trial he cannot do so, then the courts will regard damages (usually in the discretion of the jury) as an adequate remedy.*[2]

The grant of both final and interlocutory injunctions is discretionary, and will be refused if damages would be an adequate remedy.

Examples
P claims that D's breach of contract will harm his business. He could not quantify his loss if it did. Damages would not be an adequate remedy. An injunction may be granted.

But if P can quantify his loss—for example, by reference to specific instances—and D can be shown to be of sufficient means, an injunction may be refused.

Injunctions are available in the majority of commercial actions: for example, actions involving insurance issues, bills of lading in shipping cases, contracts for carriage by road or sea, breach of contract, and in many situations involving corporate disputes between shareholders and the board of directors of a company, breach of copyright and passing off.

In all cases, a plaintiff must be able to show that the conduct complained of is *unlawful*: that is, he must always have a claim under one of the established legal heads such as breach of contract, negligence, breach of copyright, or passing off, to take a few examples. It is not sufficient for the plaintiff merely to show that it is "just" or "convenient" for him to have an injunction. Special rules apply, however, to the *standard of proof* in applications for interlocutory injunctions, where the court must decide on the basis of incomplete and untested evidence. As is explained in section D, the court at the interlocutory stage needs only to be satisfied that there is "a serious issue to be tried".

In most cases, an injunction is sought as the principal remedy in the action, but it also frequently happens that an interlocutory injunction is sought as *ancillary* relief in an action, for example, for damages even when no final injunction is sought at trial. Thus, a plaintiff may apply for an injunction to restrain the defendant from taking legal action in other jurisdictions, or from calling a meeting of shareholders of a company that could affect the litigation. Probably the two most important types of ancillary injunction are those granted to restrain the defendant from disposing of his assets in such a way as to defeat any award the plaintiff is likely to obtain if he is successful in an action for debt

1. P may go on to claim a final injunction at a full trial.
2. Note—you *can* get a final injunction in a libel action.

or damages; and a related procedure requiring the defendant to allow the plaintiff access to his property and that the defendant should deliver up items of property to the plaintiff. Orders of the first sort are called "*Mareva*" injunctions after the name of the case in which the principles were first formulated. Orders of the second sort are for the same reason called "*Anton Piller*" orders. Although very similar in some ways to other types of injunction, some important different rules apply. This topic is considered separately in Chapter 11.

Actions for final injunctions generally follow the same procedures as for other actions. But in the case of interlocutory injunctions special, additional rules will apply.

C. THE PROCEDURES FOR OBTAINING INTERLOCUTORY INJUNCTIONS

Some preliminary points

People often speak of "taking out an injunction" in terms that suggest a routine and effortless procedure. This is misleading. You should bear in mind the following points before committing yourself to making an application.

Applications for injunctions are not obtained merely by presenting standard forms to the court. They usually involve intense periods of preparation at short notice, instructing counsel to represent you in court, usually in front of a High Court judge, and often in the face of stiff opposition.

They are almost always expensive, reflecting the amount of work done at short notice. The expense can be in terms not only of your lawyer's time but also that of your executive staff who must frequently drop what they are doing to assist.

Which courts?

Both commercial divisions of the High Court (that is, the Queen's Bench, including the Commercial Court, and the Chancery Division) may grant an injunction in most types of case, and the county court also now has power to do so,[3] but in practice most applications for injunctions are dealt with in the High Court. Applications in the county court, contrary to what might be expected, tend to be no less expensive in their preparation, and most practitioners are, in fact, usually more familiar with applications to the High Court, which is more accessible and carries greater weight.

Both the Queen's Bench Division and the Chancery Division of the High Court have important similarities of procedure, but the chief difference is

3. But not to make *Anton Piller* orders: see Chapter 11. The power of the county court to grant a *Mareva* injunction is limited. The Family Division may also grant injunctions.

that in the Queen's Bench Division the application is made privately ("in chambers"), whilst in the Chancery Division the application is made in open court which the public and the Press may attend. This may or may not be an advantage, depending on what you want to achieve.

Urgent applications[4]

It is vitally important that a plaintiff seeking an interlocutory injunction starts his proceedings as soon as possible after becoming aware that he has a legitimate complaint.

> *Whilst he is allowed a short time in which to investigate the complaint and to marshal his case, he must move with all reasonable speed. If he does not do so the court is likely to say that he has sat on his rights and so is not entitled to an injunction, and although he may later be awarded damages, that may be too late.*

The law's delays are proverbial, but the speed at which the courts will entertain an application for an injunction that is genuinely urgent is impressive. Sometimes, a case is so urgent that the plaintiff will suffer harm that cannot later be remedied if he has to wait even a few days. In such a situation, he may apply to the court for an order without the need to notify the defendant, and even, in extreme cases, without having first issued a writ. The plaintiff must swear an affidavit setting out the facts upon which he relies. Great care must be taken to ensure that the affidavit is correct and complete. The court must be informed of all relevant issues, including any defences on which the defendant, who, of course, is not present to protect his own position, may be known to rely. Failure to bring to the court's attention material issues can lead to the later discharge of the injunction and other penalties, despite the evidence having been assembled at great speed. If the plaintiff is able to make out his case, the court will grant a temporary injunction, which will last for a brief period, usually measured in days, to preserve the position until both parties can be represented. Usually, the order so made gives the defendant the right to apply to the court on short notice to discharge the order.

In cases of absolutely extreme urgency, applications for an injunction can be made at the judge's home out of court hours, and sometimes injunctions can even be granted by the judge over the telephone without his having seen the papers.

> *The court's willingness to accommodate such urgent cases must not be taken advantage of and the applicant must be genuinely confident of his ability later to maintain the injunction when all the evidence is heard. If he cannot do so,*

4. For the sake of simplicity, the procedure dealt with here is essentially that of the Chancery Division but the overall procedure of the Queen's Bench Division is not significantly different.

then he may incur heavy penalties in damages and costs. Failure to do so may result in the injunction later being discharged.

Less urgent applications[4]

If the application is not of such urgency, the plaintiff must give the defendant two clear days' notice of his intention to apply. At the same time, he should serve his written evidence in the form of affidavits supporting his case. Depending upon the time available, the affidavits should be sworn by the plaintiff, or, in the case of a company, by the relevant officers, and must set out in full all the facts and matters relied upon, and be accompanied by all the documents such as contracts, board minutes, internal memoranda, correspondence and other material necessary to prove his case. The defendant will have a similar opportunity to serve evidence in response.

The first hearing of the application will be listed to take place before a judge within two days of notice having first been given. If the hearing is expected to take over two hours (because of the volume of the evidence, or when the legal argument will be lengthy) the matter will be adjourned to a later day when there will be sufficient time to deal with it. Frequently, this is achieved by the defendant undertaking not to take any further steps of the sort complained of until the matter can be determined. If the defendant is not prepared to do so, the plaintiff will have to make his application there and then on the evidence available at that time. The defendant may be allowed only a limited right of reply. If the plaintiff wins, the matter is still listed for a full hearing later. If he loses, he may well decide to abandon his claim.

The hearing of the main application for the interim injunction (or the further hearing that takes place after an *ex parte* application) may take place at some time in the future, possibly not for two or three months, depending on the complexity and urgency of the case and the congestion in the court lists.

In the case of each party, the court will generally assume that what is sworn to be true in the affidavits is correct and will be proved at trial. This is because, with no witnesses being present to testify, neither side at that stage has the opportunity to cross-examine a witness under oath.

The possibility that even if an interlocutory injunction is granted the matter may go to a full trial at which witnesses will be cross-examined must be borne well in mind when preparing the affidavits, which must be comprehensive and frank. Any failure to present the evidence fairly and truthfully at this early stage can put someone in contempt of court and have serious implications later if the court finds that it was induced to grant (or decline) an injunction on the basis of incomplete or misleading evidence. This is especially true in the case of ex parte *applications. This can present a real practical difficulty for someone seeking or opposing the grant of an injunction when working under intense pressure of time.*

Once the hearing of the application for the interim injunction has been concluded, the case continues to a trial in which a final injunction is sought, following the same procedure as in any other litigation.

D. THE GROUNDS ON WHICH INTERLOCUTORY INJUNCTIONS ARE GRANTED

One problem which the court faces when asked for an interlocutory injunction is that it must make a decision affecting the rights of the parties without the opportunity of fully testing the disputed issues or evidence. To deal with this problem, the courts follow a procedure that involves the consideration of a number of what are, admittedly, short-term considerations, and it will not normally consider who is most likely to win at trial.

The court considers the following issues:

- Is there "a serious question to be tried"?[5]
- If so, would damages not be an adequate remedy for the plaintiff were an injunction to be refused? The court's usual remedy is damages, and the plaintiff must show that this usual award is inappropriate to his case.
- Even if the plaintiff can satisfy these two tests, the court then considers whether the defendant would be adequately compensated by a later award of damages if the injunction is subsequently held to have been wrongly granted because of the shortage of time and the absence of full evidence and argument.
- If damages would not be an adequate remedy for the plaintiff, will he suffer greater harm by the refusal of an injunction than would the defendant were an injunction to be granted? This is known as the so-called "balance of convenience" test and is usually the most important of the issues that the court has to decide. Evidence should be presented in the affidavits to meet this issue.
- If the court is unsure of where the balance of convenience lies, then it will generally lean towards preserving the "status quo"—that is, it will make an order that will "freeze" the position until trial.
- If the court is even then still undecided it may as a last resort take into account its preliminary assessment of the relative strengths of each party's case.

It has been held in a recent decision that the rules set out above do not preclude the court from considering the strength of each party's case as one of the main criteria in granting or refusing an interim injunction, and not just as a last

5. The "serious question" is, roughly, "could what P alleges be a claim in law?" (and not, for example, "will he be able to prove the claim?" or "is the case an important one?"). A somewhat stricter test is applied in cases in which P seeks to compel D to do certain acts pending trial than applies where P only wants to restrain D from taking certain steps.

resort, but that this should only be when it is apparent from the evidence that one party's case is clearly much stronger than the other's.

— Sometimes the defendant is able successfully to oppose the grant of an interlocutory injunction if it would in practice have the effect of granting the plaintiff a final injunction before the court can consider all the available evidence. In such cases also, the court may take account of its preliminary view of the strengths of each party's case.

Example
D has invested heavily in the development of, and has just launched, a range of fashionable clothes. If it is stopped, D argues that he cannot re-launch. P thinks the range infringes his designs and wants an injunction. D says an interim injunction would effectively kill his product: by the time the case gets to trial, his opportunity will have been lost, and all his start-up costs thrown away. He may still claim damages if he wins at trial, but the need for a full trial on the issue of the injunction may, in effect, have passed.

The courts may in such a case be reluctant to grant an interlocutory injunction unless the damage to the plaintiff is extensive and outweighs any disadvantage to the defendant, and the plaintiff has shown a very good case on the merits. But if the injunction is refused on this basis, the defendant must be confident of his case before he carries on with the course of conduct, as any sales he makes may determine the damages he must pay to the plaintiff should he lose at trial.

This interlocutory procedure generally leans in favour of the plaintiff. For example, the threshold test "is there a serious issue to be tried?" can often be met with relative ease. But, as the next section shows, there are a number of associated risks that can redress the balance.

E. RISKS AND TACTICS: SOME WORDS OF WARNING

Where an interlocutory injunction is granted the courts require from the plaintiff an undertaking to the court itself to compensate the defendant for any loss he may suffer as a result of the injunction should it later be decided at the trial that the plaintiff was not entitled to it.

Example
P thinks D's business infringes his copyright and harms his reputation. He wants it stopped. D's losses would amount to many millions of pounds. If P gets his injunction but it transpires that he had no right to it, he must compensate D in money for all his losses suffered as a result.

The plaintiff must give evidence of his ability to pay appropriate damages. In some cases, for example where the plaintiff fails to show sufficient means, the court will not accept the undertaking, and the application, although otherwise perfectly in order, will fail.

If the plaintiff cannot afford to pay the damages that may be awarded to the defendant in respect of the plaintiff's undertaking, he may have to put up with the defendant's conduct until trial and, if then successful, claim a final injunction and damages for the loss sustained in the period until the trial.

In this situation, the plaintiff will not have to give an undertaking in damages and therefore incurs no risk of liability to the defendant at trial. But although this course has some attraction, it is not generally regarded as a tactically strong one, and a claim for a final injunction not coupled with an application for an interlocutory injunction may not be taken seriously.

It can, however, also put the defendant in a difficult position if the plaintiff does not seek an interlocutory injunction: if the defendant does not discontinue his dealings, and loses at trial, he may have continued nevertheless to incur liability to the plaintiff, in addition to liability for any damages that may already have arisen, for any damages arising over the period until trial. However, he may not, on the evidence available at the outset, be able properly to assess to what extent he is at risk. If, of his own accord, he stops the conduct complained of and then wins at trial, he almost invariably has no remedy in damages against the plaintiff.[6]

If the case goes to trial and the plaintiff loses, he will usually also have to pay the legal costs of the whole action including the application for his interlocutory injunction, and the defendant's costs.

The plaintiff, having won an interlocutory injunction, must then proceed quickly with his action. If he does not, even if the defendant takes no steps to have the injunction discharged, the plaintiff may later have his case struck out for delay and have to account to the defendant in money for any damage that the defendant has sustained by the grant of the injunction. This can be very significant: it is of great importance, therefore, that the plaintiff, having obtained his injunction, proceeds with his action if he cannot settle.

F. THE SETTLEMENT OF APPLICATIONS FOR INTERLOCUTORY INJUNCTIONS

An application for an interlocutory injunction does not necessarily have to be contested: the defendant may always, if he wishes, compromise the application if he is prepared to agree to the proposed injunction or to offer other terms which are acceptable to the plaintiff. In such a case, the defendant may give *undertakings* to the court instead of submitting to an injunction. The undertakings are formally recorded in an agreed order of the court, and have the same effect as an injunction, and can be enforced against the defendant in

6. In some very rare cases the court has ordered an action for a final injunction to be struck out unless the plaintiff was prepared to apply for an interlocutory injunction until trial and to give an undertaking to pay damages; but such an order is not normally made, and the defendant usually has to make a difficult choice as to whether to continue to do the thing complained of.

the same way: see section H, below. The defendant will usually give the undertakings "without prejudice" to his right later to argue that he was under no liability.[7] In certain circumstances it may be sensible for the defendant to adopt this course, as it avoids the court making early adverse findings and will avoid the costs of a contested hearing.

It is possible and often sensible for the parties to agree at the hearing of the interim injunction to a compromise that will bring the entire case to an end (including the claim for a final injunction). This is often the object of the exercise for the plaintiff, and avoids many of the problems already identified. However, the fact that the court usually makes no ruling on the strengths and weaknesses of the parties' cases can create uncertainties that prevent a settlement being reached at this stage.

G. COSTS[8]

Contrary to what might be expected, if the plaintiff wins an application for an interlocutory injunction, or successfully opposes the grant of one, he will not usually be awarded his costs at once. This is a corollary of the fact that the courts have made an order on the basis of incomplete and untested evidence and will not pre-judge the issue as far as "the merits" are concerned. Accordingly, if the plaintiff's application is successful, the costs will normally be "in the cause"—that is, whichever party wins at the final trial will obtain the costs he has incurred at the initial stage. Alternatively, if the application fails, the plaintiff will probably not be ordered to pay the costs of the interlocutory hearing, provided that he had reasonable grounds for proceedings.

H. THE ENFORCEMENT OF INJUNCTIONS

The penalty for failure to comply with an order for an injunction is generally a fine or, in serious cases, committal for contempt of court.[9] A party in default may also thereby incur liability in damages to the plaintiff.

As soon as the injunction has been granted, it is very important that the order is sealed by the court and served upon the defendant. This is especially true in the cases of *ex parte* injunctions when the defendant has no knowledge of the making of the order and can neither be expected to comply with it nor be in contempt of court until it has been served upon him. The order should ideally be indorsed with a "penal notice" which informs the defendant that he may be committed for contempt of court if he fails to comply with the order. If the order is served on the defendant (or in the case of a company, its officers)

7. This is a consequence of the fact that at the outset the court does not usually consider who is most likely to win at trial. See also Chapter 4, fn 6.

8. See Chapter 24 for a full account of the rules concerning costs in legal proceedings.

9. See Chapter 38.

and the defendant later breaches its terms (or his undertaking to the court) an application can be made for the defaulter to be committed for contempt. Although the court has power to commit a defendant to prison, this sanction is seldom adopted in the first instance of a contempt, and commonly the court will accept the offer of an apology provided that there are thereafter no further breaches. If there are further breaches, the courts take a more serious view.

INJUNCTIONS

PROCEDURAL GUIDE

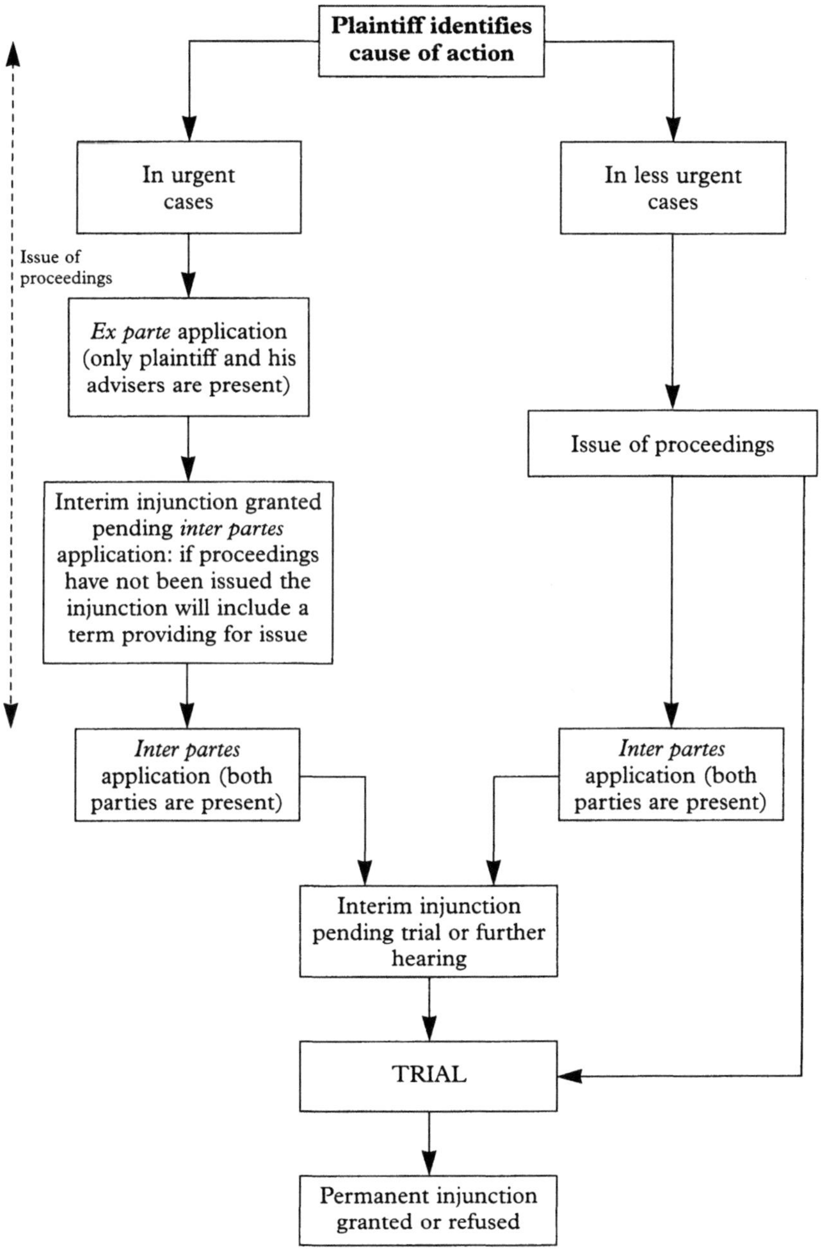

CHAPTER 11

MAREVA INJUNCTIONS AND ANTON PILLER ORDERS

This chapter explains how the courts will, at the outset of a claim, assist a plaintiff in preserving property that is claimed in or is relevant to the action, and prevent a defendant from dissipating his assets or otherwise taking steps that would defeat the purpose of the action.

A. INTRODUCTION

This chapter describes two specific types of injunction that are designed to preserve property and assets pending the trial of an action. It should be read in conjunction with Chapter 10, which explains the general principles of injunctions. The object of this chapter is to describe the special features of the *Mareva* injunction (a "*Mareva*") and the *Anton Piller* order (an "*Anton Piller*") and, to the extent that they depart from or add to the principles set out in Chapter 10, to identify such differences. It should be noted at the outset that both *Marevas* and *Anton Pillers* are orders made in the course of proceedings in which the plaintiff seeks relief over and above the injunctive relief granted by these orders. For example, he may seek the return of property or damages as his main relief. *Marevas* and *Anton Pillers* are orders *ancillary* to the main action; but the procedure for obtaining them has many features in common with the procedure in applications for other interim injunctions.

Marevas and *Anton Pillers* are among the most powerful weapons available to a litigant. *Mareva* injunctions can be obtained against foreign as well as English defendants and can extend either to assets within the jurisdiction of the English courts or to assets anywhere in the world (a "worldwide *Mareva*").

A *Mareva* is designed to prevent a defendant from dissipating his assets or moving them abroad or from one foreign jurisdiction to another, with the intention of defeating any judgment made later in the plaintiff's favour.

An *Anton Piller*, which has been described as "the nuclear weapon of the law", imposes an obligation on the person on whom it is served to allow the plaintiff and his lawyers (under the supervision of an independent solicitor) to search his premises and to seize certain specified items, primarily to preserve evidence which might otherwise be destroyed or removed from the jurisdiction.

To reflect the fact that these remedies are extremely serious, the plaintiff undertakes very significant risks when applying for them. Financial penalties can accrue to the plaintiff if he obtains a Mareva *or* Anton Piller *that is subsequently discharged once the court has given fuller consideration to the matter.*

Marevas and *Anton Pillers* are still relatively new weapons in the legal armoury. Both have been considerably refined over the past few years and recently the courts have laid down new directions governing their operation and future development. These are explained in this chapter.

B. *MAREVA* INJUNCTIONS

Obtaining a *Mareva*

A *Mareva* is initially an "interlocutory injunction"[1] (or "interim injunction") which a plaintiff seeks from the court without warning the defendant (an "*ex parte*" application). As the object of the order is to prevent the dissipation of assets by the defendant, it is important to retain the element of surprise and so prevent the defendant from doing before the application is heard what the application seeks to prevent.

If the plaintiff's application succeeds, the injunction will usually apply until the trial of the underlying dispute, or until further order. The defendant has the right to apply to the court at any time to have the injunction varied or discharged.

The effect of a *Mareva*

As soon as the order is made, the injunction takes effect. The assets of the defendant as specified in the order immediately become frozen and any dealing with them otherwise than in accordance with the terms of the order is potentially a contempt of court.[2]

The standard form of a worldwide *Mareva* injunction provides that a defendant must not:

(i) Remove from the jurisdiction any of his assets which are in England or Wales whether in his name or not or jointly owned, up to a specified value.
(ii) Dispose of or deal with or diminish the value of any of his assets whether or not they are in the jurisdiction or in his own name or jointly owned, up to the value specified.

In practice, no one will know that a *Mareva* has been granted until he has

1. See Chapter 10.
2. See Chapter 38.

been informed. Accordingly, as soon as the order has been obtained, the plaintiff's lawyers must serve a copy on the defendant and on any third parties who hold, or are believed to hold, assets of the defendant: an obvious example of such a third party is the defendant's bank. Once a third party has notice of the order it must freeze any assets of the defendant which it holds, although in the case of banks, various indulgences are normally granted, such as certain rights of set-off against any money which the bank holds to the credit of the defendant.[3]

What assets can be the subject of a *Mareva*?

Usually money is the principal asset which a plaintiff aims to preserve, but the injunction can cover any property and has been used to preserve a wide range of assets including aeroplanes, hovercraft, ships, and the proceeds of a bond.

When can a plaintiff apply for a *Mareva*?

As with any interlocutory injunction, the court will grant a *Mareva* when it appears "just and convenient" to do so. There are seven conditions that must normally be satisfied:

(i) The plaintiff has a cause of action which the English courts have jurisdiction to hear or which is the subject of existing legal proceedings abroad, whether in Convention or non-Convention countries.[4]

Examples

P, a bank, makes a substantial loan to D. P becomes concerned when he later hears that D has failed to meet his financial obligations in respect of certain other lenders, although D has never defaulted under his agreement with P. P further learns that D is in the process of reorganising his assets and has been transferring them to another company outside the jurisdiction. In these circumstances, P would not be able to obtain a *Mareva* injunction because, despite his fears as to the risk of D dissipating his assets, P has no cause of action against D, since D has done him no wrong.

The facts are as above, but if D has failed to pay a number of interest instalments to P, P now has a cause of action against D (for breach of contract) and, as long as the other conditions are also fulfilled, he would be entitled to apply for a *Mareva*.

P, a company incorporated in Canada, brings in Canada an action against D, a resident of Canada with assets in England. P may apply to the English courts for an injunction to restrain the dissipation by D of his assets in England (provided of course that P can satisfy the usual rules).

The jurisdiction to grant interim injunctions ancillary to proceedings in foreign courts will probably be cautiously exercised.

(ii) If successful at trial, the plaintiff would receive judgment for a sum of money (that is, a debt or damages).

(iii) The plaintiff has a good arguable case.

3. See Chapter 36 for an account of special issues relating to banks.
4. See Chapter 6, section L.

- The plaintiff need not show that he is likely to win, but the test is likely to be more difficult to satisfy than in the case of other types of interlocutory injunction.

(iv) The plaintiff has grounds for believing that the defendant has assets within the jurisdiction.

- It is not necessary to establish conclusively that there are assets within the jurisdiction. It will usually be enough to demonstrate circumstances which indicate that such assets do exist. (But see below for an account of the court's approach to assets held abroad.)

(v) The plaintiff has grounds for believing that there is a *real risk* that the defendant will dispose of his assets within the jurisdiction or remove them from the jurisdiction so that they are not available or traceable when judgment is given.

- In considering this matter, the court will take into account factors such as the defendant's conduct and reputation generally, whether he has evaded or attempted to evade other judgments, and whether he is based in a tax haven.

(vi) The plaintiff has made full and frank disclosure of all material facts.

It is extremely important that the plaintiff brings all material matters to the court's attention. This means telling the court not only about the plaintiff's claim but also about the defendant's response or likely response and defence to it. One of the easiest ways in which defendants can discharge Marevas *is by showing the court that the plaintiff has failed to mention all relevant matters. This may well lead to the discharge of the injunction even in cases where the plaintiff's claim, and the likelihood of the defendant dissipating his assets, are strong.*

(vii) The "balance of convenience" favours granting rather than refusing an injunction.

- The court will balance the prejudice to the plaintiff if the injunction is refused against the prejudice to the defendant (and any third parties) if the injunction is granted. Where the balance will lie depends upon all the facts of the particular case.

Example
D has breached a contract with P. The damages P is likely to win at trial are very substantial. P knows that D has certain assets in the jurisdiction which are machine parts which D is about to export for inclusion in machines being constructed abroad. The scrap value of the machine parts is not significant compared with their value to D as essential parts of the completed machines. In this case the "balance of convenience" might well lie against P.

Marevas can also be used in aid of enforcing foreign judgments in the United Kingdom. The first condition, that the plaintiff has a cause of action, will be met automatically in such a case, but the remaining conditions will still need to be satisfied before the injunction will be granted.

In appropriate circumstances, it is possible to obtain a *Mareva* which applies to the defendant's assets outside the United Kingdom. In exceptional cases, this may be possible even where the defendant has no assets in England. In view of the opportunities available for the movement of monies internationally, this is plainly of great importance to a plaintiff, especially the concurrent right to discover details of the nature and whereabouts of the defendant's assets. Because of the possible problems entailed by the exercise of this wide jurisdiction, the English courts impose restrictions on the applicability of such orders, so that they may only affect third parties, such as foreign banks holding the defendant's assets, if the orders are declared valid by the foreign court (see Chapter 36).

It is now possible to obtain a *Mareva* (or other ancillary relief) in aid of English proceedings, or proceedings pending in another country.[5] This was previously only possible in Convention countries, but since 1997 such a remedy has become available in non-Convention cases as well. The court may now grant, whenever it is just and convenient to do so, a worldwide *Mareva* injunction in support of foreign proceedings.

In criminal cases, the police can sometimes obtain a similar injunction over assets which they reasonably believe to be stolen or fraudulently obtained.

What obligations are imposed on the party applying for a *Mareva*?

The plaintiff has to give the court two undertakings, the financial consequences of which could in some circumstances be severe for the plaintiff should his claim against the defendant ultimately fail.

— First, he must give an undertaking to pay damages, should it subsequently transpire that the *Mareva* was wrongly granted, to compensate the defendant for any loss suffered by him as a result of the grant of the *Mareva*.

— Secondly, he must undertake to pay any costs incurred by third parties who hold assets of the defendant and who are therefore to ensure compliance with the order. In the case of a bank which is given notice of a *Mareva* in respect of one of its customers, the process of implementation can be expensive, especially if the bank is required to trawl through its records in order to ascertain what assets it holds on behalf of the defendant. Because of this, the fuller the information that can be provided to the bank, the better.

5. See Chapter 6 for a statement of the relevant law, and above.

Should a third party require any variation of the order, or directions from the court as to how he should proceed, the plaintiff will have to pay his costs reasonably incurred.

Although highly effective in an appropriate case, a Mareva *can be a risky remedy for the plaintiff to invoke given the potential financial exposure under the undertakings in damages and costs.*

What if you are a creditor of someone who is subject to a *Mareva*?

If a debtor's assets have been frozen by a *Mareva*, other creditors will not thereby be disadvantaged. The injunction itself does not give the successful applicant priority over other debtors, nor does it overrule the laws of insolvency.[6] The order of the court granting the *Mareva* will normally include conditions permitting payments out of the defendant's otherwise frozen assets to meet certain liabilities (see below). If the order does not contain wording which covers the debt owed to you, it is possible to apply to the court to seek permission for the necessary payment. In order to succeed, you would have to show two things:

- that, but for the *Mareva*, payment would have been made out of the frozen funds; and
- that there is no ulterior motive for the making of the payment out of the frozen funds.

Example
P has obtained a *Mareva* against D (a company). D is indebted to its parent company, A Limited, under an inter-company debt arrangement. A Limited attends court to ask for repayment out of D's frozen assets. A Limited is well aware that by obtaining payment in full from the frozen assets it will essentially deprive P of the ability to enforce any judgment against D. In these circumstances, the court may consider that an ulterior motive existed and that a variation to the *Mareva* to enable payment of the inter-company debt should not be allowed.

As a creditor, you may well be able to claim from the plaintiff your costs of applying to the court under his undertaking to the court to pay third party costs.

The terms of the court order

Apart from preventing the defendant from disposing of his assets, there are a number of other provisions which will usually be included in a *Mareva*.

- The plaintiff's undertakings in damages and costs will be set out, as will any indulgences permitted to the defendant allowing him to use funds or other assets for certain limited purposes. A failure to include such provisions in an order will mean that the defendant himself will be entitled to apply to the court to vary the order. If granted, it is

6. See Chapter 33.

highly likely that the plaintiff will be called upon to pay the defendant's costs of the application.

— The defendant will, under the terms of a typical order, be allowed to withdraw limited sums to pay for his normal living expenses and to pay for legal advice relating to the injunction and the defence of the underlying claim; he should also be permitted to pay his ordinary business debts.

Other orders which may be granted with a *Mareva*

The court has wide powers to ensure that evidence is properly preserved and it may grant certain other orders in addition to a *Mareva*.

The court may and often will on application by the plaintiff order the defendant to demonstrate the exact nature and extent of his assets, and to this end he may be required to produce an affidavit of means. However, the court will not allow the plaintiff to initiate a "fishing expedition" so as to determine whether in fact the defendant has assets in the jurisdiction; nor will the defendant be forced to make statements about matters that may interfere with his privilege against self-incrimination.[7]

If the plaintiff can show that the defendant is likely to dispose of goods deliberately to deprive the plaintiff of his rights and that the goods in question probably belong to the plaintiff, then the court may make an order for the "delivery up" of the goods. The items will be handed over either to the plaintiff's lawyers or to some other receiver appointed by the court for safe-keeping.

In extreme cases, the court may be persuaded to make an order preventing a defendant from leaving the jurisdiction, although this is a separate order and not, strictly speaking, a part of the *Mareva*.

It is not uncommon for an *Anton Piller* to be combined with a *Mareva*. *Anton Pillers* are examined in greater detail in the following section.

C. *ANTON PILLER* ORDERS

Obtaining an *Anton Piller*

Anton Pillers are most frequently used in the context of cases concerning the infringement of copyright and trademarks, the misuse of confidential information or fraud.

An *Anton Piller* is even more drastic than a *Mareva* since its effect is to order the person upon whom it is served to permit the plaintiff to enter his premises and to remove those assets (usually documents) specified in the order. Its

7. See section D, below.

purpose is to preserve evidence which there are grounds to believe the defendant might otherwise destroy before trial.

> *Obtaining and executing an* Anton Piller *is often an extremely time-consuming, and therefore costly, exercise. It is a drastic remedy, to be used only in the most extreme circumstances where the evidence is compelling. Similar undertakings to the court need to be given as with a* Mareva, *so the financial risks for the plaintiff can be considerable.*

The order is obtained without giving prior notice to the defendant, as with a *Mareva*. Because of its extreme nature, the court will only grant an *Anton Piller* when there is a genuine risk that, if the defendant is given advance warning, he may destroy or remove the relevant material.

The effect of a typical *Anton Piller*

The order is not equivalent to a search warrant, since, if entry is refused, the plaintiff has no right to exercise any force.

However, a defendant who refuses entry will be in contempt of court and the plaintiff is then entitled to apply for the committal to prison of the individual concerned or for any of the other remedies for contempt.[8]

An *Anton Piller* will normally require the person on whom it is served:

- — to deliver up specified documents/materials to the person serving the order; and/or
- — to permit the person serving the order to enter on to the premises to search for and to remove the articles and documents specified in the order; and/or
- — to provide immediately to the person serving the order any information specified in it; and/or
- — not to destroy or part with possession of the specified documents or articles; and/or
- — to keep secret the fact that the proceedings in question have been commenced, usually until the date of the court hearing specified in the order; and/or
- — to swear an affidavit stating that he has no specified articles in his possession and/or setting out his knowledge of the whereabouts of such items.

The order may also require the plaintiff to arrange for the insurance of any items removed.

8. See Chapter 38.

When can an *Anton Piller* be obtained?

In order to qualify for an *Anton Piller*, the applicant has to persuade the court of three things:

- That there is clear evidence to show that the defendant has relevant documents/materials and that there is a real possibility that he may destroy such material beforehand if given prior notice of the application.
- That he has an extremely strong case against the defendant.
- That the damage which is being/will be done in the absence of an order is extremely serious.

It is most important that the plaintiff makes sufficient investigations into the defendant's activities prior to applying for an Anton Piller, *since the provision of inadequate information could result in either the total failure of the application or the subsequent discharge of the order, which is likely to entail considerable costs penalties for the plaintiff.*

The court is extremely unlikely to grant an order if it considers that the motive behind the application is merely to put the defendant out of business.

Obligations of the plaintiff

As with a *Mareva*, the plaintiff must give an undertaking to the court that in the event that an *Anton Piller* is subsequently shown to have been wrongly granted, he will compensate the defendant for any financial loss suffered as a result of the order.

The court will want to be sure that the plaintiff is capable of meeting any such obligation to pay damages and in some circumstances (especially if the plaintiff is a foreign company) he will be required to provide some form of security, either by means of a payment into court or by the lodging of a bond or other appropriate financial instrument.

The plaintiff must give full disclosure of all material facts. The question of materiality is one for the judge and not for the plaintiff. Even innocent failure to disclose relevant details can result in the discharge of the order, with unfavourable cost consequences for the plaintiff.

Service and execution of the order

Once the order has been obtained it usually has to be served upon the relevant individual and executed under the supervision of an independent solicitor, who is familiar with the operation of *Anton Pillers*. If the person receiving the order is likely to be an unaccompanied woman, one of the people attending at the premises must also be a woman. Very strict compliance with the terms of the order is necessary.

Upon service, it is necessary to explain to the recipient:

— the effect of the order and the consequences of non-compliance; and
— that he should contact his lawyer as soon as possible; and
— that he is entitled to apply to court to discharge the order.

If the recipient permits entry on to the premises the supervising solicitor together with those specified in the order (normally the plaintiff's lawyers) can enter and remove the relevant documents and material.

— If a breach of the peace is anticipated, the police are often asked to attend at the premises as well, although if this is envisaged it is prudent to inform the judge granting the *Anton Piller* of such a proposal.

No material which is obtained as a result of the execution of the order may be disclosed to third parties without either the defendant's or the court's authority.

Discharge of the order

The defendant can apply to discharge the order usually upon giving the plaintiff 24 hours' notice.

Orders may be discharged on the grounds that insufficient or inaccurate factual information has been provided by the plaintiff to the court upon their initial grant, as well as disputing the legal grounds on which the order was made.

— The court also retains a power to discharge an order on the basis that production of the documents or assets would result in the defendant incriminating himself. This is based on the so-called "privilege against self-incrimination": see section D, below.[9]

Other options

Anton Pillers may not always be the best remedy for a plaintiff. For example, where the defendant is suspected of counterfeiting goods it might be more appropriate to inform the Trading Standards Officers, who may be prepared to conduct their own raid on the relevant premises.

Although this would undoubtedly result in a saving on costs, one difficulty is that it is not normally possible to gain access to items removed by these

9. This topic also arises in the case of discovery of documents, and is considered in Chapter 18.

officers, which might otherwise have been vital evidence in support of the plaintiff's case against the defendant.

D. THE PRIVILEGE AGAINST SELF-INCRIMINATION

One of the fundamental qualifications to the rule that a party must disclose material to an opponent is that to do so might expose him to the risk of criminal proceedings. The obligation to comply with *Marevas* and *Anton Pillers* could interfere with this privilege. The general rule is that, provided that there is a genuine risk of the defendant being exposed to a criminal prosecution, he need not comply with those parts of such orders as may involve a waiver of this privilege. This could excuse him from the obligation to disclose details of his assets.

This rule threatened at one time to upset the whole basis of *Marevas* and *Anton Pillers*, but it has been abrogated in a number of important respects. Thus, in proceedings that could give rise to certain serious charges under the Theft Act 1968, or which relate to intellectual property or passing off claims, the privilege will not apply (although certain restrictions will be imposed on the use to which material and information disclosed may be put in related criminal prosecutions). However, some defendants in civil fraud cases take the point that they may be charged with being part of a criminal conspiracy (which is not caught by the exceptions mentioned above and in respect of which the privilege has survived), and thereby may still defeat the purpose of *Marevas* and *Anton Pillers*. In such cases, the courts may require the defendant to be informed before the order is executed that he has a right to avail himself of the privilege against self-incrimination and provide that certain parts of the order are only to be executed insofar as the privilege is not claimed. Unless such a provision is included, an order containing provisions likely to require a defendant to incriminate himself is liable to be set aside.

Note, however, that the privilege is against *self-incrimination*, so that, for example, a defendant company that is alleged to be the "alter ego" of a personal defendant must usually answer questions even if the answers may tend to incriminate that person.

CHAPTER 12

SUMMARY JUDGMENT

The courts recognise that it is inappropriate to force a plaintiff to face a full trial where there is no arguable defence or dispute. In such cases, he may apply for judgment without a full trial. This is called "Summary Judgment", and is described below. The main steps involved are shown in a chart on page 98.

A. INTRODUCTION

Not all cases have to be pursued to a full trial. The procedure known as "summary judgment" (sometimes referred to as "Order 14"[1]) provides a cost-effective and speedy procedure for obtaining a judgment in a claim to which there is no genuine defence, and no other reason why there ought to be a trial.

Summary judgment is a remedy that is available only to plaintiffs.[2] Where the defendant considers the plaintiff's claim is bad and wishes to dispose of it quickly, then (unless he can identify a point of law the answer to which will finally dispose of the entire claim—see section G of this chapter) he must apply to have the claim struck out.[3]

In order to succeed, the plaintiff must demonstrate on oath (by filing an affidavit) that the defendant has *no arguable defence* at all: the standard of proof is high and there is little useful purpose to be served by applying for summary judgment in cases where there is a clearly arguable defence. In such cases, the wisest course is to proceed as fast as possible to trial.

The procedure is available in the majority of cases, including claims for a final injunction,[4] but cannot be used for certain defamation claims, or in actions that have not been begun by writ.[5] It used to be the case that proceedings involving claims of fraud could not be subject to this procedure; this rule has now been abolished but it is considered to be extremely difficult to persuade

1. So-named because the rules for this procedure are set out in Order 14 of the Rules of the Supreme Court.
2. Note, however, that a defendant who has a counterclaim may also adopt this procedure in relation to that counterclaim; and see section G, below.
3. See Chapter 13.
4. See Chapter 10.
5. There is a similar procedure for claims for specific performance of obligations relating to property. Such claims are described in Chapter 23.

a court to give summary judgment in such cases, as a defendant accused of fraud has a generally recognised right to have his defence heard on oath at trial.

There is a similar procedure available in the county court: see Chapter 28.

B. TACTICS

If the plaintiff's claim is clearly very strong, an application for summary judgment should be considered at the outset.

A successful application will give the plaintiff an enforceable judgment within a very short time and at relatively low cost.

Merely making the application will send a clear signal to the defendant both as to the merits of the plaintiff's claim and his readiness to pursue it. This may encourage an early settlement without the need for a hearing.

As is explained below, a defendant must swear an affidavit verifying his defence if he is to be given leave to defend. It is often thought to be tactically helpful to a plaintiff to be able to see his opponent's case on oath at an early stage, even if judgment is not given until trial, as the defendant will be committed to the evidence given earlier.

Whilst an application for summary judgment is an effective step in appropriate circumstances, the alternatives and potential disadvantages should not be forgotten.

The principal alternative is insolvency proceedings, which may sometimes provide a more effective procedure for recovery of undisputed debts.[6]

If the application fails, you will have incurred additional expense and, in some circumstances, where, for example, the defendant appeals from any order made against him, the application will have delayed the final determination of the dispute. There is also a risk that the unsuccessful outcome and/or any adverse judicial comments made at the hearing may increase your opponent's confidence in his defence, thereby reducing the prospects of settlement.

C. TIMING

Although such an application can be made at any time after the defendant has

6. See Chapter 33.

acknowledged service of proceedings,[7] it is usually made either before or shortly after the service of the Defence.

Where an application for summary judgment is made, the defendant does not have to serve a Defence (if he has not already done so) until the determination of the summons.

- The plaintiff must decide whether to make the application before or after the defendant has served a Defence. Much will depend upon how confident the plaintiff is that there is no defence to the claim: in some circumstances it may be preferable to delay consideration of a summary judgment application until you have seen what is said in the Defence.
- Because an application for summary judgment effectively freezes the litigation timetable, the progress of the action may be delayed considerably if the application is made and fails. For example, a defendant who fails at this stage may go through lengthy appeals that may seriously delay the trial. You should, therefore, normally apply for summary judgment only when there is plainly no defence.

D. PROCEDURE[8]

The application is made by summons supported by an affidavit stating that there is no defence to the claim. Sometimes the affidavit will be very short, although if a Defence has been served or you know from correspondence what the defence will be, it will usually be sensible to expand the affidavit to say why that defence will fail.

The defendant then deposes in an affidavit to details of the defences on which he will rely or the reasons why a full trial is necessary.

The plaintiff will usually have an opportunity to reply to the defendant's affidavit.

If the defendant's affidavit sets out the facts which support an available defence, there will be little point in proceeding with the application. The court will not usually decide between conflicting accounts of the facts at a hearing for summary judgment.

E. GENERAL PRINCIPLES ON WHICH THE COURT ACTS

If the defendant satisfies the court that he has reasonable grounds to defend

7. See Chapters 5 and 8.
8. A chart detailing the procedural steps appears at the end of this chapter.

the claim, summary judgment will be refused and the defendant will be given leave to defend.

Leave to defend will usually be given if the defence depends on resolving a substantial factual dispute requiring cross-examination of witnesses at trial, especially where the defendant has not had access to those witnesses in preparing his defence. If, however, the defence rests solely on a question of law or the meaning of a document, the court may decide that a trial is unnecessary and determine that question there and then (see section G, below).

The defendant will often plead a *cross-claim* against the plaintiff.[9] He may, for example, admit that he owes the amount claimed from him, but rely on a claim of his own for the same or a greater amount. The effect of a cross-claim of this sort in the context of an application for summary judgment will depend, broadly speaking, on whether the cross-claim is for a debt or damages and on how closely it is linked to the plaintiff's claim.

If the cross-claim is for a simple debt or arises out of the same transaction as the plaintiff's claim, it is a set-off and it will usually provide a defence entitling the defendant to unconditional leave to defend.

Example
P sells goods to D, who refuses to pay for them. D satisfies the court that the goods are defective and that, as a result, he has a cross-claim for damages against P. If that cross-claim equals or exceeds P's claim for the price, the court will give D leave to defend.

If the cross-claim is for damages and relates to an entirely separate matter, it may not be a defence but a *counterclaim*, and judgment may be given to the plaintiff. In these circumstances, however, it is possible for the court in appropriate cases to order that the plaintiff should not enforce the judgment until the cross-claim has been dealt with.

Example
P sells goods to D, who refuses to pay for them. D satisfies the court that he has a cross-claim for damages against P arising out of breach of an unconnected distribution agreement. Summary judgment may be given to P, possibly subject to a stay on enforcement.

The rules relating to set-off do not usually apply to actions brought on cheques or bills of exchange. The courts regard such instruments as equivalent to cash and will not allow a defendant to dispute liability on any grounds other than fraud[10] *or illegality, which has to relate to the obtaining of the cheque rather than to the underlying transaction.*

F. POSSIBLE ORDERS

If the defendant is unable to satisfy the court that the matter ought to be tried, judgment will be given to the plaintiff.

9. See Chapter 9 for a fuller consideration of the nature of cross-claims.
10. There is one other exception, that of "total failure of consideration", but this is rarely applicable.

If the defendant does demonstrate a credible defence, the plaintiff's application will fail and the defendant will be given unconditional leave to defend. The suspension of the usual litigation timetable will then be lifted and the court will commonly give directions as to how the case should go forward thereafter.

If the defendant satisfies the court that he may have a defence, but the court thinks that the case is borderline and the defence weak, then it may impose conditions on the defendant's leave to defend. The most common condition is payment into court by the defendant of all or part of the amount claimed by the plaintiff. The money will remain in court until the dispute has been resolved.

Judgment may be given to the plaintiff, subject to a stay of enforcement pending the hearing of the defendant's counterclaim.

— A plaintiff may also couple his request for summary judgment with an application for an *interim payment*. This differs from a payment into court in that the plaintiff actually receives his money at once, rather than having to wait until the trial of the action. Further consideration is given to this subject in Chapter 15.

G. DETERMINATION OF QUESTIONS OF LAW OR CONSTRUCTION

In some cases, it may be possible to isolate a question of law or a question as to the meaning (or "construction") of a document, the answer to which will determine finally the entire claim.

If none of the facts giving rise to that question are in dispute, either party can apply to have the question answered and the case disposed of straight away.

The procedure for obtaining summary judgment on a point of law or construction is similar to that outlined above, the principal difference being that either party may apply and that both parties must either consent to the use of the summary procedure or at least have the opportunity to argue their case before the court decides the point.

SUMMARY JUDGMENT

PROCEDURAL GUIDE

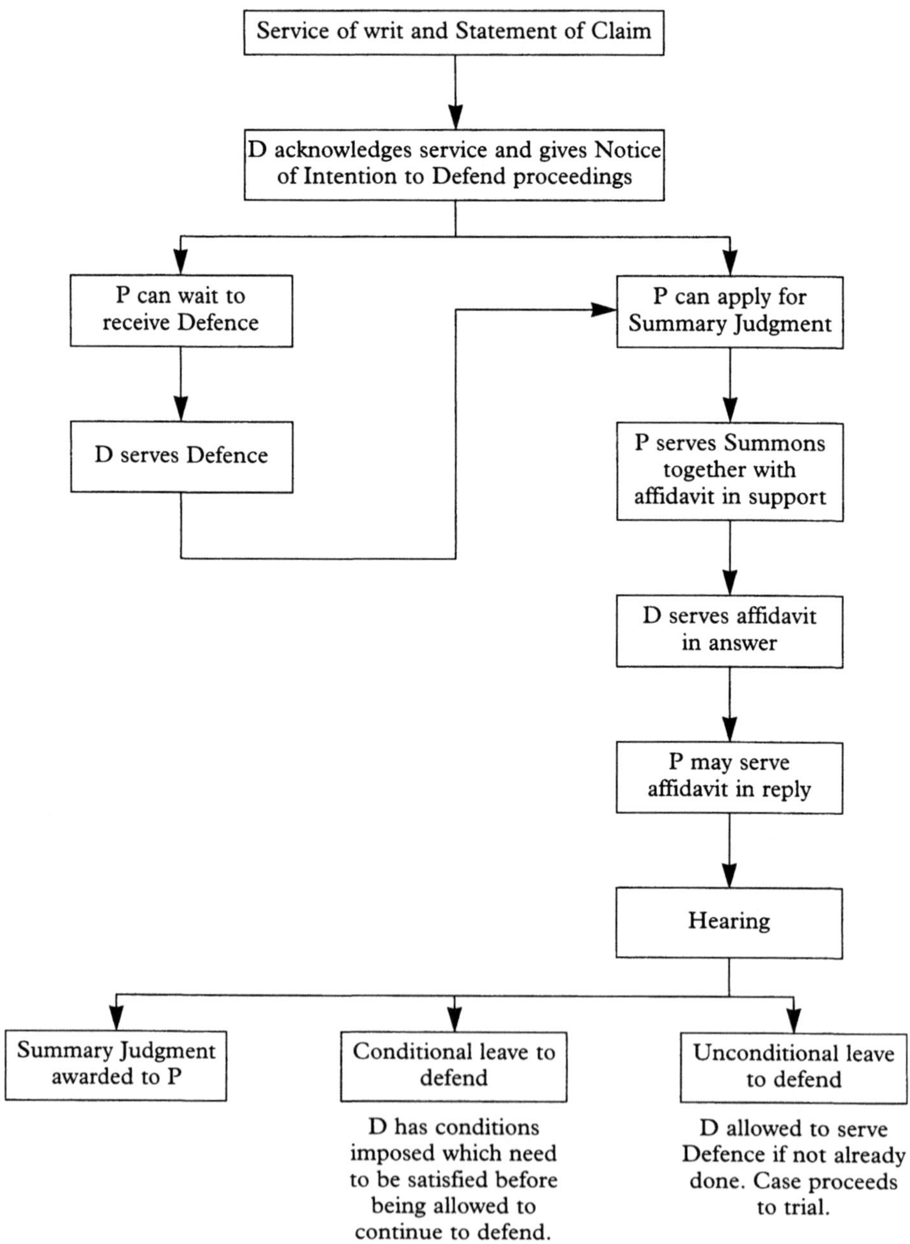

CHAPTER 13

APPLICATIONS TO STRIKE OUT A CLAIM

Chapter 12 describes the procedure whereby a plaintiff may obtain summary judgment in cases where there is no real defence to his claim. The nearest equivalent procedure for a defendant who does not consider that the plaintiff's claim should go to trial is to apply to have the plaintiff's claim struck out.

A. INTRODUCTION

Strike out applications are most commonly made by defendants in cases where they consider that the claim made against them, or a part of it, is bound to fail. As such, they provide a similar remedy for defendants to summary judgment for plaintiffs.[1]

Such applications are not, however, a mirror image of applications for summary judgment. In practice, an order striking out the plaintiff's claim is only likely to be granted in the clearest of cases.

Where there is some doubt in the court's mind, the court will not strike out the claim even if it thinks it very unlikely to succeed. There is no equivalent in a strike out application to conditional leave to defend given in an application for summary judgment. The court cannot give the plaintiff leave to continue with his claim conditional upon his depositing a sum of money in court: a conditional order refusing to strike out a claim will not be made.

B. GROUNDS FOR STRIKING OUT CLAIMS

The defendant may apply to court for an order striking out the writ or the whole or part of the Statement of Claim if:

— it is plain that the pleadings shows *no arguable case in law*: that is, where, even if at trial the facts alleged can be proved to be true, it

1. Note that this is a different procedure from that applicable when the defendant seeks summary judgment on his counterclaim: see Chapter 12.

would make no difference because there would still be no arguable case; or

- the case is *frivolous* or *vexatious*: for example, if the plaintiff is trying to re-open a suit that has already been decided; or
- the claim raises an issue that would *prejudice, delay or embarrass a fair trial*; or
- the case is *an abuse of the process of the court*: for example, the court is wrongly being used as the means of achieving a purpose in which the court cannot or should not be involved or where the plaintiff has been guilty of persistent and deliberate delay.

There is often an overlap between the various grounds for striking out a claim and, for tactical and procedural reasons, more than one ground is usually relied upon.

C. TIMING AND PROCEDURE

An application to strike out a claim can be made at any stage in the proceedings. The application should usually, however, be made promptly and, if possible, before a Defence is served.

Unlike an application for summary judgment, an application to strike out a claim does not automatically suspend any of the procedural time limits for the service of a Defence. Because of this, the defendant will need to seek, either by agreement or from the court, an extension of time for service of his Defence until after the strike out application has been heard if it is brought before he serves his Defence.

The procedure is similar to that for applications for summary judgment.[2] The principal difference is that affidavit evidence should not be filed if the only ground on which the strike out is sought is that the claim shows no arguable case in law. This is because the court must assume that the facts pleaded are correct but even so could not amount to a valid claim in law.

D. POSSIBLE OUTCOMES AND TACTICAL CONSIDERATIONS

As previously stated, an application to strike out a claim, or a part of it, will either succeed or fail in its entirety. There is no middle course. In cases of doubt, the application will be dismissed.

Even where a Statement of Claim is bad on its face, if the defect can be cured by an amendment, the court will usually give leave to amend and allow the claim to continue.

2. See Chapter 12.

Since the usual objective of a strike out application (namely to dispose of a bad claim once and for all at an early stage) is the same as for an application for summary judgment, very similar tactical considerations will apply.[3]

3. See Chapter 12, section B.

CHAPTER 14

PREVENTING ABUSES OF THE PROCESS OF THE COURT: DELAY AND NON-COMPLIANCE

The courts will not generally allow cases to be started after a relevant limitation period has expired, or to be started and then forgotten; nor will they allow either party to fail to comply with their procedural obligations during the life of a case. In such circumstances, application may be made to prevent such abuse of the court's process.

A. REMEDIES FOR DELAY

Limitation periods: starting proceedings

Reference is made in Chapter 4 to the existence of certain time limits, either contractual, equitable or statutory, within which most types of lawsuits must be started. If the action is not begun within this period then, unless some very convincing reason can be made out—and even then, only in certain exceptional cases—the defendant will be able successfully to plead the expiry of the limitation period as a complete defence.

Similar principles apply to a defendant who is counterclaiming. For these purposes, he is in the same position as a plaintiff.

Delay after the start of proceedings[1]

Even where a case has been brought within the relevant time limit, a plaintiff cannot then afford to delay: he must press on quickly with the case, to avoid the risk of being debarred from litigating further.[2] Equally, a defendant or other party must follow the procedures within the time limits set down, at the

1. The procedures are roughly similar in the High Court and the county court, but note that in the latter there is a further rule applicable in some cases under which a claim is automatically struck out where there has been no application to court to fix a date for trial within 15 months of the close of pleadings.
2. In practice, many of the time limits for taking steps are too tight to enable most cases to be prepared properly, and the solicitors frequently reciprocate in extending these periods: but only up to a point, and within reason.

risk of his Defence (and Counterclaim, if he has one) being struck out. This rule applies in two ways.

(i) Delay by either party in complying with interlocutory orders

In relation to interlocutory matters, a persistent failure by any party to comply with an order of the court may be penalised by an order that the action or Defence be struck out. Here, even if there is still time left before the right of action becomes statute-barred (that is, before the time limit for bringing the case has expired), it will not automatically follow that a plaintiff can bring a new action on the same facts: the defendant may still be able to strike out that action as an abuse of the process of the court on the grounds of the earlier delay, if the defendant can show prejudice.[3]

Example
P takes action against D for damages. At the hearing of the Summons for Directions, he is ordered to give discovery within six weeks. He does not. D will apply again on one or more occasions for a further order compelling compliance. If P's delay is persistent and there is no excuse, his claim may be struck out. Although it is possible for a new writ to be issued, that claim may itself be struck out if the earlier delay was serious and prejudicial to D.

This rule applies to both plaintiff and defendant, depending upon who is obliged to comply with any particular order.

There are no hard and fast rules in this situation—much will depend on the history of the person's conduct, and the court has a very wide discretion in the matter to do what it thinks right. In practice, the courts have tolerated considerable delays, and it is rare for pleadings to be struck out. However, the courts are set to adopt a stricter attitude in the future.

(ii) Delay generally: "want of prosecution"

In relation to the case as a whole, different and more clear-cut rules apply. The rationale is that the court will not allow a plaintiff (or a defendant who is counterclaiming) to start an action, force his opponent to set to work, and then go slow, leaving that opponent with the worry and cost of litigation hanging over him indefinitely.

There are three matters on which the court must be satisfied before it will order a case to be struck out for delay:

- That the right of action has become statute-barred since the case began. It is pointless to strike out if the plaintiff could issue a new writ.[4]
- That the plaintiff has been guilty of inordinate and inexcusable delay

3. See Chapter 13.
4. Although, if he did, he might nevertheless be struck out for abusing the process of the court.

in fighting the case. In practice, you will need to show a high level of deliberate delay before the delay satisfies the test.

— Most importantly, that the delay has prejudiced the chance of a fair trial. Usually, this involves showing that key witnesses have died, that memories have faded, or documents have been lost. But in some cases, you can win on other grounds: for example, if you are a professional man with an allegation of negligence hanging over you, you may be able to prove prejudice for that reason alone.

Although you will not be debarred just because you delay the issue of your writ until the very last possible occasion, any later delay in prosecuting the claim, provided it has caused more than minimal prejudice, may entitle your opponent to strike out the claim. You must, therefore, get on with the action as fast as possible.

Delay in litigation is generally a bad thing, because even if your case cannot be struck out, you will prejudice your credibility and prospects of settling, and damage your chances of winning at trial: for example if important evidence in your favour is no longer available or your opponent's finances suffer a set-back in the meantime.

B. REMEDIES FOR NON-COMPLIANCE

During the course of litigation, the parties are subject to duties that must be performed if the case is to be fairly tried. These duties are in addition to the general obligation to proceed with due despatch. For example, there are mutual obligations to give discovery of documents,[5] to serve pleadings[6] and to serve witness statements. The court on application by the party complaining may impose penalties on the recalcitrant party, as follows:

(i) Requiring the party in default to comply with the obligation at risk of his claim or defence being struck out in whole or in part.
(ii) Ordering him to pay the costs of and occasioned by the default.
(iii) Finding him to be in contempt of court.[7]

5. See Chapter 18.
6. See Chapter 8.
7. For a detailed account of the rules of contempt of court, see Chapter 38.

CHAPTER 15

INTERIM PAYMENTS

This chapter describes how the court may order a payment of damages before trial, to protect the plaintiff against possibly protracted litigation. A chart showing the principal steps involved appears on page 110.

A. INTRODUCTION

An *interim payment* is a payment that a defendant is ordered to make to a plaintiff before trial on account of any damages, debt or other sum which may be awarded at trial. The purpose of an interim payment is to prevent or reduce the financial hardship which the plaintiff may suffer by being kept out of his money until a judgment (and possibly until the enforcement of that judgment) that may be some years away. A common example of such hardship is that suffered by the plaintiff in a personal injury action. The procedure may also be used to reduce hardship where a landlord who seeks possession of premises is receiving no benefit from the land despite the tenant remaining in occupation pending the resolution of the dispute. The procedure is capable of applying, however, to any claim for a debt or damages, and is available either in the High Court or in the county court.

B. TIMING

As the purpose of applying for an interim payment is to mitigate the plaintiff's hardship in having to wait for his money, the application should normally be made at the earliest opportunity, that is, once service of the writ has been acknowledged. However, an application can be made at any stage before trial.

Further applications may be and often are made as circumstances and the plaintiff's needs change, irrespective of the success or failure of the initial application.

C. PRINCIPLES

There are three situations in which an interim payment in a claim for damages may be awarded:

— Where the defendant has admitted liability but disputes the value of the claim.
— Where the plaintiff has obtained judgment on liability but the amount of money due has yet to be quantified by the court.
— Where the court is satisfied that, if the action proceeds to trial, the plaintiff would be likely to obtain judgment in a substantial sum.

It is not necessary for the plaintiff to have obtained judgment to be eligible for an interim payment.

In the third of these three situations, an interim payment will not be ordered unless the court considers that the plaintiff is likely to recover *substantial* damages. The meaning of "substantial" depends upon the plaintiff's needs, but the court will not award interim payments of trivial amounts.

Interim payment applications are sometimes combined with applications for summary judgment.[1] Even if summary judgment is refused, an interim payment may still be ordered if the court considers that the defence is borderline or weak and so gives only conditional leave to defend.[2]

If, however, a credible defence is pleaded and the defendant is given unconditional leave to defend, he cannot be ordered to make an interim payment.

In fixing the amount of any interim payment a relevant factor that the court will also take into account is whether the defendant may suffer any irremediable harm that cannot be made good by an eventual repayment. The court will take account of the fact that, even though it thinks it likely that the plaintiff will succeed at trial, there is a chance that the plaintiff will lose (in which case the interim payment will have to be refunded).

There are special rules that apply in relation to *personal injury* actions, where an order for an interim payment will not be made unless the defendant is either:

— insured in respect of the plaintiff's claim; or
— a public authority; or
— a person whose means and resources are sufficient to enable him to make an interim payment.

1. See Chapter 12.
2. Alternatively, and more usually, the defendant may be ordered to pay into court the whole or part of the sum claimed: see Chapter 12.

The making of an interim payment is confidential and will not be referred to, nor be made known to, the trial judge until all issues of liability and damages have been resolved.

D. PROCEDURE

The application is made by summons supported by an affidavit which verifies the amount claimed and the grounds for the application. Where an application for summary judgment is made, the interim payment application will usually form part of the same application.

The defendant may then serve an affidavit of his own setting out any grounds on which he opposes the application.

At trial, the court will make adjustments to the final award to take into account any interim payment, and can in appropriate cases order repayment.

INTERIM PAYMENTS

PROCEDURAL GUIDE

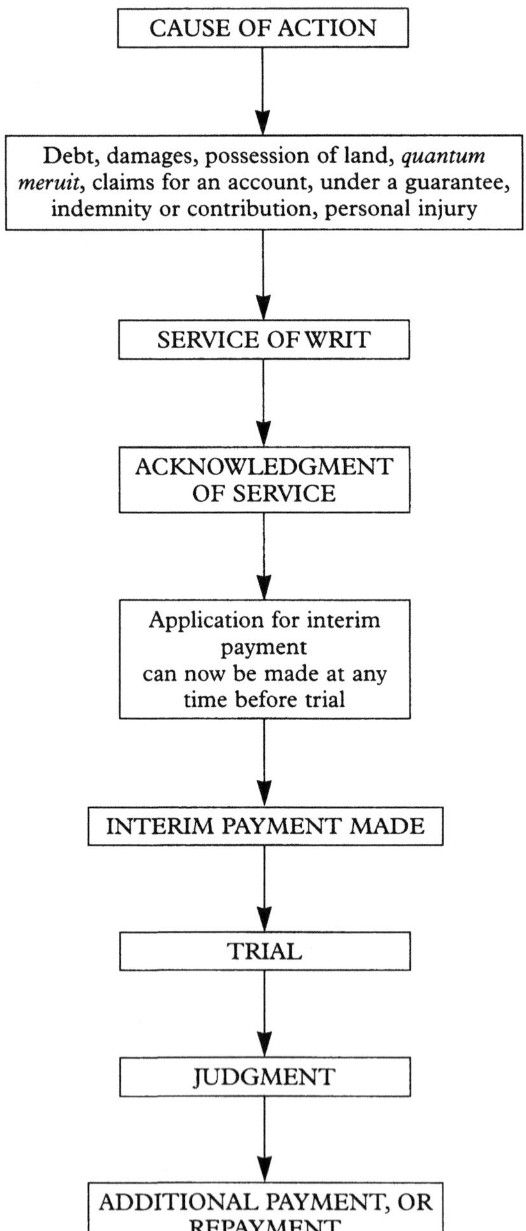

CHAPTER 16

SECURITY FOR COSTS

This chapter describes the rules whereby the courts may protect a defendant from incurring legal costs in certain cases where the plaintiff, if unsuccessful, may be unable to reimburse him.

A. INTRODUCTION

A defendant may, on satisfying certain conditions, obtain an order from the court requiring the plaintiff to give security for any costs that the plaintiff may have to pay to the defendant if the plaintiff loses the case.[1] Security is given by the plaintiff paying the appropriate sum into court or providing it by some other means, such as a bank guarantee.

The court's power to award security for costs is discretionary and it will be exercised having regard to all the circumstances of the case. However, where the likelihood of the plaintiff succeeding, or of the defendant failing, is strong, security for costs may not be ordered.

B. WHEN A DEFENDANT CAN APPLY FOR SECURITY

The most common situations are:

- Where the plaintiff is an individual resident outside the European Union.
- Where the plaintiff is a limited company incorporated in the United Kingdom and/or is resident in another European country and there is reason to believe that it would be unable to comply with an order to pay the defendant's costs.

1. See Chapter 24.

Generally, security will not be ordered against an individual who is resident within the European Union, whatever his means.

Note that it is not necessarily sufficient to satisfy the conditions set out above. The court may still refuse to give security where, for example, the application is being made to stifle a proper claim, or where the plaintiff's lack of funds is the result of the defendant's wrongful conduct, or where there is a co-plaintiff resident in the jurisdiction who could meet an order for costs.

C. HOW A DEFENDANT MAY APPLY FOR SECURITY

Before applying to the court the defendant should send a written demand to the plaintiff with a statement of the costs claimed supported by a draft bill setting out the costs that are estimated to be incurred usually up to and including the stage of discovery of documents or, if that stage has already been reached, until the trial.

If no agreement between the parties can be reached, the application is then made by summons supported by an affidavit verifying the draft bill of costs and the circumstances which give rise to the application.

D. WHEN TO MAKE AN APPLICATION FOR SECURITY

An application for security for costs may in theory be made at any stage of the proceedings.

But any delay in making such an application may be relevant to the exercise of the court's discretion and may be an important factor where it has led, or may have led, to the plaintiff acting to his detriment.

E. THE ORDER FOR SECURITY

The earlier an application is made, the more speculative may be the estimate of the costs likely to be incurred, and the more inclined the court is to scepticism, and to limit the security ordered to be given. It is therefore not unusual for a discount to be applied by the court to any early estimate of costs.

Once the court has decided that security for costs should be given, it then fixes the amount and directs the mode and the time for compliance. The order will also usually provide that the proceedings be temporarily suspended until such security is provided.

Where the court refuses a defendant's request for security and the decision is not appealed, it is final. Furthermore, where an order for security is made by consent, or the application has been unopposed, the plaintiff may be unable to argue that the court does not have jurisdiction to hear further requests for security. It is normally possible for a defendant to make more than one request for security for costs.

F. WAYS OF PROVIDING SECURITY

If the plaintiff agrees to give security, the money is normally paid into an interest-bearing joint bank account opened in the names of the solicitors for both parties. If no agreement can be reached either on whether security should be given or as to its amount, then the court, if satisfied that an order should be made, will direct one of the following methods:

- The *payment into court* of a sum of money: this is the more usual and convenient way of providing security for costs.
- The provision of a *bank guarantee* from a bank within the United Kingdom.
- A *bond*: this is usually given by two sureties who have been approved by the court.

G. PENALTIES FOR NOT GIVING SECURITY

Initially, the plaintiff may be able to extend the time within which he has to give security if he has a good reason for doing so. Otherwise, if security is not given the plaintiff's claim is stayed pending compliance and may ultimately be dismissed in the case of continuing default.

H. SECURITY FROM A DEFENDANT

There is no provision requiring a defendant to give security for costs even if that defendant is not resident in the jurisdiction.

However, where a defendant makes a counterclaim which amounts to a cross action,[2] *the court will consider an application for security against the defendant and will deal with it according to the principles set out above.*

I. INTEREST

Interest accrues on money paid into court pursuant to a court order at the daily court rate.

Alternatively, it is open to the parties (see section F, above) to agree that the sum ordered by way of security should be paid into an interest-bearing deposit account opened in the joint names of their legal representatives in a bank of their choice so that a current market deposit rate may be obtained.

J. RETURN OF SECURITY

Where a plaintiff can show a material change in circumstances since the date of the order, for example, his coming permanently to reside within the jurisdiction, the court may discharge the order and return the security to him.

Successful plaintiffs are entitled to have returned to them money paid into court as security for costs notwithstanding a stay of execution pending appeal.

2. See Chapter 9.

CHAPTER 17

EVIDENCE

The court determines a case according to the law and to the evidence that the parties submit. Evidence, broadly, is either oral and given by witnesses of fact and expert witnesses; or documentary. The practices and procedures concerning such evidence are dealt with in Chapters 18, 19 and 20. In this chapter, the general rules of evidence that will apply before and at the trial are explained. In section E, the rules that apply to affidavits (used in pre-trial summonses[1]) are described.

A. INTRODUCTION

The rules of evidence specify what facts and matters must be proved, which party has to prove them, and how they may be proved.

The rules are extremely complex and it is not possible to do otherwise than summarise them in this chapter. The various elements of the rules of evidence are dealt with under the following headings:

- Types of evidence: *oral*, *documentary*, and *real*.
- The *nature* and *standard* of proof.
- Particular problems.

B. TYPES OF EVIDENCE

There are three main types of evidence that may be adduced (that is, brought before the court), and each is considered in turn. It should be stated at the outset that the nature of English litigation is such that evidence must in the ordinary course be disclosed by the party relying upon it before trial, so as to avoid the dangers of "trial by ambush".

(i) Oral evidence

The principle of *orality* lies at the heart of the English legal process and, as a general rule, any fact required to be proved by a witness in any action begun

1. See Chapter 5.

by writ[2] must be proved by the examination of witnesses orally, and in open court. Oral evidence is given by *witnesses of fact*[3] and *expert witnesses*.[4] The bulk of a witness's evidence will already have been disclosed in a witness statement, or expert's report, described in Chapters 19 and 20. In court, the witness will swear[5] that the evidence in his statement is true, and then he will be *cross-examined* upon it and any other relevant matters. The procedures involved in this process are explained in Chapter 22.

(ii) Documentary evidence

In commercial disputes, a great deal of evidence is likely to be documentary. The documents used in evidence at trial are selected from the documents exchanged at the stage of discovery.[6] Such evidence covers a very wide range of material, and includes papers, tape recordings, films, microfilms, video recordings, computer disks, e-mail and anything that records information.

(iii) Real evidence

This comprises physical objects such as buildings, items of property, animals, vehicles or locations.

C. THE RULES OF EVIDENCE

(i) The standard and burden of proof

The *burden* of proof concerns the question of who must prove any particular point in the action. In a general sense, the plaintiff must "prove" his whole case, but within a large trial there arise many subsidiary matters in respect of which the burden shifts. For example, the defendant need not support with evidence a denial of some fact or matter asserted by the plaintiff (although he will often try to do so), but if he positively asserts some statement, then he must make good that assertion by evidence.

The *standard* of proof concerns the degree to which the court must be satisfied as to the proof of matters in issue. In *civil* cases, this is "the balance of probabilities", that is, that it is more likely than not that the assertion is true; and is less strict than that applicable in *criminal* trials, where the standard is "beyond all reasonable doubt".

2. For the rules relating to Originating Summonses, see Chapter 26.
3. See Chapter 19.
4. See Chapter 20.
5. The oath is "I swear by Almighty God that the evidence that I shall give shall be the truth, the whole truth, and nothing but the truth". The witness may also affirm.
6. See Chapter 18.

(ii) Relevance and admissibility

All evidence must be both *relevant* and *admissible*. All relevant evidence can be adduced unless it is inadmissible.

Evidence may be inadmissible, for example, to prove the intention of a party in entering into a contract; and "without prejudice"[7] communications are generally inadmissible. Evidence of opinion is normally inadmissible except where given by an expert witness with the leave of the court (see Chapter 20, section D). However, as is explained in section D below, the rule against *hearsay* evidence in civil proceedings has now been abolished.

Evidence is *relevant* if it is probative or disprobative of some issue in the action that requires proof. Even if, however, the evidence is relevant and admissible, the question still remains of what *weight* the court should attach to it. Often, both parties will produce evidence that satisfies both the relevance and admissibility rules, in which case the court must evaluate the strength of the testimony and documents and decide who is telling the truth and which documents are credible. This is the purpose of the *oral* nature of the hearing, and is probably the factor that gives rise to the greatest degree of uncertainty in the trial procedure.

D. PARTICULAR PROBLEMS

(i) Oral evidence

The general rule explained above, that matters in issue that are required to be proved by witnesses must generally be proved by oral testimony, can create a number of problems. These arise principally where a witness cannot or will not give evidence. Where the witness is merely unwilling, the problem can be solved in a practical sense by the service of a *subpoena*,[8] although this method is far from ideal if the party calling the witness does not know what the witness will say. Sometimes it is possible to commission the evidence of a witness who is abroad.[9]

The problem was particularly acute in cases involving *hearsay* evidence. Such evidence is testimony not of what the witness himself saw or heard or did, but of what he heard *others* say they saw or heard or did.

The general rule in litigation is that evidence of factual matters must be given orally by those with first-hand knowledge. Previously hearsay evidence was generally inadmissible. The reason was that evidence must be subject to cross-examination before it is considered to be reliable. However, recently[10]

7. See Chapter 21, section B.
8. See Chapter 19.
9. See Chapter 6.
10. The new law was introduced by the Civil Evidence Act 1995, which simplifies earlier more complex rules that permitted hearsay statements being used at trial, and which were unsatisfactory because frequently infringed.

the rule against hearsay in *civil* proceedings has been abolished, and a simplified procedure introduced that allows such evidence to be used.

The procedure requires, broadly, that a *notice* be served on the opposing party stating an intention to rely on a statement made by someone who will not testify. The party relying on the statement must give details of the statement and the reason why the maker will not be called.

The court will not necessarily have to accept the evidence, but may assess it according to several general criteria as to *weight*, including whether it is reasonable or practicable for the witness whose statement is submitted to testify: if he is, there is in this case a right for other parties to call the witness for cross-examination; whether fraud or misrepresentation is alleged in connection with this statement; whether the statement was made contemporaneously with the events it records; the manner in which the statement was submitted; and whether the statement involves "multiple" hearsay. The emphasis is on the value and weight of the evidence, rather than on the form in which it is given. Although admissible, such evidence cannot (except in the case referred to above) be subject to cross-examination, and will be unlikely ever to carry as much weight as that which has been subject to cross-examination.

(ii) Documentary evidence

Documentary evidence gives rise to some special problems, which are of particular importance in complex commercial actions involving great numbers of documents. These problems relate both to the *nature* of the evidence, most of which is hearsay and is not direct proof of the matters recorded in the documents, and to the *practice* that has grown up of producing photocopies of documents to the trial judge.

Two particular problems arise in the case of *photocopy* documents: whether the copy is "the best evidence", that is, whether the *original* is available; and whether the document is *authentic*. It used to be the rule that in court proceedings the "best" evidence had to be produced, and this entailed an obligation to produce the originals of all documents on which reliance was placed. That rule no longer applies, so that photocopies are invariably used unless some issue such as the authenticity of a signature is in doubt. In practice, most of the documents now relied upon at trial are photocopies, although any party may still have the right to call for production of original documents that are said to be in the other party's possession.

In High Court cases,[11] a party is, except in certain circumstances, deemed to admit that all documents, whether original or copy, that are disclosed in the other side's list[12] are authentic, in the sense, for example, that they are not forgeries, and such documents need not, therefore, be strictly proved by the party producing them.

11. In county court cases, the rule is slightly different.
12. See Chapter 18.

Note, however, that merely accepting that a document (whether an original or a photocopy) is authentic, in that it is what it purports to be, does not amount to acceptance of the truth of what the document states. It is still necessary to prove that statements contained in the document are true. Such (hearsay) statements must it seems be proved by a witness who can speak from first-hand knowledge, or by a statement served in accordance with the rules set out above.

Example

In a claim for breach of contract, a copy document is produced to the court that states that the maker of the document told his counterpart that he admitted he was bound by the contract, that statement being now disputed. No issue is taken as to whether the document is genuine, but the maker must testify as to his conversation, the document not being direct evidence of it, or a notice be served under the rules stated above.

(iii) Evidence given in other proceedings

In many situations, relevant statements or notes of interviews may have been taken by other parties, often the Serious Fraud Office, the Bank of England, the police or a Department of Trade and Industry inspector. These may sometimes be used in evidence in other proceedings, possibly under subpoena, but their main worth is normally to ensure that what the witness testifies to in court is consistent with what he has said before. The statement by itself will not necessarily be evidence of the facts recorded in it, except perhaps in accordance with the hearsay rules set out above.

E. AFFIDAVITS

In almost all court hearings before trial, and in proceedings begun by Originating Summonses,[13] evidence is adduced by *affidavits*. This is true whether the hearing is before the master, a judge or the higher courts. Affidavits are sworn statements of fact[14] produced in support of whatever issue is before the court. It often happens that documents material to the application are produced to the court as exhibits to an affidavit. Affidavits may, for example, be used in applications for an injunction, for summary judgment, to strike out a claim, to seek specific discovery of documents, or to seek more time in which to comply with an obligation. An affidavit made by a witness who testifies at trial may form the basis of cross-examination.

13. See Chapter 26.

14. Strictly, argument and opinion should be omitted, but the practice nowadays is more relaxed and they are often included.

CHAPTER 18

DISCOVERY

This chapter describes the obligations that relate to discovery of documents.

A. INTRODUCTION

It is fundamental to English civil litigation that all documentary and other evidential material that may be relevant to the issues which the court has to decide should be made available by the parties before trial. The court regards this approach of "cards on the table" as the best way of ensuring that justice is done, and will assist a party who can show that his opponent is withholding important material.[1]

Accordingly, it is a strict obligation of all parties to English litigation to disclose to their opponents *all documents or other evidential material which they have or have had in their possession, custody or power which may be relevant to the issues*. This process is called "discovery".

B. PROCEDURE

Discovery involves each party[2] preparing and serving on the other parties a list of all documents (and other material) that are or have been in that party's possession, custody or power relating to the matters in question in the action. Normally lists of documents are exchanged simultaneously. The list will identify the documents by date, type, sender and recipient, usually in chronological order.

The party on whom the list is served is then entitled to inspect all the documents still held by the party serving the list, unless they are privileged from production for inspection: see below, section G. It is possible for the

1. This approach is in marked contrast to the procedure in civil law jurisdictions, and reflects the adversarial nature of English litigation which involves a hostile and untrusting attitude to the opponent's case. In the United States of America, the process of discovery is more extensive still and includes lengthy pre-trial depositions of witnesses as well as disclosure of documents.

2. The obligation extends to co-defendants, but only to third parties once formal directions to that effect have been given.

inspecting party to insist on inspecting the actual documents referred to on the list of the disclosing party, although in modern litigation inspection is sometimes effected by providing photocopies of whatever documents on the list are required by the other party. Photocopying charges are payable by the party requesting the copies.

In a party's list of documents he must state whether the document is original or a copy. If no challenge is made, the other party is deemed to admit that a copy is a true copy, or that the original is what it purports to be. It is necessary to be vigilant about this as, if a party discloses only a copy of a document of which he has, or of which he might be expected to have, the original, an opportunity to exploit a weakness may be lost.

Recently, computer systems have been created to facilitate the process of discovery. These are still at an early stage of development, and no truly acceptable substitute for manual systems may be possible.

C. THE IMPORTANCE OF DISCOVERY

Although the responsibility for disclosing all relevant documents lies with the parties to the litigation, the court regards it as the duty of the lawyers acting for the parties to satisfy themselves that their clients have properly complied with all their discovery obligations. These obligations are important and the court may impose sanctions on any party (or his lawyer) who does not comply with them.

In larger cases, discovery may involve many thousands (or even millions) of documents, and it can be the most time-consuming and expensive part of the litigation process apart from the trial itself. A failure to deal with discovery properly at the first attempt may lead to extensive preliminary skirmishes in court, with the parties applying for court orders forcing their opponents to disclose particular documents or categories of document. Such skirmishes can be protracted and expensive.

Discovery is an important watershed in many cases. Once discovery has been completed the lawyers can assess the strengths and weaknesses of their clients' cases, and should be able to give more reliable advice on the chances of success at trial.

It is equally as important for a party to know that he or his opponent has documents that are damaging to his own case as to be aware of documents that assist. Knowing at an early stage the problems associated with your case enables you to take an informed decision as to whether or not, or how, to progress the litigation.

If decisive documents are revealed for the first time on discovery, this may well have the effect of bringing the parties to the negotiating table.

D. WHEN DISCOVERY TAKES PLACE

As is described in Chapter 8, the initial stages of litigation involve the parties setting out their case in writing, mainly in the form of a Statement of Claim, Defence and Reply. These written pleadings define the issues in dispute, and service of the last of them marks the "close of pleadings". The issues having been defined, the process of discovery follows. At that point the parties are able to determine which documents and what other material is relevant to the issues and what is, accordingly, disclosable.

Discovery should take place automatically within 14 days of the close of pleadings. In the normal case, however, the volume of documents is such that it is impracticable for the parties to complete their obligations to give discovery so soon after close of pleadings, so there are normally extensions of time either agreed by the parties or granted on application to the court.

Any document referred to in a pleading (or affidavit) must be produced for inspection (within four days) if another party requests it. This is a separate obligation from the general discovery obligation.

As is explained in section K below, in certain situations it may be possible to obtain pre-action discovery, or, by a separate action, discovery against someone who is not a party to the action to ascertain the identity of those liable for damage caused by them to the plaintiff.

E. WHAT DOCUMENTS AND OTHER MATERIALS ARE DISCOVERABLE

The rules of discovery cover anything which records in a permanent form information that is relevant to the issues in the action. These may include:

- Any form of written document, including correspondence, accounting records, order forms and invoices, board minutes, diaries, notebooks and handwritten notes.
- Photographs, plans and drawings, video tapes and tape recordings.
- Computer disks, e-mail and microfilms.

The basic rule is that material is discoverable if it contains, holds or reveals some form of recorded information that is relevant to the issues in the action or which could put a party on to a course of enquiry that is likely to be relevant to those issues.

All copies of documents which may exist have to be disclosed. This is especially relevant in complex commercial cases involving numerous personnel each of whom has maintained his own file.

There is a duty to search for documents and to ensure that everything is found and disclosed. This may involve checking archives, contacting former directors or employees, searching computer disks, calling for personal and office diaries, following up circulation lists and, where there is reference in one document to another document, checking that you have that other document.

When litigation starts, or comes into prospect, you will need to contact: anyone involved in the transaction at any location or branch from which the company operates; anyone who may have kept their own files; anyone who received documentation or memoranda relating to the transaction; anyone who attended any meetings and may have made their own notes or kept diary entries; anyone else who may have relevant documents, such as the company secretary and the accounts department.

It is vital that, at the moment when litigation seems likely, all these steps are taken, and especially that no documents are destroyed or lost.

F. "POSSESSION, CUSTODY OR POWER"

Documents must be disclosed if they are or have been in your *possession, custody or power*. Accordingly, it is not sufficient simply to disclose those documents that may be in your own files. There may be documents held on your behalf (for example, by your accountant or solicitor or some other agent) for which you can call (that is, which you have power over) that should be disclosed.

It is not necessarily the case that this would entail disclosing documents held by an associated company, because you may have no power to compel production by that associated company. Your lawyer can advise on whether documents held by a particular party are within your custody or power.

It is important to note that the obligation to give discovery extends to the disclosure of documents that are no longer in your possession, custody or power. Thus, if documents have been destroyed or lost or for whatever reason are no longer in your possession, it is still necessary to disclose them in your list of documents, or to describe them as a category of documents if they are not capable of individual specification.

G. WHAT DOES NOT NEED TO BE DISCLOSED

Relevance

It is not necessary to disclose any items that are not *relevant* to the issues in the proceedings.

An item is relevant if it contains information that may either directly or indirectly enable the other party either to advance his own case or to damage the case of his adversary *or that may fairly lead him to an avenue of enquiry that may have either of these two consequences.*

Documents relating to the amount of a claim (as opposed merely to liability) are also considered relevant and so should be disclosed.

Privilege

Certain items are *privileged* from production. These are described in more detail below, but will include communications with your own lawyers, notes of their advice, and instructions to counsel. These documents do not have to be given to your opponent, but they must be listed, so as to offer him the opportunity to contest the claim to privilege.

The test of whether or not a particular item is privileged is complex, and it will usually be for the lawyers to determine whether a particular item can be described as privileged.

The two main categories of document that are privileged are:

- Confidential documents which have come into existence at any time for the purpose of giving or receiving legal advice ("legal advice privilege").
- Documents created for the sole or dominant purpose of the litigation ("litigation privilege").

Legal advice privilege covers, for example, a letter written by a client to his lawyer seeking advice, the reply to such a letter, and any notes made by the lawyer or the client of legal advice given. Care should be taken to avoid making unnecessary photocopies of such letters, because such copies may not themselves be privileged.

Litigation privilege covers, for example, any documents prepared by a client or a third party for the use of his lawyers at the request of the lawyers and for the sole or dominant purpose of the litigation.

Documents passing between solicitors and counsel will also normally be privileged, as will correspondence between a lawyer and a witness, as well as witness statements (including drafts) and drafts of experts' reports[3] that have not been disclosed already.

Legal advice privilege may also apply to the work-product of an in-house lawyer. Special care must, however, be taken in such cases because an in-house lawyer may perform a variety of different roles, not all of which will attract privilege. Thus, where an in-house lawyer also serves as a company secretary, or director, or as a compliance officer, work that he produces in such capacity will not be privileged. It is important that each document produced clearly states in what capacity the writer is acting, so as to prevent any documents or communications that are privileged from becoming integrated with those that are not.

3. See Chapter 20.

Correspondence between the parties direct (or between their lawyers) which is covered by the "without prejudice" rule will also usually be inadmissible as evidence and privileged.[4] These are, broadly, documents that are brought into existence for the purpose of or in connection with the negotiation of a potential settlement of the dispute.

It is probably also the case that "without prejudice" documents in earlier cases are protected from production in later cases.

Example
P sues D for breach of contract; D tries to settle on a "without prejudice" basis with P. The talks fail but D then sues X for damages alleging X was responsible to P for the same losses. It is likely that the "without prejudice" correspondence between P and D will be privileged in the later action.

Correspondence between a party to the litigation and a third party after the litigation has commenced will not normally be privileged.

Difficult questions arise in relation to documents such as reports of internal investigations. It is only if the investigation was for the *dominant* purpose of actual or reasonably prospective litigation that notes and reports and other documents created in the course of the investigation will be privileged. If the dominant purpose was the reorganisation of the company's procedures to prevent a recurrence of the incident, the documents must be disclosed even if the possibility of litigation was part of the reason for the enquiry.

It is necessary therefore to take the greatest care in the production of internal investigative reports and to avoid recording any unnecessary information that may be damaging or confidential.

The board minutes of companies can create special difficulties. Where a board minute records legal advice, a minute of that advice will usually be privileged. However, if the minute also records the board's assessment of that advice, the rest of the minutes may not be privileged. The minutes ought, therefore, to be carefully drafted so as to separate the record of the legal advice from any discussion of it, or from other board discussions that may be discoverable. Caution should be exercised in deciding how much of any such discussions should in any event be recorded.

It is often difficult to distinguish documents that are privileged from those that are not. Some documents may arguably fall into either category, depending on the circumstances in which they were produced. The following categories of document require special care, as they may well not be privileged:

— Copies of privileged documents that are not produced for privileged purposes. For example, a copy of a lawyer's letter of advice sent to a company's bankers or accountants will not necessarily be privileged.

4. The term "without prejudice" is explained in Chapter 21, and Chapter 4.

- Copies of non-privileged documents obtained or made by a party for a privileged purpose. For example, a copy of a non-privileged document made by a party does not become privileged simply if he sends it to his lawyer for use in litigation.
- Reports prepared partly for an internal investigation, and partly for use in litigation. Only if the report is prepared for the *dominant* purpose of litigation will it be privileged.
- A reference to legal advice in board minutes or other reports. These will usually be privileged, except where the reference is for the necessary purpose of communicating that advice.
- Correspondence with parties such as witnesses, unless entered into for the dominant purpose of litigation.
- References to litigation in company accounts.
- Letters from a company's solicitors to the auditors of the company.

H. PARTLY IRRELEVANT OR PARTLY PRIVILEGED DOCUMENTS

Where parts of documents are privileged or irrelevant those parts may be masked in the document disclosed so as not to be apparent to the other party. For example minutes of board meetings of companies and company reports may be in part relevant and in part irrelevant; only those parts that are relevant and not privileged need to be produced. The rest may be concealed, but the fact of the concealment has to be drawn to the attention of your opponent so he may contest the approach.

> *Note that it is possible inadvertently to waive legal privilege, by disclosing on a non-privileged occasion a document that is covered by privilege: for example, by giving to a bank or an accountant a copy of your lawyer's letter of advice, or by referring in court to your discussions with your lawyers. This may be very harmful, as the result is almost certainly to waive privilege in the document disclosed, but possibly also in other documents of the same nature or relating to the same transaction to which the first document refers.*

I. CONFIDENTIAL DOCUMENTS AND DISCOVERY

A party to litigation cannot avoid giving discovery of relevant documents even if he regards them as confidential. The courts, however, may in their discretion mitigate the severity of this rule and permit a party to withhold production of confidential documents if satisfied that the interests of the opposing party do not outweigh the claim to confidentiality. Usually, the courts will lean in favour of upholding confidentiality in documents that involve the affairs of parties not directly involved in the litigation; but, in cases where the confidentiality applies only to a party to the action, the courts will probably order production.

In some cases, the courts will impose restrictions on the production of confidential information, so that, for example, only a party's lawyers may have access to the material. Occasionally, production may be ordered to be given only to the court.

J. LIMITS ON DISCOVERY

In certain, often large, cases the court may limit discovery.[5]

Although the rules of discovery are wide, the courts will only order disclosure of such documents as are necessary either to dispose of the case fairly, or to save costs. The courts resist extravagant or oppressive demands that would impose unreasonable burdens on the party without any corresponding benefit to the other.

It is important to remember that discovery applies to documents relevant to the issues already pleaded in an action. It is not permissible to use the process of discovery to "fish" for materials that may reveal additional claims not previously identified.

In some cases *Public Interest Immunity* may be asserted by a public body involved in the process. If the court is of the view that disclosure of particular material would be injurious to the public interest and that this outweighs the general public interest that documents needed for trial should be disclosed, the court may order that such material need not be disclosed. The party wishing to give discovery of documents should notify the public body beforehand so as to give it the opportunity to seek an order from the court. The court will then carry out a balancing exercise as between the two competing claims and may order or refuse the disclosure as is just.

A party may claim that the production of documents may expose him to the risk of criminal proceedings. In these cases, he may claim the *privilege against self-incrimination*. It should be remembered that such a claim is not generally approved of by the courts, and may not succeed, for example, where the prosecution authorities confirm that they will not press charges. The rule does, however, have real application in cases of commercial fraud involving *Mareva* injunctions and *Anton Piller* orders where obligations are imposed on a defendant to disclose documents and information that may expose him to a risk of criminal prosecution: see Chapter 11, section D.

5. This is because in some very large cases the parties tend to abuse the process and to apply for far more extensive disclosure than is necessary, to divert the opponent from the real issues.

K. PRE-ACTION DISCOVERY

Normally, discovery is ordered only after the case has begun and will not be ordered by the court to enable a prospective plaintiff to discover whether he has a claim. But in some exceptional cases a plaintiff may be entitled to discovery before the proceedings have been issued.

- In *personal injury* cases, medical records may be obtained to enable the plaintiff to consider whether there is a case for negligence against a doctor or hospital authority.
- Although the court will not usually force a person who is entirely innocent to disclose documents or information that may help a plaintiff to bring an action against someone else, it is possible for a prospective plaintiff to bring an *action for discovery* against someone who, whilst not being personally responsible for any wrongdoing, may have facilitated or become unwittingly mixed up in the wrongdoing of another. These actions are known as *Norwich Pharmacal* actions, after the case of that name. The action is intended to lead to the disclosure of material that would identify to the plaintiff the person who was responsible for the wrong done to him. It may also be possible to use this rule to obtain from others discovery during the course of an action that has already begun, and against a defendant wrongdoer who has knowledge of others who are responsible with him. An example of the application of the rule is the case of an action to force the disclosure of a journalist's sources.

This rule is discretionary and is subject to serious limitations under the law of contempt of court[6] *especially in relation to the disclosure of journalists' sources. In such cases, the court will only order disclosure of material (including such sources) where it is necessary in the interests of justice or national security or for the prevention of crime or disorder. The rule is also subject to the privilege against self-incrimination (see Chapter 11, section D).*

- The *Norwich Pharmacal* rule should be distinguished from the "mere witness" rule: although a "mere witness" can be forced by a subpoena to give evidence at trial, he cannot be forced to give information or documents before trial. The fact that a witness knows the identity of a wrongdoer will not normally be sufficient to bring him within the *Norwich Pharmacal* principle. (See also Chapter 36, section C for an account of the application to the rule in banking cases.)
- Note also that the courts may in certain exceptional circumstances give an order for disclosure of documents in aid of an action to trace

6. See also Chapter 38.

assets into the hands of another party, such as a bank. See Chapter 36, section C for a fuller account of this procedure.

L. DANGERS AND PRECAUTIONS

It is important to realise that the obligation to give discovery continues throughout the action. Documents which are created right up to and during the trial are disclosable. If such documents come into existence after the exchange of lists of documents, they have to be disclosed in a supplementary list.

Care must be taken not to create prejudicial documents which may become discoverable at any stage in the litigation.

Legal advice (either from outside or from in-house lawyers) should not be disseminated internally in such a way that it loses its cloak of privilege. Board minutes discussing the litigation, internal memoranda and even rough notes may become discoverable and may be damaging.

Example
If a document is produced by your opponent and you write on it "We have a problem with this point, because our witness will not deny that he said what they allege", that may then become discoverable to your opponent unless you can claim privilege for it.

A litigant must be careful with correspondence with its insurers, and with its parent company. Admissions may be made in a statement to insurers or to a parent or associated company, and these may be disclosable in litigation.

It is advisable to ensure that all individuals within a company are aware of the pitfalls with respect to internal communications and to communications with outside parties.

Once litigation has started it is wrong and dangerous to destroy documents which may be relevant, whether the destruction is part of a routine policy or is carried out on an individual basis. Destruction could be dangerous because it may involve the loss of documents which would have been of assistance in the proceedings and/or it may lead the court to draw adverse inferences about what may have been in the documents which were destroyed or about your conduct and probity.

In some circumstances the destruction of documents can be a criminal offence. This is usually for reasons that do not concern the process of discovery.

M. PRACTICAL MEASURES

There are other points of which employees or members of your organisation should be aware in the event of a dispute arising. In particular, files should not be arranged in a different order, because this may make it difficult for the lawyers to place properly an undated or unsigned document, or to put particular items into context. The original sequence of the contents of a file may itself be relevant.

Notes in similar forms to those at the end of this chapter could appropriately be circulated and made part of company policy, to ensure that all relevant documents are retained.

N. USE TO WHICH DOCUMENTS DISCLOSED ON DISCOVERY CANNOT BE PUT

To protect parties to litigation from the possible consequences of wrongful disclosure a party who obtains documents from his opponent on discovery is generally permitted to use them and the information contained in them *only* for the purposes of conducting the case in which the documents were discovered. The documents cannot be used for another purpose unless they have later been read out or referred to in court.[7]

Despite this protection, in some cases litigation may result in sensitive and commercially useful information being disclosed to a trade rival. In cases of particular sensitivity, the court may place restrictions on who may inspect documents, for example by confining inspection to solicitors or independent persons, and express undertakings more extensive than normal may be required.

O. SUBSEQUENT PROCEDURES

Interrogatories

As already seen, the usual rule in civil litigation in England is that the parties will know in advance of the trial what documentary and expert evidence will be adduced by their opponents. They will not usually, however, know until quite shortly before the trial begins what *oral* evidence will be given. In certain situations, the parties are, after the service of witness statements, allowed to *interrogate* an opponent as to factual matters that are relevant to the proceedings.

7. This rule applies to documents disclosed pursuant to a legal obligation, for example, to give discovery, and does not apply, therefore, to documents that have been exhibited to an affidavit that is served voluntarily.

- Each party may serve on the other without leave of the court not more than two[8] *written interrogatories* or sets of questions which are drafted to ascertain what a party's evidence will be on important issues. The opponent must give his replies in writing under oath.
- If the other party objects, the matter is decided by the court, which will order the interrogatories to be answered provided that to do so is in the interests of a fair trial or will reduce the costs of the proceedings.

Interrogatories will be refused by the court if it considers that the request is a "fishing expedition" or where privilege[9] is claimed for the information sought, or where the information may equally be provided by Further and Better Particulars.

Notices to admit facts and to produce documents

In addition, a party who needs at trial to prove certain facts may serve on his opponent a *notice to admit* some or all of those facts or *to produce* documents. If the admissions are not made or the documents not produced, in circumstances where the court considers that the other party should have complied with the notice, the party refusing will have to bear the costs of the proof, regardless of the outcome of the trial.

P. RULES CONCERNING BANKERS' BOOKS

In addition to the rules relating to *subpoenas* and *pre-action discovery*[10] special procedures apply to documents held by a bank. An application supported by an affidavit may be made to the court to obtain access to and copies of many internal records of bankers, such as statements of account, that are relevant to the issues in and necessary for the just determination of the litigation.

8. Further interrogatories may be raised with the leave of the court.
9. See section G above.
10. See also Chapter 36 for a further consideration of particular aspects of disclosure in relation to bankers' records.

FORMS TO ASSIST DISCOVERY

This is a suitable form* to be circulated to all company staff at the outset of litigation.

A dispute has arisen with [ ] in relation to [ ] and litigation now seems likely. [Brief details of claim.] In the event of litigation the company will have to disclose to [the opposition] all documents relevant to this transaction which are or have been in its possession, custody or power even if they are damaging and confidential. This obligation will continue up to and during the trial.

Some documents will be exempt from production because they are privileged, such as correspondence with lawyers for the purpose of giving or taking legal advice or correspondence with third parties for the dominant purpose of the litigation. But this privilege can be lost if a privileged document is used or copied for a non-privileged purpose or if the litigation is only part of the purpose for which a document is produced. It is important therefore that you follow these guidelines to avoid prejudicing the company's position.

Do not destroy any documentation relating to this transaction.

Search for and locate any documentation relating to this transaction including:

correspondence, memoranda, drafts and manuscripts,
notes of meetings,
all copies,
diaries,
microfilms, tape recordings and transcripts, photographs, drawings,
films and videos.

If this documentation is in storage please make arrangements for retrieval.

Do not approach third parties for documents or copies relating to this transaction unless this has been cleared by the legal department.

Do not rearrange or edit relevant files.

Do not create any new documents relating to or concerning this matter, including internal memoranda, unless requested to do so by the legal department.

Do not copy any existing documents which may be relevant to this transaction.

Do not make manuscript notes on any relevant documents.

If you are approached by third parties, for example by the police, insurers, regulatory or similar bodies, auditors, accountants, or the Press, refer the matter to the legal department or seek advice from them.

This is a form* of wording suitable for incorporation into a company's policy manual or staff guide.

To ensure that relevant documentation will be available in the event of a dispute, it is this company's policy not to destroy documentation until [six] years have elapsed. To ensure that documents can be located and retrieved when necessary you are asked to adhere to the following:

> Whenever a transaction has been completed, carefully collect all documents that you have created or received. Documents include originals and copies of minutes of meetings, notes, correspondence and memoranda; drafts and manuscripts; diaries, microfilms; tape recordings and transcripts; and videos, films and photographs.
>
> When you have no further need for these documents they should be sent to storage.
>
> Keep a careful note of where the file(s) are stored and ensure that if you leave the company you make the whereabouts of the file(s) known to [your departmental head].
>
> Do not keep papers at home or otherwise outside the office.
>
> Never destroy documents until you have discussed this with [your departmental head].

* These forms first appeared in an article published in the October 1993 edition of PLC Magazine, and are reproduced with their permission.

CHAPTER 19

WITNESSES OF FACT

This chapter describes the rules relating to the disclosure of the evidence of witnesses of fact who testify voluntarily, and explains the procedures to compel those witnesses who are unwilling to do so to attend at trial.

A. INTRODUCTION

Once the issues in the action have been defined in the pleadings, and the documents relevant to those issues have been disclosed, it is possible to identify which witnesses of fact are necessary to prove a party's case. These witnesses fall into two broad categories: those witnesses who will testify willingly, and those who will not.

Witnesses who testify voluntarily

The procedure followed is that the solicitor interviews the witness and takes a draft "proof of evidence", which is a detailed account of what the witness can say in relation to the issues in the action. In some cases, counsel may be asked to read the draft and comment.[1] The witness is asked to confirm that the draft is accurate, or to make any amendments that he thinks appropriate.

— The statement will be privileged from disclosure in the litigation, and need only be disclosed if helpful to your case. Note that statements prepared by the parties themselves will not necessarily be privileged. It is, therefore, prudent to ensure that statements are made to lawyers.

There are now rules requiring the statements on which a party wishes to rely at trial to be exchanged with the other party in good time for the hearing, so that he will not be taken by surprise by what the witness says at trial.

— This innovation is something of a mixed blessing. Previously, it was considered madness to disclose such statements, as to do so told your

1. See Chapter 3, section C for the conditions to which this is subject.

opponent too much of your case; but now the advantages of this new open approach tend to be reduced by the service of statements so heavily "lawyered" and anodyne as to be uninformative and, sometimes, misleading. The current tendency for statements to be partisan and argumentative, and to contain hearsay[2] evidence, is frowned upon by the courts which are increasingly vigilant about such abuses. In future, it is possible that large parts of a witness's statement may not be allowed.

The rules regulating the way in which the witness gives his evidence at the hearing are dealt with in Chapter 22.

Note that a witness may also give evidence in *interlocutory* matters, in which case he does so by swearing an *affidavit*, which stands in place of a witness statement, although in very unusual circumstances he will not be cross-examined upon it at the hearing in which the affidavit is deployed in evidence. He may, however, be cross-examined on his affidavit at the later trial, usually to draw out any inconsistencies between it and his oral testimony.

B. SUBPOENAS

(i) Types of subpoena

Not all witnesses are willing to attend court. Sometimes, for example, because of the constraints of an individual's profession, a witness is unable to attend court voluntarily. In such cases, a litigant will need to obtain a writ of subpoena. The purpose of a subpoena is to compel a witness to attend trial under threat of punishment. There are two types of subpoena:

Subpoena ad testificandum

This is to compel a witness to attend trial to give oral evidence.

It is usually regarded as a dangerous practice to compel a witness to testify before it is known what he will say. The procedure involves a calculated risk, and should not usually be followed unless absolutely necessary.

Subpoena duces tecum

This is to compel a witness to attend court with documents, sometimes as well as to give oral evidence.

It is important to specify exactly what documents are sought. It is not permissible

2. See Chapter 17.

to "fish" for documents that you think or hope a witness may have; nor should the subpoena be oppressive in the sense that it seeks categories of document that a witness will not have or which will cause him great time and expense to produce.

(ii) Court rules

Once a subpoena has been issued it must be served within 12 weeks and at least four days before the date on which the attendance is required.

A subpoena must be served personally on the witness. At the same time "conduct money" must be tendered. This is an amount of money sufficient to repay travelling costs.

A subpoena will not usually include details of the time of the hearing. It is the duty of the issuer of a subpoena to advise the witness of the time of the hearing.

Remember that the documents requested have to be produced to the court, rather than to the party issuing the subpoena. This can be dangerous if the documents the witness produces may be unhelpful to your case, as they cannot be kept private.

It is possible for the proposed witness to dispute the *regularity* of the subpoena. A dispute most often arises in the case of a *subpoena duces tecum* in which it is asserted that the scope of the documents required is oppressively wide.

Example
A bank's employee is served with a *subpoena duces tecum* to attend a hearing and to bring with him all the bank's papers relating to the specific matters in issue in the case. The bank may seek to set aside the subpoena on grounds such as that the subpoena has not adequately identified the documents required or that the call for documents is so extensive and oppressive that the bank should not be burdened with such a task. The bank might also seek to claim that it should not be required to disclose its confidential documents.

It is a contempt of court[3] to fail to comply with a subpoena, and a witness who fails to attend court to testify may also incur civil liability for damages to the party who sought his attendance.

In the past, a party issuing a *subpoena duces tecum* had to wait until trial before he could get access to the papers. Nowadays the practice has changed, so that he can usually have access much earlier, by making an application to accelerate the trial date. This involves a fiction, as the trial is not actually heard at the hearing for the production of documents, and the only matter in issue at this early hearing will be the production of the documents or the witness's application to set aside the subpoena. In this way, *subpoenas duces tecum* have become almost an additional part of pre-trial discovery.

3. See Chapter 38.

C. LETTERS OF REQUEST

In certain cases, it is impracticable to bring to trial a witness who is overseas, and it is possible to arrange for his testimony to be given abroad. The procedures involved are explained in Chapter 6. This may sometimes be done by video-link.

CHAPTER 20

EXPERT WITNESSES

Many cases turn on questions of what are the normal practices and procedures in specialist walks of life. This chapter explains the basic rules by which evidence of such matters is brought before the courts.

A. INTRODUCTION

A general rule in litigation is that evidence may only be admitted of factual matters through witnesses who can speak from their own direct knowledge. Opinions are normally irrelevant and inadmissible. An exception to this rule is the case of *expert witnesses.*

Evidence from expert witnesses is often an essential element of a litigant's case, especially if the dispute involves issues of technical complexity. Lawyers from overseas jurisdictions are often required to give evidence of foreign law. Doctors, accountants, engineers, architects, surveyors, bankers and brokers are all frequently called to give their opinion on the facts in issue. Such matters often concern professional standards in negligence cases.

B. WHAT IS AN EXPERT?

An expert is an individual who can satisfy the court that he has adequate depth of experience, understanding and ability in a given subject to justify the court listening to and taking account of his opinion on the matters to be tried. Generally, this is achieved by reference to the witness's formal qualifications and experience. On occasions, it may be necessary to have more than one expert witness. This may be as a result of there being more than one area of technical complexity relevant to the case or where two expert witnesses can combine their skills to present more complete expert evidence to the court.

Examples

In a personal injury case where the injury sustained has led to brain damage, expert evidence may be required from a physician, a neurosurgeon and an occupational therapist.

In a case concerning the value of defective machine parts it may be appropriate to instruct an expert concerning the manufacture and function of the parts and also an expert who, while he may not have the technical qualifications of the first expert, has numerous years of experience of actually trading in such machine parts.

In construction disputes, which involve numerous different disciplines, architects, surveyors and engineers may all be required as expert witnesses.

C. CHOOSING AN EXPERT WITNESS

There are two chief points to consider when choosing an expert. The first is the field in which expert evidence is required. The second is the need to instruct the right person for the job. It must be remembered that a judge has to, and can only, assess the evidence put before him. It must, therefore, be assumed that weight will be given when assessing that evidence to the respective levels of qualification of the opposing experts. For this reason, it is usual for the parties to instruct one of the leading experts in the field, and it can be a false economy to involve someone who lacks the relevant experience, or who has not testified as an expert witness before.

However, the use of expert witnesses has developed to the point where there is now effectively an industry of people whose livelihood is that of acting as expert witnesses in litigation. Sometimes, the instruction of such "professional witnesses" can be advantageous, but care should always be taken to ensure that the witness has recent personal experience of the practices in issue. It is preferable to select someone who, whilst skilled at trial technique, also actually earns his living by working in his field of professional competence.

D. THE COURT'S RULES ON EXPERT WITNESSES

The court will not, in general, permit expert evidence to be used unless leave for expert evidence has been obtained from the court. The court will usually accept an agreement between the parties as to such matters, but will expect that the numbers of expert witnesses are kept to a sensible level. Leave will generally be limited to a specified number of experts only, in areas the relevance of which has been justified to the court. It is usually the case that the number and nature of experts will be agreed by the litigants.

The courts now tend to be more restrictive in their approach to experts, and will not give such orders as freely as before. This is in response to a tendency by practitioners automatically to call experts "just in case" they may be necessary.

Expert evidence cannot be relied upon unless the expert's report has been disclosed to the other side before trial. The purpose of this rule is to allow each party to know in advance what the expert will say on highly technical matters on which advice will be needed from the other party's expert witness.

It is generally considered to be bad practice to serve an expert's report unilaterally: the most sensible procedure is to exchange a report, thereby denying your opponent the opportunity to serve a report that amounts to little more than a criticism of your own.

It is generally possible to update or revise an expert's report after it has been served, if new facts have emerged.

The court usually directs that there should also be a meeting of opposing experts with a view to the experts seeking to narrow the points of issue between them.

There is no requirement that expert evidence which is not intended to be relied upon at trial need be disclosed. Accordingly, if an expert's written report is unfavourable, while it may clearly give rise to a re-evaluation of the merits of continuing with the case, it need not be disclosed and a second, more favourable, report can be obtained from a different expert and relied upon at trial, provided the report is made in good faith. A litigant should be careful when arranging experts' reports on his own account. They will be disclosable to the other party unless commissioned for the "dominant purpose" of litigation. If the dominant purpose is, for example, to enquire into and rectify a faulty system, the report will be discoverable, even if critical of your case.[1]

Sometimes it may be tactically desirable to serve an expert's report on the opposing party at the outset of the action if that report is so conclusive and of such substance that it will be likely to encourage the other party to settle the action. This can be a somewhat hazardous practice and should be regarded as exceptional.

The lawyers usually identify, retain and brief the expert, and work with him in the preparation of his report; but it should be stressed that although the expert should ideally be integrated as a member of the litigation team, he must be completely neutral and independent in his approach.

It has recently been emphasised by the courts that an expert must prepare his own report. Cases in which a client's lawyers have, in effect, written the report for the expert are heavily frowned upon. In practice, an expert's report is prepared in conjunction with the lawyers, but their role has to be confined to briefing the expert on the facts and defining the issues for his opinion, which must be his independent product uninfluenced as to form or content by the exigencies of litigation.

Note also that great care must be exercised when drafting instructions to an expert witness. Although instructions sent by a lawyer will normally be privileged, any reference in the expert's report to those instructions may waive that privilege. This may lead to a line of cross-examination of the witness as to the nature and scope of his instructions, which should be avoided.

1. See Chapter 18 on discovery of documents generally.

CHAPTER 21

SETTLEMENTS, PAYMENTS INTO COURT AND DISCONTINUANCE

The English legal system favours the settlement of disputes. If "ADR"[1] has been attempted and failed, it should still be possible for a claim to be settled, and this is often the parties' main objective. Most lawyers try to achieve the objective of a favourable settlement by the use of pre-trial tactics. This chapter concerns the legal and practical rules by which cases can be settled before trial. There is a chart that sets out the main steps involved on page 149.

A. INTRODUCTION

Of all actions which are commenced, probably not more than five per cent reach trial. Although there is no particular time or stage either before or after legal proceedings have commenced when settlement may be achieved, it often happens that a settlement is reached at one of three important stages in the life of a lawsuit. The first is before the proceedings are begun; the second is after pre-trial discovery and disclosure of evidence; and the third is just before the trial is due to begin. These stages represent the most decisive periods in litigation: when the parties are about to commit themselves to litigation; when they have ascertained the strengths of their cases; and when they are about to incur the costs of trial. It is possible, however, to settle cases at any time.

The courts encourage the settlement of disputes so that there can be "an end to litigation",[2] and the rules of litigation provide a number of ways in which parties can try to settle their dispute in a way that need not prejudice their cases should the attempt not succeed.

B. MEANS OF ACHIEVING A SETTLEMENT

"Without prejudice" negotiations

The "without prejudice"[3] rule means that (provided no settlement has been

1. See Chapter 2.
2. The judiciary is promoting the consideration of alternative dispute resolution, see Chapter 2.
3. See Chapter 4, section F.

reached) nothing that is or has been said during negotiations concerning settlement either orally or in writing will be admissible in evidence should the matter come to trial, unless the parties consent.[4]

Negotiations for settlement should, therefore, always be conducted on a "without prejudice"[5] basis: usually the process is initiated by a "without prejudice" letter or meeting. In either case, the "without prejudice" protection allows the parties to make proposals for settlement which necessarily involve express or implied concessions or admissions whilst reserving their ability to maintain denials of liability in court should those proposals not be accepted. If the matter does go to trial the judge will not know of the admissions and his perception of the merits of either side's case will be unaffected.

However, this does not mean that your opponent will not learn something of your own opinion of the strength of your claim or defence from "without prejudice" proposals and unless your approach is carefully considered it may become harder to settle the claim on terms favourable to you.

It is not strictly necessary to confirm any agreement made on a "without prejudice" basis by an open agreement in order to make it effective, but it is obviously prudent to do so.

As soon as a "without prejudice" offer has been accepted the "without prejudice" protection falls away, a settlement is reached and the agreement becomes binding on the parties.

Payments into court

Whereas "without prejudice" negotiations can take place at any time, the procedure for making a payment into court is only available to the defendant once proceedings have commenced, and is appropriate where settlement has for any reason not proved possible. For example, the plaintiff may simply be unwilling to discuss settlement, or he may be prepared to do so only on terms that are thought by the defendant to be unreasonable and to bear no relation to what he is likely to win at trial. In such circumstances, the defendant can protect his position as far as the future legal costs of the case are concerned by using the mechanism of the "payment into court".

Where a claim is for a debt or damages[6] (that is, where the judgment will result in an order for the payment of money) the defendant may pay into court the sum of money which he is prepared to offer to settle the claim. For reasons explained later in this section, although applicable and useful in all claims for debt or damages, the procedure is most appropriate where the plaintiff's claim is for an uncertain amount, or where it comprises different limbs not all of which are likely to succeed: that is, where the plaintiff may be awarded different,

4. See Chapter 4 for the rationale behind this rule, and Chapter 18 on discovery generally.
5. See Chapter 4.
6. See Chapter 23 for a description of the awards that the court may make at trial.

and therefore uncertain, sums depending on the way his case is assessed, rather than where he is claiming a fixed sum that the court will either award in full or not at all. In such cases, the plaintiff cannot be sure what sum he will be awarded if he wins, and the defendant by this procedure can force the plaintiff to take a realistic attitude to his case.

If negotiations have foundered and the defendant considers that judgment is likely to be awarded against him at trial for some amount but not necessarily for all that he is claiming, this is an effective device to bring about a settlement at the amount of the sum paid into court or, if that is not possible, to protect the defendant from further adverse costs. By making the payment into court and giving notice of it to the plaintiff, the defendant puts the plaintiff at risk as to costs should he refuse to accept the payment-in and proceed to trial.

A payment into court is made at the administrative offices of the court and is not notified to the judicial officers, such as the master or trial judge, until after the trial has been concluded, except for the purposes of removing the payment from court in those cases where leave to do so is required: see later in this section. Only the other parties to the action receive notice of the payment-in.

> *Note that the amount of the payment-in has to include the interest that is likely to be awarded at trial, and also carries the additional commitment to pay the costs incurred by the plaintiff up to the date of the payment-in: it must be remembered that if the plaintiff accepts the amount paid into court within the time limit, the defendant must also pay, in addition, the plaintiff's costs up to that date: see below.*

If the plaintiff accepts the payment-in within 21 days of receipt of the notice of payment-in, the proceedings are brought to an end there and then and he is entitled to recover his costs from the defendant together with interest accrued on the amount paid into court, up to the time when he gave notice of acceptance.

If the plaintiff does not accept the payment-in, it is not treated as an admission of liability on the part of the defendant: the case will proceed to trial and, as stated earlier, the judge will not be told of the payment-in until the case has finished.

It will make no difference if at trial the plaintiff recovers more than the amount paid in. If, however, the plaintiff recovers the amount paid in or less, the court, in exercising its discretion as to which party should pay the costs, is obliged to take into account the payment-in and its amount. This usually means that the plaintiff, even though he may have "won", will only be entitled to reimbursement of his legal costs up to the date of the payment-in, but not after. Further, the defendant will be entitled to have his costs from the date of the payment-in paid by the plaintiff.

Example
P is advised that, if successful, his claim is worth £100,000 but that the chances of success are 70%. D pays into court £60,000. If P accepts the payment into court he would receive £60,000 plus his "taxed" costs.[7] If P does not accept the payment-in, proceeds to trial and is awarded £55,000 he will only be entitled to his costs up to the date of payment-in and will have to bear his own costs incurred thereafter and pay the taxed costs incurred by D from the date of payment-in. The net result is that P may at trial receive a total of £55,000 for his claim but he may have to bear the brunt of both parties' costs from the date of the payment-in, despite having "won".

Whether to accept a payment into court involves a difficult decision for a plaintiff, especially where the payment-in has been made early in the proceedings and is in a sum close to that which he has been advised he will be able to achieve at trial. The party's lawyer will be able to advise on the chances of success, the likely costs consequences of proceeding to trial and the likelihood of any further payments into court being made.

A payment into court can be made before or at the same time as acknowledging service of the writ, at any time up to trial or, indeed, after the trial has begun.

A payment into court can be increased at a later date.

A payment into court, once made, can only be withdrawn by the defendant in very exceptional circumstances.

A plaintiff needs the leave of the court to accept a payment-in after 21 days from the date of the payment-in, but cannot remove a payment-in once the judge has begun to deliver his judgment.

Similar rules apply in the case of a defendant's counterclaim.

The calculation of the amount of the payment-in is often difficult. The procedure is mainly relevant when the plaintiff is seeking damages the amount of which is in the discretion of the court and where, therefore, the plaintiff must be unsure what precisely he will be awarded. But for that reason, so too will the defendant be unsure what to pay into court. His offer to the plaintiff will probably have been rejected, but he still wants to settle. The trick is to identify that sum that is sufficiently close to what is likely to be awarded but not too high. In view of the uncertainties of litigation, it is by no means easy to select the right figure.

In cases where the plaintiff will either win all of his claim or nothing, the calculation is even more problematic, and involves, in effect, an estimate of what sum would be sufficiently tempting to the plaintiff, having regard to the plaintiff's overall chances of success. If the payment-in is not accepted, it will probably have no effect on the costs of the trial.

7. See the explanation of taxed costs in Chapter 24.

"Without prejudice save as to costs"

In a claim for debt or damages the defendant can make a payment into court of money.

However, where the claim is not for money, such as where part or all of the claim is for an injunction or a declaration or specific performance of a contract, the defendant cannot make a payment into court. The same applies to Contribution and Third Party[8] proceedings. In such circumstances, written offers made "without prejudice save as to costs" can be made.[9] The effect is the same as in relation to payments into court. The defendant writes to the plaintiff offering a set of terms and agreeing to pay the costs of the case to date. If at trial the plaintiff betters those terms, he will normally be awarded his costs. If he does not, he must usually bear the defendant's costs from the date of the offer.

An offer made "without prejudice save as to costs" will be of no effect where a payment into court could have been made. Where the plaintiff claims money, the defendant must make a payment into court.

C. EFFECT OF SETTLEMENT

Where the parties to a dispute have reached a settlement following the issue of court proceedings, the new agreement should preclude them from taking any further steps in the existing proceedings (except for the purpose of enforcing the terms of settlement).

The existing proceedings still need to be disposed of and there are a number of ways of achieving this. Proceedings can be *stayed*, *discontinued*, *withdrawn* or *dismissed*, and the settlement agreement should adopt one of those methods. Each method is slightly different and your lawyer will be able to tell you which one is suitable in your particular circumstances.

D. CONFIRMING A SETTLEMENT

If "without prejudice" negotiations have led to an agreement before proceedings have been commenced and the negotiations were oral it is prudent to confirm the agreement in writing. In complicated matters it is common for a settlement agreement to be prepared by lawyers.

If a settlement is reached after proceedings have been commenced then an agreement is required to record the terms and confirm the method of disposing of the court proceedings. Normally, this is by a court order, made with the consent of the parties, recording the terms of settlement.

8. See Chapter 9.
9. A so-called "*Calderbank*" offer, named after the case in which the practice was first approved.

In either event, it is possible to insist that the settlement and/or its terms remain confidential so that it is not recorded on the court file.

E. FULL AND FINAL SETTLEMENT

It is always advisable to make express provision in a settlement, whether before or after proceedings have commenced, that the terms are to be in full and final settlement of all claims that either party has or may have against the other in relation to the dispute. This releases the parties from the threat of future related litigation.

Care should be taken not inadvertently to release from liability parties with whom you are not settling. In such cases, rather than "releasing" a party, the agreement should be expressed as a "covenant not to sue", which ought to preserve the ability to proceed against other parties also liable with those with whom you have settled. This is relevant where, for example, the plaintiff wants to start another action against a new party who he thinks is liable for the same loss. If he does, his "without prejudice" discussions with the party with whom he has already settled may remain so for the purposes of the new action.

F. DISCONTINUANCE AND WITHDRAWAL

A party is not obliged to continue with his claim, or every part of his claim. If he wishes not to proceed with some allegation or claim relief, he may *withdraw* it; and if he wishes not to proceed with the whole of his claim, he may *discontinue* it. The right to do this is generally subject to obtaining the permission of the court, which is normally given on condition that the costs wasted by the process that is being withdrawn or discontinued are borne by the party responsible. The fact of the discontinuance will not usually of itself debar future claims being brought for the same relief against the same defendant, but the court may impose such a stipulation when giving leave to discontinue. Sometimes, as part of a settlement, the parties will agree to the discontinuance of the claim. In this case, the discontinuance should by contract expressly preclude the right of future action on the same facts against the defendant.

Distinguish this situation from those where by agreement the court dismisses a claim: in such a case, no further action may be taken against the other party.

SETTLEMENTS, PAYMENTS INTO COURT AND OFFERS "WITHOUT PREJUDICE SAVE AS TO COSTS"

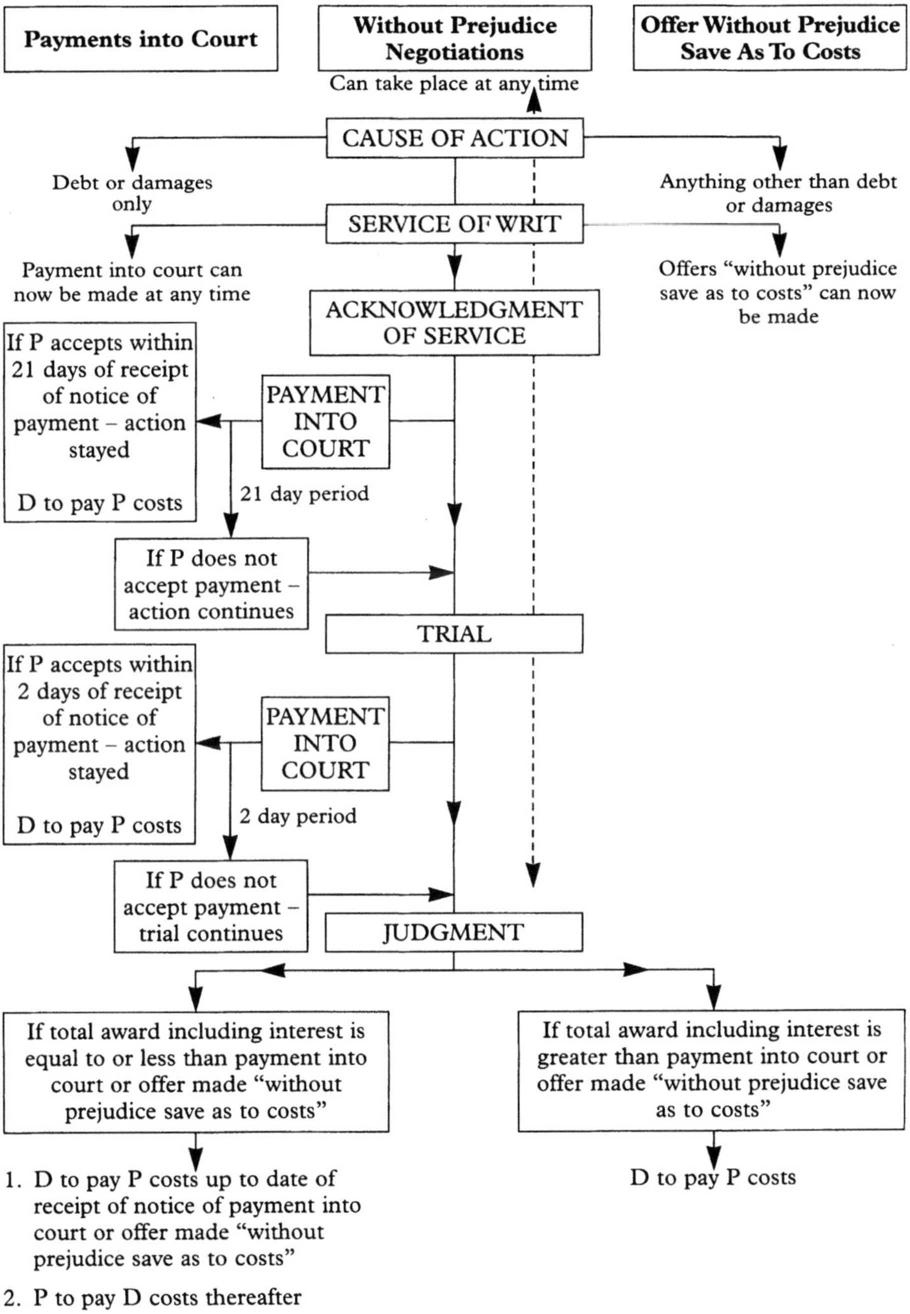

CHAPTER 22

PREPARATION FOR TRIAL AND TRIAL MANAGEMENT

Here we explain what in practice is involved in preparing for trial and what procedures are followed in court during the hearing.

A. INTRODUCTION

It has been pointed out that the course of litigation is split into two chief phases: *pre-trial* and *trial*, although in a sense it is true that these two periods merge because a litigant ought always to be preparing for trial if he wishes to maintain the tactical initiative and force a favourable settlement.

In this sense, preparing for trial is a process continuous from the outset of a case. There is no single date or time when a conscious decision is made to prepare for trial. Your lawyers, when conducting any litigation on your behalf, will always have in mind the possibility that the case will go to trial and that it will be necessary to prove or defend the allegations that have been made.

Preparations for trial begin in earnest once the pre-trial period is completed. That phase sees the preliminary steps taken that enable the parties to identify the matters in dispute and to assess the strengths and weaknesses of their cases by reference to the evidence, both factual, in the form of witness statements and documents, and of opinion, in the form of experts' reports. Once these preliminary steps have been concluded, the case is set down for trial and there then follows a period of intense preparation and tactical exchanges. Settlement talks are frequently initiated; last-minute amendments of the pleadings are made; and further documents disclosed or demanded.

The immediate pre-trial period is intensive for the lawyers, and a large proportion of the costs in litigation is incurred at this stage. If you are seriously considering compromising the proceedings, the period immediately before the preparations for trial commence can be a good time to approach the other party.

B. PRELIMINARY ISSUES

In certain cases, for example, where:

- — a single issue of law can be isolated from all the other issues in the action and its resolution may determine the whole case; or
- — all the facts in the case are agreed and the only dispute is one of law,

the parties may sensibly decide to have that legal issue dealt with by argument as a "preliminary issue". For example, the issue may be whether or not a notice was served in accordance with a contract, or whether an employee had been employed for a necessary period, or whether words published are capable of bearing a defamatory meaning; and may be quite separate from any other issues, and may if resolved make the rest of the proceedings superfluous. The court may hear the preliminary point at or at some time before trial, and only go on to deal with the remaining issues if its judgment makes it necessary. In this way, costly proceedings may be avoided.

C. THE TIMING OF THE TRIAL

The date of the hearing of the trial will have been determined many months and (in a major case) possibly several years earlier. Following the directions that are usually given at the Summons for Directions, the plaintiff's lawyers will have set the case down for trial by lodging at court the appropriate documents. The court will then have allocated the case to a particular list, depending upon the nature of the claim. It is possible to apply for a fixed date for the trial, so that the parties will know when the case will come on for hearing. This may be useful, for example, when a number of witnesses will be needed at the trial. The *Clerk of the Lists*, an official of the court who deals with the court trial calendar, may decline to allocate a fixed date to the trial. He may direct that the case "floats" in the *General List*, when the hearing date will be determined by the number of other cases in the General List, and whether those cases settle. The case may be transferred to the *Warned List* which contains those cases that will be shortly called on for trial.

In very urgent cases, it is possible at the hearing of the Summons for Directions for the lawyers to apply to the court for an order for an expedited trial. The effect of such an order is that the case will "leapfrog" other, less important, cases and be listed for an early trial. This, however, is a rare procedure.

D. BRIEFING COUNSEL[1] FOR THE TRIAL

Although solicitors now may have rights of audience in the higher courts, and often appear at preliminary hearings prior to the trial, it remains usual to instruct counsel to appear at the trial. Counsel specialise in advocacy and have considerable training and experience in the oral presentation of a case to the court. They are skilled and experienced in the cross-examination of witnesses and in responding to questions raised by the judge. Where the case is of particular complexity or importance to clients, the lawyers will instruct leading counsel (that is, a Queen's Counsel) as well as a junior.

The brief delivered to counsel contains all the papers which are relevant to the case and enables him to prepare for the trial. It is good practice to deliver the brief to counsel well in advance of the trial to give counsel plenty of time to prepare for the hearing, although this has certain financial consequences (as to which, see below).

When your solicitors deliver the brief to counsel for the trial, they also incur a liability to pay the *brief fee* (which must be paid by the client). This fee will have been negotiated in advance by the lawyers with counsel's clerk and it covers the cost of counsel's preparatory work for the trial and the first day of the hearing. Once the brief has been delivered to counsel, the brief fee will be payable even if the case settles before the trial starts, although it may be possible to negotiate a reduction in the brief fee with counsel's clerk. It may seem unfair that the brief fee is payable even if the case settles, but counsel will have spent a considerable amount of time preparing for the hearing, and counsel's clerk may have turned away other work and kept counsel's diary free for the duration of the hearing. In large cases it may be possible to negotiate a brief fee payable in stages, so that, if the case settles, only those stage payments that have already been made are irrecoverable.

The brief fee covers only the first day of the hearing, but most trials last longer than one day. For subsequent days in court, it is normal to pay counsel a further daily fee (known as a "refresher"). The brief fee is almost always the largest single payment made to counsel in the course of an action.

The delivery of the brief can be a useful negotiating weapon for the plaintiff. It enables him to impose a deadline on offers of compromise, after which date the brief for trial will have to be delivered, and the case will become correspondingly more costly for the defendant to settle.

E. PREPARING THE BUNDLES FOR TRIAL

The obligations upon parties and their lawyers to give discovery ensure that a substantial amount of documentation is produced in the course of the

1. See Chapter 3 for a description of the roles of solicitors and counsel in litigation.

proceedings. However, by the time the case reaches trial, it may be evident that much of this documentation is irrelevant to the issues which remain in dispute. The lawyers will try to agree volumes of the documents (referred to as "bundles") which will be used at the trial and also a "core bundle" of the essential documents that will be most frequently referred to. This agreed core bundle will contain the source documents relevant to the dispute, in chronological order. There will also be other designated bundles, for example a bundle of witness statements, a bundle of pleadings, a bundle of experts' reports and a bundle of the relevant legal authorities. The plaintiff's lawyers are responsible for producing these bundles, which can sometimes run to many volumes. Multiple copies will need to be produced for the judge, the lawyers and the witnesses, and considerable photocopying costs will be incurred. The plaintiff may be able to reclaim a proportion of those costs from the defendant, if he is successful.[2]

In practice, the bundles contain photocopies of documents, and not the originals. Thus, except in cases where the authenticity of a document is in issue, the parties rely almost exclusively on copies, and in practice it is extremely rare for a point ever to turn on whether a document is an original or not.

The inclusion of documents in the bundles does not amount to an agreement as to the matters recorded in the documents. These still have to be proved by a witness.[3]

Apart from the bundles of source documents, other documents in agreed form may be produced to assist the court, such as a chronology of the important events and a *dramatis personae* listing the relevant people involved in the dispute.

F. OTHER PREPARATIONS

There are usually a great number of sundry practical matters which have to be undertaken by the lawyers when a trial is approaching. For example, *subpoenas* may need to be served to compel witnesses to attend a hearing,[4] witnesses will need to be notified and reminded of the hearing date, and travel and accommodation arrangements made for the witnesses if necessary. In large cases, shorthand writers will need to be booked to produce a daily transcript of the hearing. It is also necessary for the lawyers to present to the court before trial a "skeleton argument" setting out the chief points of their legal submissions.

It may also be immediately prior to trial that the defendant decides to make a *payment into court*.[5] This has important costs consequences, and will concentrate the plaintiff's mind on whether he really wishes to proceed to trial.

2. See Chapter 24.
3. Or, it seems, by a Civil Evidence Act notice: see Chapter 17 on evidence generally.
4. See Chapter 19.
5. See Chapter 21.

G. ADJOURNMENTS

It sometimes happens that one or both of the parties wants the trial adjourned. Although this is sometimes permissible, it should not be assumed that the judge, to whom the application to adjourn is made, will grant it unless good cause can be shown. Sometimes a brief postponement will be allowed to give time for settlement talks to take place or for further investigations to be carried out following the late discovery of important matters, but an adjournment to a later date for reasons of one of the parties' convenience will not usually be permitted.

H. THE TRIAL

The following will be present at the trial:

The judge

In civil litigation (that is, not in criminal proceedings) the liability of the parties and any damages awarded as a result of that liability are determined by the judge alone. There is no jury.[6] The judge usually has some members of the court staff, such as an usher or a clerk, to assist when documents need to be handed up to him. If you are a witness, you should address a High Court judge as "my Lord" and a county court judge and Official Referee as "your Honour".

Solicitors and counsel[7]

Solicitors' and counsel's roles at the trial have already been explained.[8] If leading counsel has been instructed, junior counsel will sit behind him and provide general assistance to him, researching points of law, finding additional legal authorities, annotating the bundles and dealing with any points arising overnight. The solicitors will sit behind junior counsel (or in front of leading counsel) and will act as a general support team, ensuring that the witnesses are present at the correct time, that counsel have all their papers, that their bundles are updated as necessary, dealing with miscellaneous problems arising from the hearing, and reporting to the client.

Witnesses

These fall into two categories: witnesses of fact and expert witnesses. It is not usually necessary for a witness to be present throughout a trial as the lawyers

6. The only exceptions are defamation actions, where a jury may still sit; and cases involving allegations of fraud, in which a jury may in theory sit but almost never does.
7. For a fuller discussion of this topic, see Chapter 3.
8. See Chapter 3.

will have agreed a timetable beforehand to decide which witness will be appearing at a particular time. In civil cases, a witness usually may be present in court throughout the hearing.[9] An expert should be present to hear the evidence of his counterpart, and of the witnesses of fact relevant to his testimony.

The parties

It is not always necessary for the client to be present in court (unless perhaps he or she is a witness), but it may be desirable so that instructions can be given promptly to the lawyers (for example if a settlement offer is made in the course of a trial), or if a particular witness needs to be contacted urgently with the client's assistance. If a client cannot be present in court, it is essential that the client remains in contact so that instructions can be given if necessary.

Members of the public may freely enter and leave the court and listen to the case unless a special order has been made by the court restricting public entry, when the court sits "in chambers".

An interpreter

In cases where evidence is given in a foreign language, an interpreter should be present to translate the testimony into English and into the foreign language.

Shorthand writers

Although all court proceedings in the High Court are centrally recorded, the facilities for obtaining from the court a transcript of the evidence and argument are limited, and it is sensible, especially in those trials that are expected to last for a long time, to engage an independent firm of shorthand writers who can produce an overnight transcript of the day's proceedings, so that evidence can be checked and documents analysed on the basis of an accurate note of what was said in court.

I. TRIAL PROCEDURE

In England trials are predominantly oral and adversarial in nature. The judge does not play an investigatory role.[10] Reforms introduced over recent years have tended to shift the emphasis towards written submissions and evidence, but the procedure is still fundamentally oral in terms of the giving of evidence and the making of legal submissions.

It is up to the plaintiff to prove his claim and accordingly the plaintiff's

9. In criminal trials, they must not be.
10. See Chapter 1.

counsel usually begins the trial by making an opening speech outlining the facts and indicating areas of dispute between the parties, the legal principles involved, and the areas where a ruling will need to be made. The pleadings and bundles of documents will be considered and reviewed.

The plaintiff's counsel then calls his witnesses. This is called "examination in chief". Where a witness statement[11] has been produced for that witness (which will be the case unless the witness has been served with a subpoena), the court will generally allow that statement, or part of it, to stand as the evidence in chief of that witness, and it will not be necessary for the plaintiff's counsel to conduct an extensive oral examination of the witness. It is important to remember that counsel may not cross-examine his own witness (see the following paragraph). The reason for this is that a party calls a witness as a witness of truth and is therefore bound to accept the answers given. The consequence is that if a party's witness gives an answer that is unhelpful, he cannot be challenged upon it.[12]

The defendant's counsel will *cross-examine* the plaintiff's witness on what he has said in his statement and/or the evidence he has previously given to the court. The witness has access to the trial bundles and may read all documents that are referred to. Cross-examination has several purposes: to elicit information not dealt with or not dealt with fully in chief; and to test the truthfulness of the witness's testimony, or to cast doubt on it, or to question the witness's general tendency to tell the truth. It is important to remember that whilst counsel may not ask "leading questions" of his own witness (that is, ask questions that suggest the answer sought) this is permissible in the case of cross-examination. Furthermore, in cross-examination there is greater freedom generally about the type of questions that may be asked, and these can be relevant, for example, to issues such as the credibility of a witness, or his conduct in other matters. A witness may also be cross-examined on any affidavit he has sworn earlier in the proceedings.

The plaintiff's counsel has the opportunity to re-examine the witness, for example to seek to correct something which the witness may have said on cross-examination, or to rehabilitate evidence that has been shaken, although it often happens that damage done in cross-examination cannot easily be repaired.

After all the plaintiff's witnesses have given their evidence, the defendant's counsel will then call his witnesses. He will not normally make an opening speech. The plaintiff's counsel may then cross-examine those witnesses and a procedure will be followed similar to that described earlier.

An advocate is obliged to challenge every part of the witness's evidence which conflicts with his own case, and to put to his witness his own case on matters within the witness's knowledge, and to put any point that can properly be made.

11. See Chapter 19.
12. In some very rare cases it is possible to have the court declare that one's witness is "hostile" and thereafter to cross-examine him.

Both the plaintiff's and the defendant's counsel will then make closing submissions to the judge. The defendant's counsel speaks first, followed by the plaintiff's counsel. They each cite the legal authorities on which they rely, and are obliged in addition to refer the court to those that do not help their case as well as those that support it.

J. TRIAL MANAGEMENT

The courts and the lawyers are very aware that litigation in general and trials in particular are expensive. The increasing trend is for the lawyers, with the assistance of the court, to try to reduce costs by seeking to agree issues in advance of the trial. Before the trial there will have been a Summons for Directions or review hearings, at which the lawyers and the court will have considered questions such as the length of the trial, the number of witnesses to be present at the trial and the order in which they are to be called. Orders will have been made for witness statements and experts' reports to be exchanged, so that each party is aware prior to trial of the case which it must meet. In exceptionally large and important cases, it is possible to apply for a judge to be assigned to the case, and he will preside over all pre-trial hearings as well as the trial itself. This ensures continuity and can assist the parties greatly to manage the case.

Trial management can only be achieved with the co-operation of all the parties and firm intervention and supervision from the judge. Given the nature of litigation, it may not be possible to agree certain issues in advance, and it may be a party's tactic to be unco-operative or to procrastinate.

K. JUDGMENT[13]

When counsel have concluded their closing submissions, it will be time for the judge to determine the case. In a complex case the judge usually reserves judgment (that is, postpones giving his decision) until a later date. In those circumstances, the judge will usually prepare a lengthy, detailed and reasoned judgment. In more straightforward cases, the judge may inform the parties of his decision immediately, and provide a reasoned judgment at that time or subsequently.

When judgment has been given, various applications may be made by counsel to the judge. For example, the successful party will apply for costs to be awarded in his favour against the unsuccessful party.[14] The unsuccessful party may apply to the court for a stay of execution to prevent the judgment being enforced immediately.[15]

13. For a discussion of the types of judgment that may be made, see Chapter 23.
14. See Chapter 24.
15. See Chapter 29.

Where a payment into court has been made, application to remove the money will be made.[16]

The unsuccessful party may seek leave to appeal from the judge in those cases when leave to appeal is necessary.[17]

L. SPLIT TRIALS

In many cases, there are two main issues for the court to decide: whether the defendant is liable as claimed; and, if so, for how much. Often, this second issue is complex and involves considerable expert and factual evidence that would be wasted if prepared before the defendant had even been found liable. Therefore, it is usual for the trial of such issues to be split so that only if the plaintiff establishes liability do the parties later go on to a second trial on the amount of damages to be paid. This can involve long delays but can also save costs if the plaintiff should lose on the issue of liability.

M. THIRD PARTY PROCEEDINGS

Where the defendant has himself joined other parties to the action, or where two or more defendants claim against each other, the court will usually try all the issues in the proceedings, with the third party claims being dealt with immediately after the main action.

16. See Chapter 21.
17. See Chapter 25.

CHAPTER 23

REMEDIES AND JUDGMENTS

This chapter explains the main remedies which are available to a successful party.

A. INTRODUCTION

The court may make a number of interlocutory orders during the progress of a case to trial. For example, it may order *discovery* of specific documents; or allow *extensions of time* for performing obligations; it may grant *interim injunctions*; or it may *strike out* parts of the pleadings. Those orders have largely been explained in earlier chapters.

At trial, the court has the power to make a variety of awards depending on the nature of the case. For example, a plaintiff may seek financial compensation for a loss which he has suffered; he may seek the return of specific property of which he has been deprived as a result of the defendant's wrongful act; he may seek to stop the defendant from pursuing a wrongful act or course of action; he may seek an account of the profits earned from an infringement of his rights; he may seek a declaration from the court as to his rights in respect of an agreement; or he may seek a combination of these remedies. The following are the orders most frequently made. Some the court will make automatically on proof of the case by the plaintiff; others lie in the discretion of the court.

B. DAMAGES

Damages are the pecuniary compensation paid by a defendant to a plaintiff to compensate him, insofar as money can, for the wrong which the defendant has committed. The object of an award of damages is to give the plaintiff compensation for the damage, loss or injury he has suffered.

Heads of damage

Damages fall into a number of categories, as follows:

- *General damages*: this is compensation for loss that is presumed to flow from a breach of contract or other wrong.
- *Special damages*: these relate not to what is presumed to have been caused, but to what has been proved to have been suffered in any particular case. Examples include out-of-pocket expenses, and specific costs of medical treatment.
- *Unliquidated damages*: these must be fixed by the court as the correct amount to award in all the circumstances of the case. Most claims for damages fall into this category, despite plaintiffs' attempts to mischaracterise their own assessments of loss as liquidated damages.
- *Liquidated damages*: these are outside the court's discretion, and are those agreed upon by the parties, in advance of any dispute, as being payable in the event of breach of agreement. Examples are claims where an agreed scale of damages is laid down in a contract. It should be noted that not every such agreement is upheld by the courts, and it is necessary to demonstrate that the fixed amount is a genuine estimate of loss.

Limitations upon an award of damages

A plaintiff is not able to recover for every loss which he has suffered. He may not recover damages that are too remote from the breach or wrong; nor, for example, for that part of the loss caused by his own negligence (known as *contributory negligence*); nor for loss which was not caused by the defendant; nor for loss which is too uncertain to quantify. The law also expects a plaintiff to take all reasonable steps to reduce the loss consequent upon the defendant's wrong. This rule is known as the *mitigation of damages*.

Judgment on the award of damages, interest and costs

The court may order interest to be paid on damages, and may award costs[1] in favour of the successful party.

The court will not usually order damages to be paid until the end of the trial, but in certain cases the court will order an interim payment of damages[2] to be made.

In a limited range of contractual claims, primarily those concerned with a failure to pay money, a plaintiff has a *right* to claim interest. In other cases, the court has a *discretion* whether to award interest. In contractual claims, the court will consider whether the breach of contract has deprived the plaintiff of money which he would otherwise have had available for his use. In general, there is no fixed rate of interest, and the court may award different rates depending on the nature of the claim. In commercial cases, for example, the court may order

1. See Chapter 24.
2. See Chapter 15.

interest to be paid at a rate in accordance with the current bank lending rates, or may choose an alternative commercial rate. In debt claims and claims for liquidated damages, the court may order interest to be paid at the rate provided by the contract and will almost invariably order *simple* interest, although in rare cases it may order *compound* interest. (Note that arbitrators have the power to award compound interest in any case.[3])

The court has a discretion to decide from what date interest should run. In debt claims, it is the normal practice to order interest to be paid from the date when the money should have been paid. Where the plaintiff has suffered economic loss, the court may order interest to be paid from the date of the loss, if this date can be identified. If the loss cannot be quantified until judgment, the court has a discretion to award interest from the date upon which the cause of action arose or any proper later date. Interest at that rate will be incorporated into the judgment. If the defendant does not pay the judgment, then interest on the judgment debt will in addition be payable from the date of judgment until the date of payment. The judgment rate[4] varies from time to time, and is currently eight per cent per annum.

The court has power to give judgment for a sum of money expressed in a foreign currency. The judgment will be for payment of the amount of the foreign currency or its sterling equivalent, converted for the purposes of the enforcement of the judgment at the time of payment, that is, the date on which the enforcement process is begun.[5] Where there is more than one eligible foreign currency in which judgment may be given, the judgment will, in the absence of agreement, be expressed in the currency in which the plaintiff's loss is felt or which most closely expresses his loss.

C. SPECIFIC PERFORMANCE

In some cases damages will not be adequate to compensate the plaintiff. Where the subject matter of a contract has special value or unique features which make damages an inadequate remedy, the court may order a defendant to perform the contract rather than pay damages for breach of the contract. This is known as an order for *specific performance.*

Examples

D contracts to sell a house to P. Shortly before completion of the purchase, D decides to sell the property to X, who has made a higher offer, and refuses to sell the house to P. In this situation, damages may not be an adequate remedy for P. He has contracted to purchase D's property and damages would merely enable him to purchase another property, rather than the particular property that he wants. The court may be prepared to grant specific performance to compel D to sell the property to P.

D contracts to sell some shares to P. The shares are not available elsewhere on the market. D

3. See Chapter 31.
4. See also Chapter 29, Part I, section B.
5. See Chapter 29.

refuses to deliver the shares. The court may grant specific performance in favour of P, so that D is compelled to transfer the shares to P, rather than pay him damages.

Limitations on the grant of specific performance

The court will not order specific performance in cases where damages would be an adequate remedy. The court has a broad discretion, and will take into account factors such as the plaintiff's own conduct, and whether the rights of a third party would be adversely affected if specific performance were ordered. There are also certain contracts where it is recognised that the court will not order specific performance: for example, a contract of employment.

D. RECTIFICATION

The court may order that a contract that does not properly record the agreement between the parties should be rectified to reflect the true agreement.

E. INJUNCTIONS

In certain circumstances damages will not be adequate to compensate the plaintiff because the remedy which the plaintiff requires is to *restrain* the defendant from starting or continuing a wrongful act or course of conduct, or to *force* him to do certain things in the plaintiff's interests, and not just to be compensated for continuing losses caused by the repetition of that wrongful act or course of conduct. In many cases, a claim to an injunction is coupled with a claim for damages.

Example
D manufactures a range of counterfeit goods which replicate exactly the range made by P, and uses the name and logo registered by P. P may restrain D by injunction from continuing to manufacture the goods, and may be able to claim damages in addition to the counterfeit goods which have already been delivered up.

In urgent cases, a plaintiff may be able to obtain an *interim* injunction to restrain a defendant from causing irreparable damage until the trial of the action. In less urgent cases, the plaintiff will seek a *final* injunction to restrain further breaches. (A fuller account of injunctions is contained in Chapter 10.)

Special types of injunction are also available as relief ancillary to that claimed in the action. Injunctions may be granted to preserve property and assets pending the trial of the action. These are known as *Mareva* injunctions and *Anton Piller* orders, and are dealt with in Chapter 11. An injunction may also be granted in aid of a tracing claim.[6]

It is also possible for the court to order that the defendant *deliver up* to the plaintiff property that should have been returned to him: for example where

6. See section G below, and Chapter 36.

the defendant has infringed the plaintiff's copyright, or unlawfully taken possession of the plaintiff's goods.

F. DECLARATIONS

In some cases, the plaintiff seeks to have his rights determined by the court by a *declaration*. This may be coupled with a claim for damages or for the other forms of relief. This is appropriate in cases, for example, in which rights to land or in respect of contracts or the interpretation of legal documents that will affect rights in the future are involved. In such cases, the court will not give a judgment by default and will always hear evidence before ruling. (See also Chapter 6, section M for a description of *negative declarations*.)

G. RESTITUTION AND TRACING ORDERS

Where it is alleged that the defendant has acquired property of the plaintiff, for example, unlawfully or for no consideration in circumstances where he has been *unjustly enriched*, the plaintiff is entitled to claim back the property or an equivalent sum in cash from the defendant. Such claims are often linked to a separate claim for a *tracing* order in which the property of the plaintiff, which has fallen into the hands of the defendant, can be traced and recovered in certain circumstances. Tracing is, strictly, not a remedy, but a mechanism for achieving a remedy. (See also Chapter 36 for an account of the role of bankers in such cases.)

H. POSSESSION OF LAND

In an action under a lease or in respect of real property, the court may order that land be returned to the plaintiff. This is dealt with in Chapter 32.

I. ACTIONS FOR AN ACCOUNT

In certain cases, the court will order the defendant to provide to the plaintiff an account of his profits arising from his use or misuse of the plaintiff's property, and to give to the plaintiff the money so accounted for. This frequently arises in cases involving breach of *copyright* or *trademark* where it is proved that the defendant is accountable to the plaintiff for earnings from the infringement.

J. ACTIONS FOR DISCOVERY

In some limited cases, it is possible to bring proceedings for discovery to assist the plaintiff in establishing whether he has a claim against another party. This is discussed in more detail in Chapter 18, section K.

K. JUDICIAL REVIEW

In addition to those awards referred to above, the court may also quash decisions or make other orders in respect of the decisions of public bodies in applications for *judicial review*. This is dealt with in Chapter 35.

CHAPTER 24

COSTS

This chapter describes the rules that govern the question of which party shall pay or receive the legal costs of litigation.[1] A chart that summarises the rules appears on page 173.

A. INTRODUCTION

As a general rule, litigants are bound, irrespective of whether they win or lose the litigation, to meet the cost of advice given and work done for them by their own lawyers.

The court does, however, have a wide discretion to order one party to contribute towards the costs of another, both of pre-trial matters and in respect of the trial itself.

B. "SOLICITOR-OWN CLIENT" COSTS

The costs of litigation, including fees payable to solicitors and to counsel and disbursements such as court fees, fees payable to expert witnesses, and general disbursements (for example, fares and the cost of photocopying documents), are called "solicitor-own client" costs. They are invoiced by the party's solicitors and payable by agreement in the normal way, irrespective of the result of the proceedings.[2]

As litigation will typically last for two, three or even more years, interim invoices for these fees are usually submitted to a client at regular intervals for immediate payment.

1. Normally, costs are payable only as between the parties to litigation, but in some rare and exceptional cases, an order for costs may be made against someone who is not a party to the action at all, for example in representative actions: see Chapter 30.

2. Note that lawyers may charge fees according to results in certain matters such as personal injury and insolvency-related claims.

C. COSTS ORDERS

Costs orders may be made for the costs of the trial itself, and also for the costs incurred in the action. These include the costs in relation to the work carried out by the lawyers in the course of all their preparations, and also the costs of interlocutory applications to court. Costs will not usually be awarded for work carried out before proceedings are commenced unless it relates specifically to the preparation of the writ and Statement of Claim.

Interlocutory orders

During the course of the proceedings, the parties will almost inevitably attend the court for pre-trial "interlocutory" applications. For example, an application may be made for an order for discovery of a particular document.[3] At each of these applications, the court will make an order dealing with who is to pay the costs of that application. The most common orders are:

- *Costs reserved*: The party in whose favour an order for costs is made at trial is entitled to be reimbursed the costs of the interlocutory application unless, at trial, the court specifically orders otherwise.
- *Costs in any event*: The party in whose favour this costs order is made on an interlocutory application is entitled to be reimbursed the costs of the application whatever the final outcome of the case.
- *Costs in the cause*: The party in whose favour this order for costs is made at the trial is entitled to be reimbursed the costs of the interlocutory application at which this order was made.
- *Plaintiff's costs in the cause* or *Defendant's costs in the cause*: The plaintiff or defendant, as the case may be, is entitled to be reimbursed the costs of the interlocutory application at which this order was made provided that he succeeds at trial; if judgment is given in favour of any other party, he will not be paid his costs, but nor will he be liable to meet that party's costs of the interlocutory application.
- *Costs thrown away*: Where proceedings in whole or part have been ineffective or have been set aside, the party in whose favour this order is made is entitled to be reimbursed the costs of those proceedings or the applicable part of them.
- *No order as to costs*: Each party will pay his own costs in respect of the application.

The general costs of trial and pre-trial work

The court has a wide discretion to order that one party should contribute towards another's costs. All of the costs "of or incidental to" the proceedings

3. See Chapter 18.

will be included. These encompass, for example, the costs of drafting a letter before action, collating evidence and conducting negotiations.

Generally, only your legal costs will be recoverable: the cost of management time spent on preparations is usually irrecoverable. Management time can sometimes be claimed as damages, but not frequently.

The general rule is that the costs of the proceedings are paid by the loser to the winner: that is to say, "costs follow the event".[4] This means that a successful plaintiff who is awarded more than nominal damages will be entitled (except in unusual circumstances) to a contribution towards the costs which he is obliged to pay to his solicitors. Equally, a successful defendant is entitled to a similar order.

An order for costs will not be made if the court considers that the party brought the litigation upon himself or has done something to occasion unnecessary litigation or acted wrongly in the course of the transaction about which the complaint was made. Equally, unnecessarily unreasonable behaviour in the course of proceedings may be penalised in costs.

Example
D is ordered to serve Further and Better Particulars of his Defence. He does not do so. P is obliged to return to court for a further order. D will be required to pay the costs of the summons.

The court, at the instigation of an aggrieved party at the end of the proceedings, may order that a lawyer pay costs which have been caused by an improper, unreasonable or negligent act or omission which the court considers it unreasonable to expect a party to bear. This is known as a "wasted costs" order.

D. WHEN RECOVERABLE COSTS WILL BE RECEIVED

Whilst an order for costs can be made at any stage of the proceedings, it will not usually be open to the parties to quantify the costs payable and enforce the order until after the trial or compromise of the action.

Recoverable costs will normally only be reimbursed after the end of the litigation, which may be two, three or even more years after the payment of interim invoices.[5]

4. There is sometimes a dispute as to what precisely is "the event" that an order for costs must follow. This can typically arise where, for example, a plaintiff has succeeded in some but not all of his claims in the action, and may be complicated by similar considerations concerning a counterclaim.

5. The court may sometimes make an order for the assessment of costs ("taxation") and payment immediately, but only if, for example, there is no likelihood of a further order being made or if a party's conduct is oppressive.

E. WHAT IS RECOVERABLE

An order for costs does not necessarily entitle you to be reimbursed all of the costs which you have paid or owe your lawyers. The costs to be reimbursed, if they cannot be agreed, will be the subject of an assessment by the court. The court will order the assessment to be carried out on one of two bases: the *standard* basis or the *indemnity* basis.

The general rule is that costs are assessed on the *standard* basis, by which the court will allow all costs that are reasonable in amount and reasonably incurred. Where there is any doubt as to reasonableness, the doubt will be resolved in favour of the paying party.

As an exception to this general rule, costs may be ordered to be paid on the *indemnity* basis, where doubt is resolved in favour of the receiving party. Such an order is used as a penalty for the abuse of process: for example, contempt of court or the improper use of procedures.

Example
P obtains an *Anton Piller* order[6] without disclosing all the relevant facts to the court. The court may order P to pay D's costs on the indemnity basis, to be taxed and paid immediately.

It used to be the general rule in High Court litigation that, on the assumption that the standard basis would be applied, around 60 per cent of the costs payable to a litigant's solicitor were recoverable. It is almost impossible to be fully reimbursed.

It has sometimes (but by no means always) proved possible to recover a higher percentage, sometimes up to 85 per cent, in recognition of the real cost of litigation.

F. TAXATION

Where an order for the costs of litigation is made, it is customary for the parties' solicitors to try to agree between themselves what sum will be paid. This is done on the basis of what each predict the court would order if the matter came before it. Frequently, no agreement can be reached, in which case the dispute must be brought before the court for adjudication.

The process whereby the court assesses the amount of recoverable costs is known as "taxation".

The procedure begins when the receiving party lodges at the Supreme Court Taxing Office a number of formal documents relating to the original action, the receiving party's "bill of costs" and his solicitor's files. It is usual for the bill of costs to be prepared by a specialist costs draftsman.[7]

6. See Chapter 11.
7. It is one of the anomalies of the system that the bill of costs is exceptionally complex and its appearance bears no resemblance to a lawyer's invoice.

The cost of preparing for the taxation and the obligation to meet a taxing fee of five per cent of the sum allowed, both of which are ultimately payable by the paying party, can be sufficient to lead the parties to agree the level of costs, rather than proceed with taxation.

The paying party may lodge written notice of his points of objection prior to the hearing. Note in particular that, in the case of a taxation of a solicitor's bill at the instance of his client, if no more than 20 per cent of the bill as disputed is "taxed off" the paying party must meet the costs of the taxation. In the case of the taxation of costs as between the parties to litigation, the paying party may protect his interests by serving within 14 days of receipt of the bill a letter offering to pay what he regards as a reasonable sum.

The taxation itself is heard by a taxing officer or master who will, in the presence of representatives of each of the parties, their lawyers and costs draftsmen, assess each item in the bill of costs, having regard to all the relevant circumstances. In particular, he will take into account factors such as the time spent, the complexity of the matter, the number of documents and the specialised knowledge required.

Of these factors, the most important is the amount of time spent. The main item taxed is the solicitors' fees, which are assessed in two stages.

- First, the court considers the appropriate *hourly charge* rate, which represents the reasonable direct cost to the solicitors of undertaking the work.[8]
- Secondly, the court takes into account matters which cannot be calculated on an hourly basis, such as the complexity of the matter, and applies a percentage uplift which is, broadly speaking, around 50 per cent for a routine case.

After taxation, the court issues a taxation certificate certifying the amount of costs allowed, which includes a taxing fee of five per cent of the amount allowed, VAT where applicable (that is, where the recipient is not registered for VAT) and interest from the date of the order for costs on the taxed amount of costs.

A dissatisfied party can, within 21 days of the taxation, apply for a review. At the review, which is usually undertaken by the same taxing officer who conducted the taxation, detailed reasons for his decision will be given. Taxations of smaller bills are heard by junior taxing officers, but dealt with on review by the more senior taxing masters. A dissatisfied party may then apply for a further review by a judge, who will be assisted by a taxing master and a

8. The court has recently held that when fixing hourly rates it may take into account that it is reasonable for a party to have used a City firm, and then refer to surveys showing the real costs to such firms of providing the service of litigation.

practising solicitor, known as assessors. An appeal from the judge to the Court of Appeal may sometimes be allowed.

G. LEGALLY-AIDED LITIGANTS

The level of costs that will be awarded to a successful party is restricted if his opponent is legally-aided.

The general rule is that a legally-aided litigant can only be required to pay such amount as "is a reasonable one for him to pay, having regard to all the circumstances, including the financial resources of all the parties and their conduct in connection with the dispute".

In these circumstances, the court is obliged to examine the means and conduct of all of the parties before making any order as to costs.

A successful non-legally-aided party, who is unable to recover costs, is entitled by way of recompense to apply to the court for an order for payment of all or part of his costs from the Legal Aid Fund. The applicant must show amongst other things that, were it not for the provisions of the Legal Aid scheme, an order for costs would have been made and that these provisions will cause him to suffer severe financial hardship.

> *It almost inevitably follows that someone sued by a plaintiff who is in receipt of civil legal aid will not be able to recover his costs if he is successful and will not be able to deploy the threat of adverse costs in the course of negotiations.*

RECOVERY OF COSTS OF INTERLOCUTORY APPLICATIONS

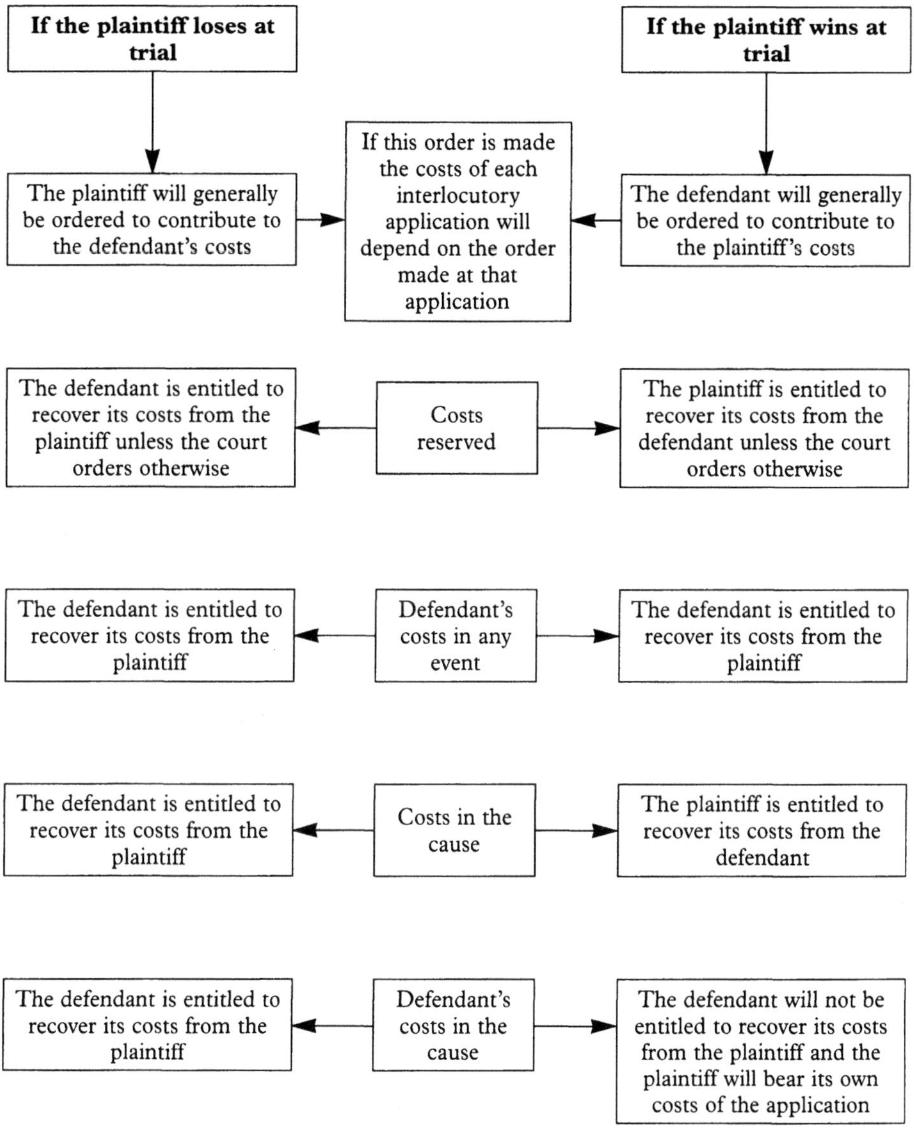

Note
This chart deals with the recovery of the costs of interlocutory applications. The costs of the trial itself will generally "follow the event", that is, the winner is paid by the loser.

CHAPTER 25

APPEALS

This chapter explains the system by which appeals from the decisions of courts and other judicial bodies are dealt with. Two charts setting out the structure of the appeal system appear on pages 182 and 183.

A. INTRODUCTION

An appeal is an application to a court from the decision of another court, tribunal or decision-making body whereby the person making the appeal seeks to overturn the decision which is the subject of the appeal on the grounds that it is incorrect. In most cases, an appeal will be from a lower court to a higher court.

The parties to an appeal are called the *appellant* and the *respondent*.

An appeal generally involves the appellant demonstrating that there is an error in the decision complained of. Sometimes, however, there is no error, and the court may be asked to *set aside* its order on another ground. For example:

— A judgment or order may be made by a court against a party in his absence. The party may apply to the same court for the judgment or order to be set aside.

— A party may obtain a judgment or order from a court through misconduct: for example, by deliberately misleading the other party or the court. The other party may bring proceedings before the same court for the judgment or order to be set aside.

Both these types of application are made to the same court which made the original order. This distinguishes them from appeals, which are generally heard by a different court.

It is often assumed by parties to litigation who are disappointed with a decision that, on an appeal, they will have the chance of having their case tried all over again. This is not so. The general rule is that decisions of bodies which exercise a judicial function are intended to be final and determinative. (See section F below for a further account of this general rule in practice.) Therefore, the grounds on which appeals can be made are generally restricted. Often, they will be limited to points of law: that is, the appellant will have to show that the judge applied the wrong legal principles in reaching his decision. It is rare for a judge's decision on a question of fact to be capable of challenge on appeal.

A decision of a court, tribunal or decision-making body generally becomes effective as soon as it is made. The fact that one party to the dispute appeals against the decision does not automatically mean that the carrying out of the decision is suspended. If a party wants the decision to be suspended, then he must ask for a stay.

B. THE SOURCE OF JURISDICTION

In English law, the rights which a party has to appeal from a decision of a court, tribunal or decision-making body are derived from statute. They are not based on the common law. The powers of various courts to hear appeals, and the rights of parties to make them, are constituted by various Acts of Parliament.

- The Supreme Court Act 1981 is the source of the constitution of the Supreme Court of England and Wales which consists of the Court of Appeal, the High Court of Justice and the Crown Court. The jurisdiction of the Court of Appeal and the High Court and their powers to hear appeals are set out therein.
- The County Court Act 1984 is the source of the constitution of the county courts, which sets out the jurisdiction of the county courts and their powers to hear appeals.

C. THE COURT STRUCTURE

The final appeal court is the House of Lords. The House of Lords deals with cases arising in civil litigation in England and Wales, Scotland and Northern Ireland.

Certain appeals are heard by the Judicial Committee of the Privy Council. The Privy Council deals with non-domestic appeals and domestic appeals. Non-domestic appeals are from decisions from the Channel Islands and the Isle of Man, from certain independent Commonwealth countries and from other countries and territories connected with the United Kingdom. Domestic appeals are from decisions of bodies such as the Admiralty Court, certain professional disciplinary committees, such as the General Medical Council, and Ecclesiastical Courts. The same judges who hear appeals in the House of Lords hear appeals in the Judicial Committee of the Privy Council. In theory, the judgments of the Privy Council do not form part of the system of precedent in England, but are of great weight and are usually followed by the other courts.

Appeals to the House of Lords are generally from decisions of the Court of Appeal. The Court of Appeal deals with decisions of lower courts in England and Wales. Its equivalent body in Scotland is the Court of Session and, in Northern Ireland, the Court of Appeal for Northern Ireland.

Occasionally, the House of Lords will hear appeals direct from decisions of the High Court. This only happens where the case involves a point of law of general public importance and where there is a binding decision of the Court of Appeal supporting the decision appealed from.

Appeals to the Court of Appeal are made from the decisions of various courts, tribunals and decision-making bodies. These include:

- The High Court and county courts, which are the courts in which most civil cases are initially decided.
- The Employment Appeal Tribunal,[1] which hears appeals from decisions of Industrial Tribunals relating to employment matters and claims under the sex discrimination and race relations legislation.
- The Lands Tribunal, which deals with applications concerning land, such as the removal of restrictive covenants affecting land.
- The Restrictive Practices Court, which deals with proceedings under the Fair Trading Act 1973.
- Commercial judges sitting as arbitrators.[2]

Appeals to the High Court are made from the decisions of various courts, tribunals and decision-making bodies. Among the more important are:

To the Queen's Bench Division:

- Decisions of inspectors under the town and country planning legislation.
- Decisions of judges in contempt of court[3] cases.
- Decisions in disciplinary hearings of some professional bodies, such as Solicitors Disciplinary Tribunals.
- Interlocutory decisions of masters in cases proceeding in the Queen's Bench Division.
- Awards of arbitrators (where appeals lie to the Commercial Court, a part of the Queen's Bench Division).

To the Chancery Division:

- Decisions concerning the liquidation of companies under the Companies Acts[4] and decisions of the Department of Trade and the Official Receiver.

1. See Chapter 34.
2. See Chapter 31.
3. See Chapter 38.
4. See Chapter 33.

- Decisions of district judges in insolvency proceedings relating to individuals and companies[4].
- Decisions of county courts in bankruptcy matters[4].
- Decisions of the Inland Revenue Commissioners in taxation and stamp duty cases.
- Interlocutory decisions of masters and district judges in cases proceeding in the Chancery Division.

To the Family Division:
- Decisions arising out of matrimonial proceedings, such as payment of maintenance.
- Decisions concerning children, such as adoption or custodianship matters.

Appeals to the county courts include appeals from:

- Decisions of district judges hearing interlocutory matters in ongoing county court litigation.
- Decisions of the Civil Aviation Authority.
- Decisions arising under equal opportunities and racial equality legislation.

D. THE APPEAL ITSELF

Procedure and powers of the appellate court

Each court which hears appeals has its own procedure governing the conduct of such appeals. The procedure deals with the mechanism by which appeals may be brought before the appellate court and the way in which the hearing of the appeals is to be conducted. Broadly, each court has its own set of rules which are made through powers vested in the court by statute.

Although the rules of procedure of the various appellate courts differ, they share certain common characteristics. These include:

- The right of each party to be given notice of the other party's case before the hearing of the appeal.
- The right of each party to be heard at the same time as the other party, so that the appellate court will hear both parties' cases before making its decision.

Similarly, the various appellate courts have the power to make varying orders in relation to appeals which come before them. Orders which may be made include:

— An order dismissing an appeal. That is, the appellate court concludes that the decision appealed from should stand.
— An order allowing the appeal. That is, the appellate court concludes that the decision appealed from should not stand. This means that the party which won the case in which the decision is appealed has now lost it.
— An order for a new trial. That is, that the case should be heard again by the court in which the decision appealed from was made.

E. LEAVE

One of the most important questions is whether a party requires the permission, or leave, of the court before it is allowed to appeal.

The House of Lords

— An appeal from the Court of Appeal to the House of Lords requires leave of the Court of Appeal or of the House of Lords. If the Court of Appeal gives leave, leave of the House of Lords is not required. If the Court of Appeal refuses leave, leave of the House of Lords must be sought and may be given.
— The initial application for leave is usually made orally at the end of the hearing in the Court of Appeal. If it is not made then, a subsequent application in writing must be made to the Court of Appeal which then hears the application.
— An application for leave to the House of Lords is made by petition. It is dealt with by a committee of three Lords of Appeal. The decision to grant leave is at the discretion of the committee. Generally, the appellant must show that the case raises a point of law of general public importance before leave is given.
— The committee deals with the petition on the basis of the documents it has received from the parties. Sometimes the parties will be asked to appear before the committee to argue the matter orally. This happens if the committee is not unanimous in its decision to grant or refuse leave.
— Where the appeal is direct from the High Court, leave of both the House of Lords and the High Court is required.

Not all decisions of the Court of Appeal can be referred to the House of Lords. In some cases, the decision of the Court of Appeal is final. These include:

— Where the Court of Appeal has refused leave to appeal to itself from a decision of a lower court.

— Where the Court of Appeal (or the High Court) has refused an *ex parte* application for leave to apply for judicial review.[5]

The Privy Council

— In non-domestic cases, the right to appeal to the Privy Council depends on the law of the country in whose courts the decision appealed from was made. Usually, leave of the court in question will be needed. Sometimes, special leave of Her Majesty in Council will be obtained. Unlike the House of Lords, the Privy Council does not have power to give leave for appeals to it.
— In domestic cases, no leave to appeal is generally required. The Privy Council grants a re-hearing of the decision appealed against.

The Court of Appeal

Leave to appeal from a decision of the High Court is generally unnecessary. The limited cases where it is necessary include:

— A decision of a Divisional Court of the High Court on an appeal to the High Court.
— An order granting or refusing relief at the hearing of an application for judicial review.
— An order of the High Court in proceedings for the grant of a new tenancy under Part II of the Landlord and Tenant Act 1954[6] (security of tenure for business tenants at the end of their leases).
— Most interlocutory orders of the High Court.
— A decision of the county court where the monetary sum in issue in the case in the county court is below certain limits or where the decision of the judge of the county court was, itself, made on an appeal.

Where leave is required, it should initially be sought from the court whose decision is appealed against. If leave is refused, then it can be sought from the Court of Appeal.

An application for leave to appeal is generally dealt with "on paper" by a single judge of the Court of Appeal without a hearing, or at a subsequent oral hearing, if required.

The High Court

In some cases leave is required and in other cases it is not. Cases where leave is required include:

5. See Chapter 35.
6. See Chapter 32.

— An appeal from an arbitrator's award (unless all the parties to the award have otherwise agreed) where the appeal is on a question of law arising in the arbitration. Leave is granted in limited cases, to reflect the overall objective that an arbitrator's award is final.

Cases where leave is not required include:

— Appeals from interlocutory orders of High Court masters or district judges.
— Where there is a statutory right of appeal.

The county court

No leave of the court is required.

F. ALLOWING OR DISMISSING THE APPEAL

There is no single set of principles which governs all appeals. This is because the decisions appealed against, and the bodies whose decisions are appealed, differ. Some appeals are by way of re-hearing: that is, the court hearing the appeal hears the whole case again. Other appeals are based on specific points arising in the decision appealed against, for example, an error of law or an error of procedure. Put broadly, an appeal in the nature of a re-hearing of a case does not take place beyond the High Court. Appeals to the Court of Appeal and the House of Lords are generally on legal points.

G. FORMALITIES

The formalities for lodging appeals depend on the rules of procedure applicable to the relevant appellate court. It is important to follow the formalities closely, in particular, time limits. All appellate courts impose limits on the time which may elapse between the making of the decision appealed against and the commencement of an appeal from it. To bring his appeal out of time, that is, late, an appellant will need the permission of the appellate court. Such permission may be refused or may only be granted on conditions. The longer the delay, the more likely it is that the appeal will not be allowed to go forward.

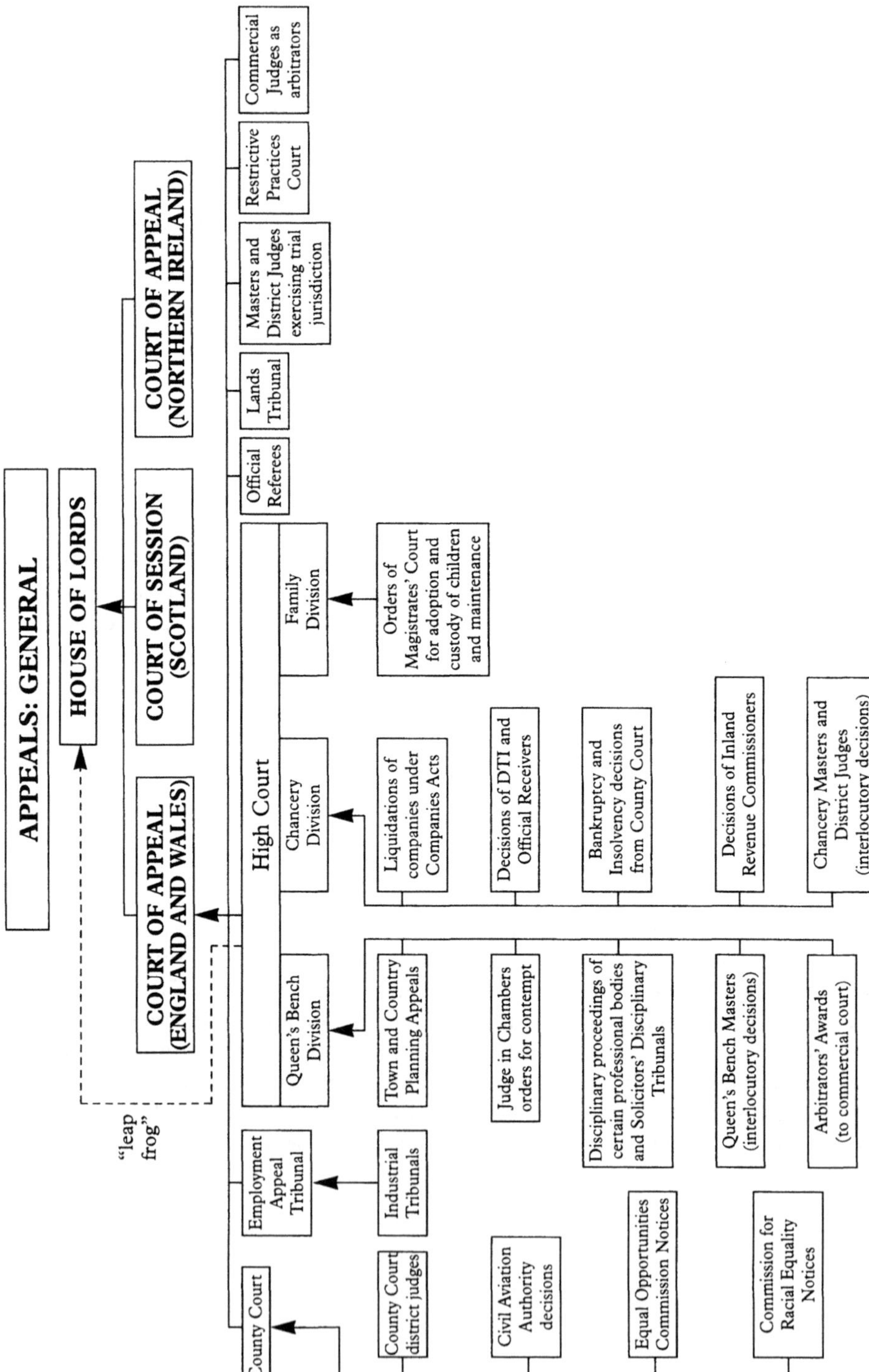
APPEALS: GENERAL
HOUSE OF LORDS
COURT OF APPEAL (ENGLAND AND WALES)
COURT OF SESSION (SCOTLAND)
COURT OF APPEAL (NORTHERN IRELAND)
"leap frog"
High Court
Queen's Bench Division
Chancery Division
Family Division
Official Referees
Lands Tribunal
Masters and District Judges exercising trial jurisdiction
Restrictive Practices Court
Commercial Judges as arbitrators
Orders of Magistrates' Court for adoption and custody of children and maintenance
Liquidations of companies under Companies Acts
Decisions of DTI and Official Receivers
Bankruptcy and Insolvency decisions from County Court
Decisions of Inland Revenue Commissioners
Chancery Masters and District Judges (interlocutory decisions)
Town and Country Planning Appeals
Judge in Chambers orders for contempt
Disciplinary proceedings of certain professional bodies and Solicitors' Disciplinary Tribunals
Queen's Bench Masters (interlocutory decisions)
Arbitrators' Awards (to commercial court)
Employment Appeal Tribunal
Industrial Tribunals
County Court
County Court district judges
Civil Aviation Authority decisions
Equal Opportunities Commission Notices
Commission for Racial Equality Notices

APPEALS: PRIVY COUNCIL

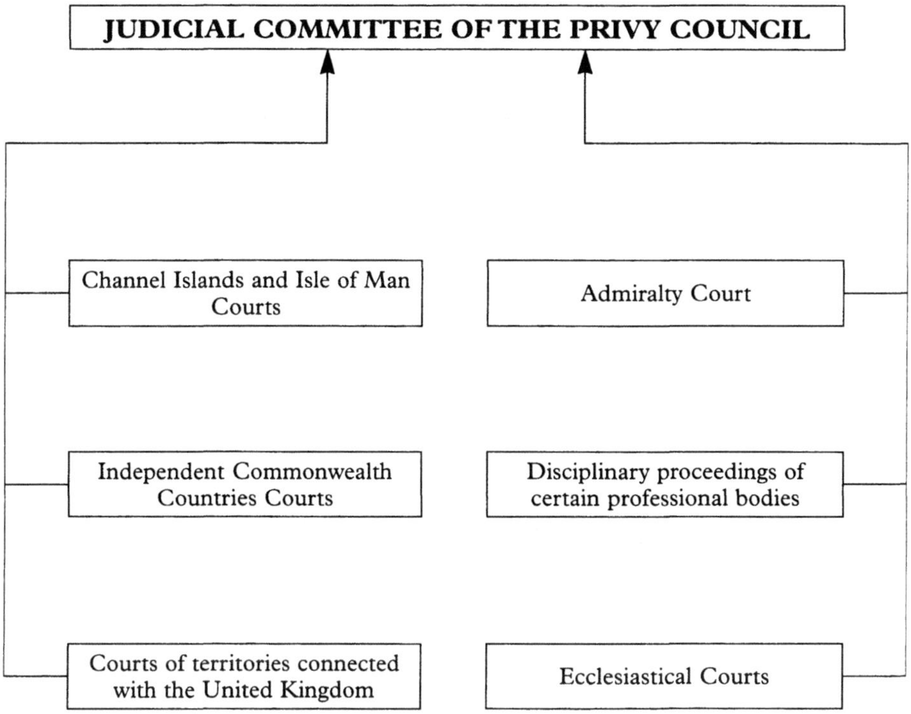

CHAPTER 26

PROCEEDINGS COMMENCED BY ORIGINATING SUMMONSES

The earlier chapters describe the rules that relate to actions begun by writ. There is a different procedure for certain other types of case that are begun by Originating Summonses.

Proceedings begun by writ typically involve considerable disputes both of law and of fact. Those cases require oral testimony which is subject to cross-examination. But other types of case involve only arguments about the interpretation of documents such as Acts of Parliament, or a deed or a will or a contract. These cases do not require detailed examination of facts, which will be largely irrelevant to the issues before the court, and a less complex procedure is laid down.

The procedure is available in both the Queen's Bench Division and the Chancery Division of the High Court, although invariably the latter is used, and in the county court.

The procedures for the issue and service and acknowledgment of service are the same as in an action begun by writ[1] but there are no pleadings or automatic discovery of documents. Summary judgment is not available in such cases.[2]

The evidence is put before the court by affidavits to which are exhibited documents relevant to the issues in dispute.

The hearing is often presided over by a master, although in a complex case he will adjourn the hearing to a judge for determination.

1. See Chapter 8.
2. See Chapter 12.

CHAPTER 27

PROCEEDINGS IN THE COMMERCIAL COURT

This chapter describes the historic role of the Commercial Court in complex civil litigation.

It is important to mention the role of the Commercial Court in modern commercial litigation. Established over a century ago, it has attracted historically some of the most able judges, who come from backgrounds in commercial law, and has been responsible for the hearing of the majority of specialist commercial cases, and for introducing innovations that have been effected later in the other courts. It was the Commercial Court that developed the practices of exchange of witness statements before trial, and skeleton arguments.

The Commercial Court is a branch of the Queen's Bench Division of the High Court, and specialises in hearing the more complex and important commercial cases, especially those involving disputes in the following areas:

— Insurance and reinsurance.
— Shipping.
— Banking.
— Carriage of goods.
— Contracts involving an international element.
— Commodity transactions.

The Commercial Court also supervises and assists the process of arbitration under the arbitration legislation, for example by hearing appeals and making orders ancillary to a pending arbitration.[1] A judge in the Commercial Court may also sit as a sole arbitrator in matters pending under the Arbitration Act 1996. To do so, he needs the consent of the Lord Chief Justice and must himself think it is proper to accept the appointment.

The judges in the Commercial Court are responsible for hearing all trials and interlocutory matters.

The Court has been distinguished by the speed, efficiency and adaptability of its procedures. Much business is attracted from all over the world by reason of its skill in handling difficult and important commercial matters.

The Court has led the way in promoting alternative dispute resolution

1. See Chapter 31.

("ADR"). The practice of the Court is to make ADR orders in appropriate cases requiring the parties to take serious steps to resolve their dispute by ADR. In the meantime, interlocutory steps may be suspended. If the attempt fails, the Court must be told why. Alternatively, a judge may himself preside over an "early neutral evaluation" of a case if to do so would be likely to assist the resolution of a dispute.

CHAPTER 28

AN OUTLINE OF COUNTY COURT PROCEDURE

This chapter sets out the circumstances in which actions may be brought in the county court, and explains the basic procedures involved in county court litigation. A chart setting out the procedures appears on page 61.

A. INTRODUCTION

The jurisdiction of the county court vis-à-vis the High Court has been described in Chapter 8. Briefly, the two jurisdictions (that is, the powers of the courts to hear and determine claims) are now largely concurrent, and with one main exception (relating to personal injury claims of under £50,000) proceedings may be *issued* in either court. In practice, however, most claims of small value (that is, less than £25,000) are *tried* in the county court. Claims begun in the county court that involve £50,000 or more will normally be transferred to the High Court. A recent innovation has led to the establishment of the Business List of the Central London County Court, which can hear commercial disputes involving up to £200,000, where the legal issues are not complex.

There are over 300 county courts throughout the country. Generally, each court may hear any case if it is a *default action*, which is basically a claim for money. If the defendant disputes the claim, the case may be transferred to the court in the place where he resides. Other actions must be commenced in the district where the defendant resides or carries on his business, where the land or property that is the subject of the dispute is situated or where the cause of action arose. The problems created by the need to correspond with the county court officials by post have been referred to in Chapter 8.

Some statutes confer exclusive jurisdiction on the county courts. This jurisdiction includes almost all cases under the Consumer Credit legislation, some actions by mortgage lenders for possession and actions by landlords under the Rent Acts and the Housing Acts 1985 and 1988. In addition, virtually all divorce cases go through the county courts.

A great many county courts have jurisdiction in insolvency matters, and some have admiralty jurisdiction in small claims up to £5,000, or £15,000 in salvage cases.

In a general sense, the procedure in the county court is very similar to that in the High Court. The same type of steps may be taken in the same sort of way, for the same type of relief. But the basic structure of county court litigation is founded upon two types of case that have somewhat different terminology from that used in the High Court.

B. TYPES OF ACTION

The two basic forms of action in the county court are the *default action* and the *fixed date action*. The first is for claims for debt or damages, including personal injury claims; the second is for other relief such as possession of land or for injunctions. In addition, there is another category of case called "matters" that includes applications for new tenancies under the Landlord and Tenant Act 1954[1] and insolvency and divorce cases.

(i) Default actions

These are begun by a Summons which is drafted by the plaintiff or his solicitor and which must be presented to the court, usually by post, for issue. Service is usually effected by the court, although the plaintiff may apply to the court for permission to effect service himself. There is no equivalent to the High Court Acknowledgment of Service, but unless the defendant pays the sum claimed within 14 days of service, admits that it is due, or files a Defence at court the plaintiff may apply for judgment to be entered.

If a Defence is served, the claim proceeds to trial, provided that within six months from the close of pleadings the plaintiff has requested a hearing date. If the plaintiff fails to do this within 15 months, or within nine months of the period fixed by the court for the making of that request, the claim will *automatically* be struck out. The claim will also automatically be struck out if the plaintiff fails to apply for judgment within 12 months of the defendant admitting liability or failing to serve a Defence. Once a Defence has been served, there is a procedure available similar to Order 14 in the High Court.[2]

(ii) Fixed date actions

These are claims other than for money alone. The Summons is presented to the court for issue and is usually served by the court or by the plaintiff if he is given permission by the court to do so. Service by post may be effected by the plaintiff in actions involving personal injuries.

In most fixed date actions, and on receipt of a Defence in default actions, and where the *small claims procedure* does not apply (see section D below), the

1. See Chapter 32.
2. See Chapter 12.

court will send automatic directions to all parties. These require most of the preparations for trial, such as discovery, exchange of experts' reports and witness statements to be completed within 12 to 14 weeks after the service of the Defence.

Automatic directions apply to all default actions and certain fixed date actions. In such cases, the court may fix a date for a pre-trial review. The purpose of this is either to dispose of the case if it is found that there is no case to answer or to be defended, or if the defendant does not appear, or to give specific directions to the parties to ensure that proper preparations for trial are made.

The remaining stages of county court litigation follow the same broad procedures as for a High Court trial, and the court has the same powers in respect of costs. Enforcement can follow the same pattern as for High Court judgments[3] and orders. The same rules and practices for settlement[4] also apply. There is a procedure available in fixed date actions similar to Order 14 in the High Court.[5] In certain cases the plaintiff, within 14 days of service, may also apply for default judgment.

(iii) Matters

These cases are begun by an *Originating Application* or a *Petition*. Examples of the former are applications under the Landlord and Tenant Act 1954.[6] Examples of the latter are insolvency[7] and divorce petitions. The cases follow a similar procedure to actions, although it is only in limited cases (for example, in those arising under the Landlord and Tenant Act 1954) that the defendant must serve a response giving his grounds of opposition. Such cases generally proceed to a pre-trial review.

C. OFFICERS OF THE COUNTY COURT

Cases are dealt with either by a circuit judge or by a district judge, depending on the value of the action and the complexity of the case. The jurisdiction of a district judge is not as extensive as that of a circuit judge, to whom certain cases are reserved. For example, in a case where the value of the claim does not exceed £5,000, it may be dealt with by either a circuit judge, or a district judge, unless it is of particular public importance or is very complicated, in which event a circuit judge will preside.

3. See Chapter 29.
4. See Chapter 21.
5. See Chapter 12.
6. See Chapter 32.
7. See Chapter 33.

D. SMALL CLAIMS PROCEDURE

Any proceedings (except actions for land) in which the claim is for £3,000 or less (or £1,000 or less for personal injury actions) are upon the filing of a Defence automatically referred for hearing by a district judge, who sits as an arbitrator. The court can also direct proceedings to be referred to a circuit judge, with the judge's consent, or to an outside arbitrator if both parties consent.

Where difficult questions of law are in issue, or where the facts or the subject matter are exceptionally complex, cases which normally fall within the small claims procedure may nevertheless be heard in open court. Conversely, a party may apply for the case to be referred to arbitration where the sums claimed are in excess of £3,000.

Where the reference to arbitration is automatic, no solicitors' charges will be awarded, except the fairly small scale costs stated on the Summons when issued, and the costs of enforcing the award.

There is no appeal from an arbitration in the small claims procedure, although a party can apply in certain situations to set aside an award.

CHAPTER 29

THE RECOGNITION AND ENFORCEMENT OF JUDGMENTS AND ARBITRAL AWARDS

Once you obtain in England a final judgment from a court or an award of an arbitrator, you may find that the debtor will not satisfy it voluntarily, or that he does not have the funds to pay a money debt, or that his assets are abroad.

This chapter explains the procedures available to you to secure the fruits of your judgment or award.

The first part of this chapter deals with enforcement procedures for judgments and arbitral awards of English origin; the second part deals with the enforcement in England of foreign judgments and arbitral awards.

A chart showing the principal methods of enforcement in England appears on page 206.

PART I THE ENFORCEMENT OF ENGLISH JUDGMENTS AND ARBITRAL AWARDS

A. Introduction

Litigants understandably concentrate on obtaining judgment at trial and it may be assumed that recovery of the award made by the court will automatically follow without any further steps being necessary.

However, it frequently happens that the judgment, which merely records the court's decision as to the rights of the parties, is not complied with and it is then up to the successful party ("the creditor") to take action to enforce his judgment if the losing party ("the debtor") refuses to comply with it.

B. Enforcement of judgments: when, where and in what amount

A judgment or order takes effect from the date it is made and generally enforcement proceedings may begin immediately.

Where the judgment or order, or part of it, relates to a sum of money, interest accrues at a statutory rate from the date of the judgment. The statutory rate varies from time to time. It is currently eight per cent. (The judgment itself may include interest up to the date of judgment at a different rate: see Chapter 23.)

Where the judgment is given for an amount expressed in a foreign currency, there are complicated rules providing for the time at which the foreign currency amount should be converted into sterling. The precise conversion date varies depending on the type of enforcement proceedings used, but will usually be at or close to the date on which the enforcement proceedings are commenced, not the date on which payment is actually made.

If enforcement proceedings are not brought within six years from the date of the judgment it may be necessary to apply to the court before the enforcement can proceed. If the action is brought on the judgment itself (as opposed to execution under it) then the action must be brought within six years from the date on which the judgment became enforceable.

Enforcement proceedings will generally take place in the court where judgment was obtained.[1]

C. Preliminary points to consider

Obviously, a plaintiff would be unwise to commence litigation without first considering whether the defendant will be able to satisfy the judgment sought. It can be frustrating to take proceedings through to trial only to find that the defendant is a "man of straw".

Note that it may sometimes be possible to obtain at an early stage an injunction that prevents a defendant from putting his assets beyond the reach of the plaintiff so as to defeat any later judgment.[2]

There is now a variety of searches which can be made to help build up a profile of the defendant's assets both prior to proceedings and before enforcement. Where appropriate it may be helpful to instruct private investigators to add depth to the profile.

— In both the High Court and the county court it is possible to fix a court appointment for the *oral examination* of a judgment debtor to ascertain what his assets are prior to enforcement.

If the debtor has no assets with which to settle the judgment, enforcement may be worthless. However, the creditor may wish to make an example of the debtor by making him bankrupt as a warning to others.

Enforcement can take place up to 12 years from the date of the judgment and thus the creditor can take advantage of the fact that a debtor's circumstances may improve with time.

1. Attachment of earnings orders can only be made in the county court. However, judgments of the High Court can be transferred to the county court for this purpose.
2. See Chapter 11.

Example
P sues D and obtains judgment for £100,000. D is impecunious and P takes no enforcement proceedings at the time. Five years later P learns that D has won the National Lottery. P can now commence enforcement proceedings for the £100,000 awarded to him together with the accrued interest.

Unless there is a risk that the debtor will dissipate his assets upon being notified of enforcement procedures it is advisable, on obtaining judgment, to send a letter before enforcement to the debtor. Such a letter should state the terms of the judgment requiring payment to be made accordingly otherwise enforcement will follow.

D. Enforcement remedies

Choosing the right enforcement remedy is a question of identifying which one is more likely to make the debtor satisfy the judgment. The choice is between insolvency proceedings and recovery of assets.

Insolvency proceedings[3]

In the case of an *individual* debtor, a statutory demand can be served on him for the judgment debt. If that is not complied with it can be followed up by a bankruptcy petition.

For a *corporate* debtor, failure to satisfy a judgment entitles the creditor to present a winding up petition without the need for a statutory demand. Prior to taking that step, it would be normal to make a written demand.

Particularly for solvent debtors who are merely dilatory in meeting their debts, insolvency proceedings are a most effective remedy. However, where the debtor is approaching insolvency the use of such proceedings may be enough to cause him to become bankrupt or, in the case of a company, be put into liquidation. This is undesirable since a judgment debtor will merely rank as an unsecured creditor of the individual or company and as a result may receive little or no return.

There are instances, however, when it may be advantageous for a judgment creditor to put a company into liquidation: for example, where he is the major creditor who is able to appoint his own nominee as liquidator, who may then use his statutory powers to reverse transactions that had taken place at an undervalue, or to institute proceedings against directors for wrongful trading.

Therefore, in circumstances where insolvency proceedings are undesirable or where the debtor is not resident in England but has assets there, it is worth considering asset-based enforcement procedures.

3. See Chapter 33.

Recovery of assets

A creditor may enforce his judgment over assets of the debtor to satisfy the judgment. Assets most commonly subjected to enforcement are as follows:

— Bank accounts.
— Property.
— Chattels.
— Earnings.

(i) Claiming money in the debtor's bank or building society account: garnishee orders[4]

The judgment creditor may request the court to make an interim order (a "garnishee order nisi") freezing the judgment debtor's bank or building society account[5] and requiring the debtor to attend a hearing in which he will have the opportunity of showing why the order should not be made *final* so as to compel the bank or building society to pay the creditor any money in the account.

(ii) Property (charging orders)

Property, being by its nature immovable, is an obvious target for enforcement proceedings.

It is fundamental to enforcement that the property is owned by the debtor. Where there are joint owners of property, it is only the debtor's interest that is liable to enforcement. For registered land a land registry search will generally reveal the identity of those persons with an interest in the property.

Enforcement proceedings over land proceed through two distinct phases. First, the creditor obtains security for the judgment debt by a *charge* over the property. Secondly, recovery is effected by an *order for sale* of the property.

(a) Obtaining security Security is obtained by a *charging order* which takes effect, if granted by the court, as if it were an equitable charge in writing granted by the debtor over his property.

As with garnishee proceedings, a charging order is obtained in a two-stage procedure with the initial *charging order nisi* made by the court in the absence of the debtor. A *charging order absolute* will only be made after a hearing at which the debtor bears the burden of showing why the charging order nisi should not be made absolute.

4. See Chapter 36, on banking litigation, for a fuller account of this remedy.
5. The bank should make no payment at this stage to either party or to any third party. Instead, it should wait for the hearing of the final order which will determine who is entitled to receive the monies. If it makes payment prematurely and that payment does not accord with what is ordered at the hearing of the application for the garnishee order absolute the bank may be liable to the aggrieved party.

The application for a charging order nisi is made with affidavit evidence in which the creditor must set out particulars of the property, the debtor's interest in it, the judgment debt and the judgment. The affidavit should also give details of any other creditors.

The application for a charging order nisi will generally be determined by the court on the strength of the affidavit evidence without a hearing. No notice need be given to the debtor. In the course of its consideration the court will weigh any evidence of the personal circumstances of the debtor and also whether any other creditor is likely to be unduly prejudiced by the making of the order. In particular, the court will not give the creditor preference over other unsecured creditors of the debtor.

If granted, the charging order nisi will give the creditor a charge over the property in question until further consideration is given to the matter at the full hearing. To secure the creditor's position before that hearing the order can be protected by registering a land charge at the Land Charges Registry (for unregistered land) or lodging a notice or caution at the Land Registry (for registered land). A date for the full hearing will be given on the order.

Once granted, the charging order nisi must be served on the debtor and, if the court directs, on any other creditor. Those served will normally have an interest in the property and will be entitled to make representations at the full hearing. Typically they will be a spouse and/or a mortgagee.

Where a debtor company is put into liquidation or an individual is made bankrupt following the grant of a charging order nisi, the court will decline to make the order absolute and the security will be lost.

If the charging order is made absolute it may be protected in the same manner as a charging order nisi.

(b) Enforcement of a charging order by sale A charging order only confers security: it does not entitle the creditor to sell the property. Therefore, once a charging order absolute has been obtained, separate enforcement proceedings must be begun to obtain court authority for sale of the property.

The application for an order for sale is supported by an affidavit. Notice of the proceedings must be given to the debtor and other persons with a legal interest in the property, again normally a spouse and/or mortgagee.

The court considers the following issues before granting an order for sale:

— The size of the judgment debt as compared to the value of the property.
— The amount of equity in the property.
— The position and attitude of other creditors to the sale, including any mortgagee.
— Whether the debtor's spouse and children reside at the property and what interest they may have in it.

— What other measures are available to the debtor to discharge the debt.

Examples

P applies for an order for sale over D's house which he jointly owns with his wife. The judgment debt is £10,000 and there is a mortgage for £50,000. D's wife and children also reside at the house. An immediate order for sale is unlikely to be made, especially if the mortgagee does not support the application.

Alternatively, where D is a bachelor living on his own, the judgment debt is £70,000 and there is no mortgage, an order for sale is far more likely to be made.

Disposal costs such as estate agency fees and land registry fees can also be recovered.

Charging orders can also be used, with some adaptation, for other assets such as shares, unit trusts or even a beneficial interest in a trust.

(iii) Chattels (seizure of goods)

Where the judgment debt is small and the debtor is an individual this is one of the most common methods of enforcement. The creditor applies to the court to be authorised to instruct a bailiff to call at the debtor's house or business premises, or wherever he has reason to believe that goods belonging to the debtor may be found, and remove and sell (normally at auction) sufficient of the debtor's goods to satisfy the judgment and cost of sale.

The technique is often more of a deterrent and rarely realises large sums because few people own valuable assets and, in any event, auction prices are low.

The bailiff will not act as a private investigator on behalf of the debtor. It is up to the debtor to direct the bailiff to where the goods may be found.

The application to the court is straightforward and there is generally no need for any hearing prior to enforcement.

The bailiff may not force entry into the debtor's property. Once inside, he may seize those goods which belong to the debtor but he may not seize certain goods such as clothes, bedding and tools of the trade, which are exempt from execution.

Once the bailiff is in possession of the debtor's goods they will be put up for public auction where prices are usually low and do not necessarily reflect the value of the goods. The sale proceeds are first used to discharge the bailiff's costs of removal and sale and the balance is then applied to reduce the judgment debt.

Disputes regularly arise as to who owns particular goods. Any third party such as a spouse or finance company may intervene and put forward a claim to the goods. If an agreement cannot readily be reached the creditor may be obliged to apply to court.

If the bailiff cannot gain entry to the premises or the debtor's goods are of insufficient value to justify the cost of removal and sale, the bailiff will make a report to the court to this effect. If it is later discovered that the debtor has goods worth seizing the creditor may re-instruct the bailiff.

(iv) Earnings (attachment of earnings orders)

The court can order the debtor's employer to make deductions from his earnings and pay them over to the creditor.

An attachment of earnings order can only be made against an employee.[6]

If the debtor leaves his employment the order is frustrated.

The attachment of earnings order fixes the weekly or monthly deductions to be made by the employer and paid to the creditor. The court will also fix an amount below which it considers that the debtor's earnings should not be reduced. This will generally be a subsistence amount which the debtor is entitled to use to support himself and his family.

The amount raised by an attachment of earnings order is normally small and the instalments may not even cover the interest on a large debt.

Difficulties often arise because the debtor may not provide the information the court needs regarding his salary and commitments. This can cause delay. However, in some cases, the threat of going to the debtor's employer may be enough to bring about a settlement offer or an informal instalment plan.

E. The enforcement of English arbitral awards in England

An arbitral award, unlike a court judgment, is not automatically enforceable. Before it may be enforced, it is first necessary to convert it into a judgment or order of the court.

There are two different methods of enforcing in England an English award.

- The first method is to sue in the High Court, on the basis of the term implied in the arbitration agreement that the respondent will honour the award of the arbitrator. It is necessary for the successful party to prove, inter alia, the validity and the terms of the arbitration agreement, that the arbitrator was duly appointed, and the fact that the award sued upon was made by him pursuant to the arbitration agreement. The court is generally only concerned with the formalities of the award, and will usually not enquire into the merits of the underlying dispute or of the award.
- The second method is to seek an order under section 66 of the Arbitration Act 1996. In this case, which is unsuitable where the defendant is expected to make substantive objections to the award, the plaintiff applies to the High Court by affidavit verifying the arbitration agreement, the award and the failure to comply, and the court,

6. This includes a director of a limited company. The self-employed and those in partnership are exempt from attachment of earnings proceedings.

if satisfied, may allow the award to be enforced as if it were a judgment, and may also order judgment to be entered in terms of the award. The court must refuse leave to enforce an award where the person against whom the award is sought to be enforced is able to show that the arbitrator lacked jurisdiction to make the award.

PART II THE RECOGNITION AND ENFORCEMENT OF FOREIGN JUDGMENTS AND ARBITRAL AWARDS

A. Introduction

Judgments and arbitral awards obtained in the national courts or from arbitration proceedings in one state are not necessarily enforceable only in that state. The law has developed to allow the judgment and arbitral awards of one state to be enforced in another state.

This chapter is principally concerned with the enforcement of foreign judgments and arbitral awards in England. The enforcement abroad of an English judgment or arbitral award, although often no different in principle, will require the involvement of lawyers in the jurisdiction in question. For that reason it is largely outside the scope of this chapter, but is dealt with briefly in section C.

B. Recognition and enforcement of a foreign judgment in England

Enforcement of a foreign judgment is a two-stage process. As a preliminary to enforcement the foreign judgment must first be *recognised* by the English courts. Once it is recognised it is treated as though it were an English judgment. It can then be enforced as if it were an English judgment using the methods set out in Part I of this chapter.

The rules and procedures to be followed before a foreign judgment can be enforced in England depend upon the terms of the relevant treaty, if any, between the United Kingdom and the foreign state in which the judgment was made.

For the purposes of enforcement, foreign states can be split into the following three categories:

(i) Signatories to the two Conventions on Jurisdiction and the Enforcement of Judgments in Civil or Commercial Matters of 1968 (known as the *Brussels Convention*) and of 1988 (known as the *Lugano Convention*) ("the Conventions"),[7] that is, members of the European Union and the Economic Free Trade Association[8].

(ii) Countries with which the United Kingdom has concluded a bilateral treaty agreement.

7. The Conventions are also dealt with in Chapter 6.

8. Not all the signatories to the Convention have yet ratified the relevant Conventions so as to bring them into force within their domestic law.

(iii) Countries with which the United Kingdom has reached no agreement.

(i) Enforcement under the Conventions[9]

Under the Conventions each contracting state must recognise judgments given in another contracting state.

Recognition should be virtually automatic and, subject to certain cases set out below, the English courts should recognise the judgment without examining the merits of the case. Once a judgment has been recognised by the English courts, it can then be enforced as if it were a judgment of the English courts.

The Conventions only apply to judgments relating to civil and commercial matters.[10]

Recognition of a judgment may be refused by the English courts:

(i) Where it is contrary to English public policy to recognise the judgment.
(ii) Where the judgment conflicts with a judgment between the same parties given in England.
(iii) Where the judgment of the foreign court is a *default* judgment and the defendant was not properly served with the proceedings.

To have a judgment recognised under the Conventions the judgment creditor should make an application by affidavit to the English court to have the judgment registered with the court. This application should be supported by an authenticated copy of the original judgment and evidence that the judgment is enforceable in the country in which it was given. This will usually be provided in the form of a certificate from the court which gave the judgment.

Once registration has been obtained and the judgment has been formally recognised by the English court the judgment creditor must serve notice of the registration on the judgment debtor. Often this will be the first that the judgment debtor will know of the registration.

A challenge can only be founded on one of the grounds for refusing recognition of a foreign judgment, for example public policy. The judgment debtor cannot contest the substance of the foreign judgment: to allow such a challenge would run contrary to the presumption in favour of enforceability.

9. The two Conventions are very similar and although there are some differences, these are not material for the purpose of this summary. The Conventions are incorporated into English law by the Civil Jurisdiction and Judgments Act 1982 (as amended).

10. Judgments relating to Revenue or Customs matters, marriages, wills, succession, bankruptcy, insolvency, social security or arbitration are not within the scope of the Conventions. The enforcement of foreign arbitral awards is dealt with separately in section E.

(ii) Treaty agreements

Many states have signed treaties with the United Kingdom which provide for the bilateral enforcement of judgments.

Although the relevant treaty will provide the basis for enforcement, the procedure for enforcement can be found in one of two Acts of Parliament ("the Acts"). Historically, the Administration of Justice Act 1920 was intended to provide a system for Commonwealth countries to enforce their judgments in England, whilst the Foreign Judgments (Reciprocal Enforcement) Act 1933 provides a similar system for non-Commonwealth countries. Although there are differences between the Acts they are not material for the purposes of this summary.

The range of judgments that can be enforced under the Acts is more limited than under the Conventions. To be eligible for enforcement under the Acts a judgment must meet the following criteria:

(i) It must be *final* (that is, not subject to appeal).
(ii) It must be for a *specific* sum of money.
(iii) It must not be in respect of *taxes* or *fines.*
(iv) It must not be obtained by *fraud* or *breach of a jurisdiction* or *arbitration agreement.*

The English courts must also satisfy themselves that the foreign court which gave the judgment had jurisdiction to give it. To satisfy the English courts, the judgment creditor must show that the judgment debtor:

(i) was resident in the country where the foreign court is located; or
(ii) had its principal place of business there; or
(iii) agreed to submit to the court's jurisdiction; or
(iv) voluntarily appeared in the proceedings.

The procedure for registering the foreign judgment with the English courts is similar to that under the Conventions, as is the procedure for challenge.

(iii) Where there is no treaty with the United Kingdom

In the absence of any treaty between the foreign state and the United Kingdom, enforcement proceeds under the common law rules.

> *Despite the development of the law in this area, a number of important trading partners, including the United States of America, Japan and the states of the former Soviet Union, have not entered into agreements with the United Kingdom regarding enforcement of judgments.*[11]

11. See section E, below, and Chapter 31 concerning the enforcement abroad of an English *arbitral* award.

At common law the relationship is analysed as if there were a simple contractual debt between the judgment creditor and the judgment debtor. It follows that the judgment creditor must begin proceedings by a writ to recover the debt.

In the absence of an allegation of fraud, there will normally be no scope for re-examination of the merits of the case and it will often be possible for the plaintiff to obtain summary judgment[12] on the strength of the foreign judgment.

The English courts will need to be satisfied that the foreign court had jurisdiction to give judgment and the principles the English courts will apply are similar to those set out in respect of the Acts.

C. Enforcing an English judgment abroad

In summary, the position is as follows:

- An English judgment will be automatically recognised and enforced by registration in the courts of a fellow contracting state under the Conventions.
- In the case of a state which is party to a treaty with the United Kingdom, enforcement will follow in accordance with the terms of the treaty as it is enacted in that state. This is provided that the courts of the enforcing state accept that the English courts had jurisdiction to give judgment. This is a matter on which advice should be obtained from lawyers practising in the country concerned.
- In the absence of a treaty, proceedings must be commenced in that country and lawyers should be consulted to establish what use, if any, can be made of the English court's judgment.

Procedure

This will be a matter for legal advisers in the jurisdiction concerned. It is likely that the foreign court will require a certified copy of the English judgment.

D. Enforcement of judgments between parts of the United Kingdom

The United Kingdom is made up of three independent jurisdictions which are:

(i) England and Wales.
(ii) Scotland.
(iii) Northern Ireland.

The general principle is that there should be free movement of judgments

12. For a description of the process of summary judgment, see Chapter 12.

among the three jurisdictions. Nevertheless, the process of registration must be followed prior to enforcement. The procedure is essentially the same as that for a foreign judgment.

There are two particular points to note:

- Enforcement cannot take place until the time limit for any appeal has expired or any appeal has been dismissed.
- The application for registration must be made within six months of the date of issue of the certificate of judgment from the original court.

E. Foreign arbitral awards[13]

(i) Enforcing in England a foreign arbitral award

The enforcement of international arbitration awards is principally governed by the *New York Convention on the Recognition and Enforcement of Foreign Arbitral Awards of 1958* ("the *New York Convention*") to which more than 80 countries are signatories, including the United Kingdom.[14]

The underlying philosophy of the New York Convention is that an arbitral award made in any state, even a state that is not a party to it, should be recognised and enforced by any contracting state so long as certain basic conditions are met.

Signatories to the New York Convention may apply two *reservations* to its application in their state both of which restrict the ambit of this general principle. These are:

- *Reciprocity*
  More than half of the parties to the New York Convention will only recognise and enforce a foreign arbitral award if it was made in the territory of another contracting state. However, most international trading nations are now contracting states and so the effect of this reservation is now of limited significance.
- *Commercial relationships*
  Contracting states may limit the applicability of the New York Convention to disputes arising out of legal relationships of a commercial nature. Contracting states may resolve this question for themselves. As a result of inconsistency among contracting states as to what is considered to be commercial, there is some uncertainty as to when enforcement will be permitted in some cases.

Under English law, which incorporates the New York Convention, a foreign arbitral award made within a state which is a party to the New York Convention,

13. See generally Chapter 31.
14. In addition to the New York Convention, there are other regional conventions, bilateral treaties and other agreements that may offer a method of enforcing a foreign arbitral award.

like a domestic award, shall with leave of the court be enforced as if it were an English judgment. Judgment in terms of the award may also be entered. Provided certain conditions applied by the New York Convention are met, recognition and enforcement are mandatory.

To obtain leave the successful party must produce to the court the duly authenticated original award and the original arbitration agreement under which it was made or certified copies of the same. A translation may also be required.

The English courts are not entitled to review the merits of the original arbitral award.

The losing party may oppose recognition and enforcement if he can show that the arbitral award was invalid on certain technical and procedural grounds, such as that it was founded on an invalid arbitration agreement or that there was a procedural irregularity in the arbitration. In both cases, the burden of proof is on the losing party to satisfy the English court that recognition and enforcement should not follow. In view of the general presumption in favour of enforcement the burden of proof is likely to be high.

In addition to enforcement under the New York Convention, it is possible for a foreign arbitral award to be enforced in the same way as may an English award, as to which see above. In such cases, which are appropriate to arbitral awards made in those countries that are not party to the New York Convention, the questions for the court are often subject to the law of the country in which the arbitral award was made.

(ii) Enforcing an English arbitral award abroad[15]

This is principally a matter for legal advice in the jurisdiction concerned. Consideration must be given as to whether:

— The foreign state is party to the New York Convention or any other agreement which provides for enforcement.
— The law of the foreign state allows the English arbitral award to be enforced as if it were a judgment of the foreign state's courts or whether further proceedings must be commenced in that state to obtain enforcement.

15. See also Chapter 31 for a consideration of the advantages of arbitration over court judgments in relation to international enforcement.

RECOGNITION AND ENFORCEMENT OF JUDGMENTS

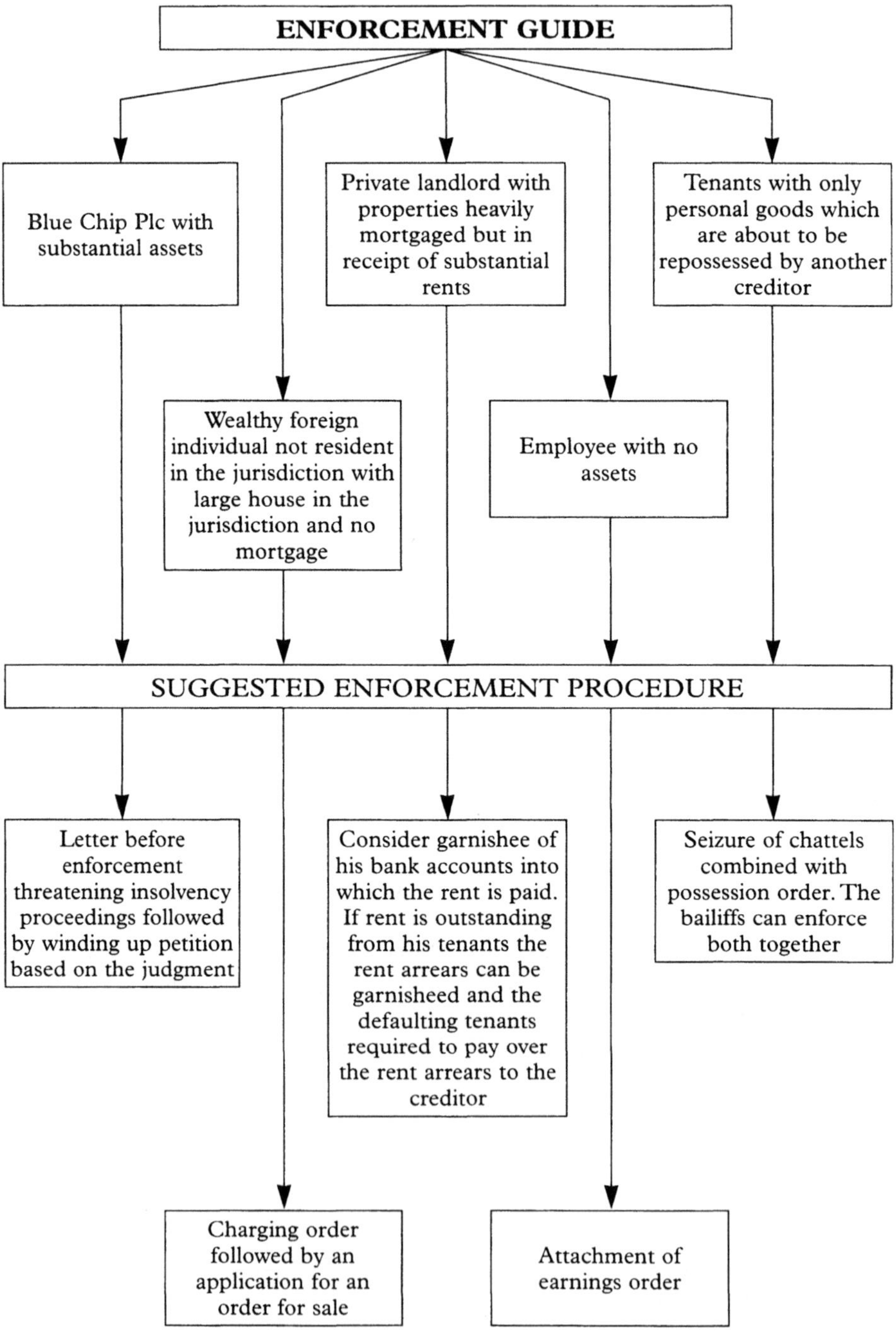

CHAPTER 30

REPRESENTATIVE AND GROUP ACTIONS

This chapter describes the rules and practices that apply in situations involving many parties that are linked by common issues and interests.

In English law there is no strict counterpart to the "class" action that can be brought, for example, in some states of the United States of America. There are, however, rules and practices of court that provide for situations in which many parties are affected by the same or very similar issues, and that enable those issues to be dealt with cost-effectively and efficiently.

Such situations typically involve national disasters such as those caused by aircraft or shipping accidents, or fires in public places; claims against pharmaceutical companies by consumers of harmful drugs; or commercial disputes involving investors in companies.

There are, broadly, *four* ways in which such multi-party claims may be brought in England:

- By "representative" proceedings.
- By *joining* many plaintiffs or defendants to the same action.
- By "consolidating" actions begun separately by many different parties.
- By the selection of "lead" actions to act as "test" cases or precedents for others in similar situations.

A "representative" action is one in which one plaintiff or defendant is selected to bring proceedings on behalf of himself and others. In such cases, the representatives and the parties represented must all have the *same interest.*

Joint plaintiffs may combine in one action, subject to the discretion of the court, provided that some *common question of law or fact would arise in all the actions and all rights to relief are in respect of or arise out of the same transaction or series of transactions.*

Where separate actions are begun by numerous plaintiffs, possibly because they were unaware of the existence of each other's claims, the court may order that the actions be *consolidated,* provided that the conditions described in the last paragraph also apply: that is, the existence of common interests and common claims to relief arising out of the same transaction.

The first three categories of case usually involve claims by one group of plaintiffs against a single defendant, or by one plaintiff against numerous defendants. The "lead" action procedure is usually most appropriate in cases in which there are multiple plaintiffs and possibly also multiple defendants, connected in the sense that each case involves similar issues. The judge nominated may play a very important role in the selection of "lead" actions in cases involving numerous plaintiffs and defendants. In this way, categories of case can be identified and typical actions singled out for trial, so that all issues may be tried and precedents created so that the court is not inundated with actions of the same or similar nature, all awaiting trial. In such cases other parties are not, strictly speaking, bound by the findings of fact in their lead cases, unless they agree at the outset, or the court so orders. Normally, however, these other parties follow the rulings made in the lead actions.

This practice was put to good effect in the *interest rate swaps* litigation, in which many banks had individual but often the same or very similar claims against different local authorities who had engaged in interest rate swaps that were later held by the House of Lords to have been beyond their lawful powers. In the subsequent litigation for restitution of monies paid to the authorities, the court appointed solicitors to co-ordinate the actions of all plaintiffs, and selected various cases involving typical facts and legal issues as lead actions so that parties could, in practice, accept the judgment of the court in those cases as binding upon them as well. Pending the hearing of the lead actions, the other actions were stayed.

In all multi-party litigation consideration should be given, either individually or as a group, to the preliminary questions of *forum* and procedure: that is, in which country ought the action(s) to be brought, and by what means? Local procedures in foreign courts may be advantageous, quite apart from the possibility of greater damages awards. This should be done at the earliest opportunity, as threshold matters such as limitation periods and local practices may determine the success or failure of the enterprise in one country but not in another.

If England is selected as the appropriate venue for the litigation, it is customary for an application to court to be made by all parties for the appointment of a judge who will deal with all interlocutory matters, and also with the trial(s). In this way, issues such as joint or several pleadings, the extent of discovery of documents, cut-off dates for the further joinder of parties, and expert evidence may all be synchronised.

All these proceedings entail a high degree of co-operation among the parties themselves, and the court. This is usually achieved by the appointment of steering and co-ordinating committees and "lead" solicitors who liaise with all parties' representatives. Although it may not always be possible to do this immediately, it is plainly sensible to co-ordinate the efforts of the whole group as soon as a common interest is identified.

In all multi-party litigation, it is necessary to provide for the payment of the legal costs. Complications may arise from the involvement of *legally-aided* parties, and for parties who join or leave the group at different times. Those cases which involve numerous plaintiffs, or where numerous different actions are consolidated, present no unusual problems: the interested parties bear and enjoy the same incidence of costs as in any litigation.[1] In a *representative* action, in which the plaintiff or defendant represents parties not joined, the result is binding upon those other parties, and the court has a further power to make an award of costs in respect of non-parties. In cases selected as *lead* actions, the selection of lead cases usually involves special arrangements for cost-sharing and bearing, approved by the judge in charge of the proceedings. Special precautions are taken to ensure that the lead or representative case does not involve a party who is legally-aided bearing the brunt of costs occasioned on behalf of clients who are not legally-aided.

1. See Chapter 24.

CHAPTER 31

ARBITRATION

This chapter explains the system of arbitration in England.

A. INTRODUCTION

In England, legal disputes tended historically to be resolved by the courts, but there is also a long tradition, which has developed increasingly since the last war, of resolving commercial disputes by arbitration. As a result, England and, in particular, the City of London, has been recognised as a leading forum for both domestic and international arbitration.[1] It has been said earlier that litigation and arbitration are, in practice, very similar in this country. Although the parties to an arbitration in England have been able to choose whether to follow an inquisitorial or adversarial procedure, frequently arbitration has seemed like litigation in plain clothes: the procedures and disciplines in practice became very similar. It has already been seen how English litigation is adversarial (and, as is shown in Chapter 40, is likely to remain so); and, although arbitration in England can follow a different course, the procedure in an arbitration, unless the parties otherwise agree, has tended also to be adversarial. In practice, however, some arbitrations adopted a sensible middle way with a procedure based on informality. This did not, nevertheless, diminish criticisms of the system and it was said to have been "highjacked" by the lawyers, who were frequently thought to have imposed upon what was intended to be an informal and truly alternative method of dispute resolution habits learned in litigation. This trend, when coupled with the role that the courts had adopted in relation to arbitration, had diminished the effectiveness of arbitration as a genuine alternative to litigation.

B. THE REFORM OF THE ARBITRAL PROCESS IN ENGLAND

For the reasons given above, the process of arbitration in England fell into disrepute both here and abroad.

1. See Chapter 2 for a consideration of alternative dispute resolution ("ADR").

The root cause of this problem was identified as the law of arbitral procedure. This comprised chiefly three principal arbitration statutes coupled with a considerable volume of case law. It was said that it was almost impossible for anyone but an expert in English law to be able to find and understand the law of arbitration in England. The statutes were said to be badly written and confusingly arranged. The relationship between case law and statute was often difficult to follow. No one could easily find out how to conduct an arbitration, and the common law dealt mainly with the supervision by the courts of the arbitral process, rather than with the process itself. As there had been little guidance on arbitral procedures, lawyers instructed to act in arbitrations tended to apply to arbitrations the established tactics and procedures of litigation. The result was thought to be that arbitration had lost its essential attributes of speed, economy and certainty. Businessmen and lay clients, especially from abroad, had little hope of knowing where they stood and were drawn almost inexorably into the arms of a legal process that arbitration had been intended to help them avoid. Equally as worrying, England was in serious risk of losing its position as a centre of international arbitration, with consequential losses of foreign revenue.

Elsewhere, reforms in arbitration procedures had been introduced. In particular, the United Nations Commission On International Trade Law ("UNCITRAL") introduced in 1985 its *Model Law* for international commercial arbitration. This was adopted by many countries as a standard code of arbitration and was widely applauded. England chose not to adopt it, but there followed in England a long public debate that culminated in the passage of the Arbitration Act 1996 ("the Act"). This was substantially brought into force in January 1997. Although it does not adopt all the provisions of the *UNCITRAL Model Law*, the Act is largely based upon it. It has been acclaimed as a major landmark in legislative reform and as a model of clarity, coherence and comprehensiveness. It has repealed all earlier arbitration statutes, codified some of the most important provisions of the common law and introduced many improvements.

C. THE MAIN FEATURES OF ARBITRATION

Before describing the main features of the Act, we give a general account of arbitration.

Arbitration is a process whereby disputes between parties may by agreement be settled in private before a tribunal of the parties' own choice (which usually has a specialist knowledge of the subject of the dispute) and which, following a fair hearing, makes an impartial and legally enforceable award in accordance with the law chosen by the parties or imposed by the law of the country in which the arbitration takes place.

Arbitrations are, generally, of two kinds:

— *Ad hoc:* in this case, the arbitrator, once appointed, controls his own procedure or follows that agreed by the parties.
— *Administered:* this is where some body or organisation other than the parties or the arbitrator determines the procedure in accordance with a system of rules created for the purpose. Examples of these are the *International Chamber of Commerce*, the *American Arbitration Association* and the *London Court of International Arbitration.*[2]

Arbitration agreements are common in disputes arising in the following fields:

— Building and civil engineering contracts.
— Partnerships.
— Maritime and commodity contracts.
— Insurance and reinsurance contracts.
— Travel and other consumer contracts.
— Rent reviews.

Arbitration is *consensual*: that is, except in fairly limited cases where arbitration is imposed by statute,[3] a party will only be able to instigate an arbitration if his opponent agrees. The agreement will either be entered into as part of a larger contract, at the time of reaching an agreement on other matters, for example, in a charterparty or a building contract, and before any dispute has arisen; or at the time when the dispute arises.

An arbitration generally begins with the appointment by the parties of an arbitrator or (where there is to be more than one arbitrator) an arbitral tribunal. This can be by private agreement, or it may be effected by one of the arbitral institutions. The arbitrator may call a meeting of the parties or representatives at which a schedule of steps to be taken should be agreed by reference to a timetable leading to the determination of the dispute either at an oral hearing involving the giving of evidence or by some less formal method at the parties' option. At the end of the process the arbitrator submits an award that is legally binding on the parties and is enforceable. There are limited rights of appeal to the courts. The award may be enforced in England and Wales or Northern Ireland, or (with some exceptions) abroad. During the process of arbitration the parties may have recourse to the courts for such assistance as is necessary for the fulfilment of the principles set out below.

2. Note that certain provisions of the Act are mandatory. As a result, the rules of arbitral institutions will only be applicable to arbitrations that have their "seat" (see section D below) in England to the extent that their rules do not conflict with the mandatory provisions.

3. For example, under the Building Societies Act 1986 and Agricultural Holdings Act 1986. Note also, that under the County Courts Act 1984, certain disputes (often involving relatively small sums of money) may be referred to arbitration under the auspices of the court: see Chapter 28.

D. THE PRINCIPLES OF THE ARBITRATION ACT 1996

The Act broadly applies to all existing arbitration agreements in writing[4] which have their "seat" in England and Wales or Northern Ireland but not to arbitrations that began before the Act was introduced. Parts of the Act also apply, for example, to certain arbitrations that have their seat elsewhere: for example, where the English courts stay court proceedings begun in breach of an arbitration agreement which requires the arbitration to take place abroad (see below); or in the case of the enforcement in England of arbitral awards; or in the exercise of the courts' powers of support of the arbitral process—for example, securing the attendance of witnesses. The "seat" is the place where the arbitration is established and has its juridical base. It may be designated by the parties, the arbitrator or institution. The fact that an arbitration has its seat in England will not, however, prevent an arbitration actually taking place elsewhere if that is appropriate. It remains possible for arbitrations having their seat in England to be administered under the rules of organisations such as the International Chamber of Commerce, except to the extent that their rules conflict with any mandatory provisions of the Act (as to which, see below).

The Act is founded on three cardinal principles. These are set out at the start of the Act.

Fairness, impartiality, speed and economy

The object of arbitration is stated to be "to obtain the fair resolution of disputes by an impartial tribunal without unnecessary delay or expense".

The autonomy of the parties

The parties to arbitration are "free to agree how their disputes are resolved, subject only to such safeguards that are necessary in the public interest" and are under a general duty to "do all things necessary for the proper and expeditious conduct" of the case.

This principle finds expression throughout the Act. The guiding objective of the Act is to achieve a fair and cost-effective resolution of the dispute between the parties by the adoption of a procedure to which they have expressly agreed. The parties have agreed to have their disputes resolved by a consensual process under their control. This involves a general right to dictate the procedure for the resolution of that dispute. This may mean that there may be no oral hearing, or that the dispute should not be subject to the strict rules of law or evidence, or that there should be no right of appeal to the courts.

4. The definition of "writing" is wider than under previous legislation and could admit cases where an oral agreement is evidenced in writing or where the parties orally agree to arbitration under the (written) rules of an arbitral institution.

In most instances the parties have the right to dictate the procedure that will apply, but in some cases the provisions of the Act are mandatory and cannot be excluded by the parties (see below). (See Section E, page 217 as to the applicable substantive law.)

Non-intervention by the courts

A corollary of the general rule of party autonomy is that the courts should not intervene in the process of arbitration but, when they do, it should be with the object of assisting the process rather than supplanting it. Thus, many of the criticisms of the old regime in which numerous appeals and references to the courts were allowed to clog the procedure have been answered.

E. THE DETAILED PROVISIONS OF THE ARBITRATION ACT 1996

It is not intended to give an exhaustive account of the detailed provisions of the Act. The following description sets out its most important provisions.

Codification of the common law

The Act codifies some of the more important features of the common law, such as the so-called "*Nema*" guidelines[5] regarding appeals from the awards of arbitrators to the courts (as to which, see section F, below), but otherwise does not interfere with the old common law rules, which will still apply provided they do not conflict with the provisions of the Act. In particular, the Act expressly preserves the old common law rules relating to the effect of an *oral* arbitration agreement (which remains permissible but will not be conducted under the Act); and the refusal of recognition or enforcement of an arbitral award on grounds of public policy.

Increased powers of the arbitrator

A fundamental cause of criticism of the old system was the fact that an arbitrator had few powers of enforcement or sanctions to impose against recalcitrant parties. Now an arbitrator has considerably enhanced powers.

The Act imposes on arbitrators a duty to act "fairly and impartially as between the parties, giving each party a reasonable opportunity of putting his case and dealing with that of his opponent" and to "adopt procedures suitable to the circumstances of the particular case, avoiding unnecessary delay and expense, so as to provide a fair means of resolution" of the dispute. Subject to those guiding principles, arbitrators are given wide powers (which, consistent

5. So-named after the case in which the old rules were somewhat inventively interpreted by the House of Lords.

with the principle of the autonomy of the parties, may only usually be displaced if the parties so agree) to determine the procedures to be followed. These powers include the right to decide on the following matters and to make the following orders:

- To rule on their own jurisdiction (unless the parties otherwise agree). This gives effect to the internationally recognised doctrine of "Kompetenz–Kompetenz" and applies to the determination of the validity of the arbitration agreement, the constitution of the arbitral tribunal and the matters submitted for determination. A ruling may be challenged through the courts, provided usually that certain time limits are complied with.
- Where and when any part of the proceedings is to be held.
- The language of the proceedings.
- Where and if so in what form the written Statements of Claim and Defence are to be used.
- The extent of discovery of documents. This is an especially important provision as it permits the arbitrator to curtail what has often been said to be a major abuse of the process.
- The rules of evidence to be applied. Equally, it was often thought that previously an arbitrator sitting in an English arbitration had to apply the English rules of procedure. Now he may decide to adopt whatever rules of procedure he thinks appropriate, subject only to the overriding guiding principles of the Act.
- Whether to apply an "inquisitorial" approach to the procedures. This should only be followed where appropriate for achieving the overall objectives of the Act.
- To award security for costs. In the past, this was an area in which the courts could also be involved, but now the arbitrator alone will have the power to make such an award.
- To give directions in respect of property pending the final determination of the process. This can include the making of orders for the payment of money or the transfer of property.
- To enforce their interlocutory (that is, interim) rulings. This may be by, for example, dismissing a claim or defence or ordering that a party in default may not advance a particular allegation or rely on certain evidence in support of it. The courts are given power to assist whatever orders of this sort the arbitrator makes.
- To grant a final injunction[6] or specific performance of a contract not relating to land or for the rectification of a contract.
- Whether there should be oral and written submissions. This can include the power to limit the amount of advocacy in a hearing and to

6. Note however that the language of the Act suggests that the arbitrator still has no power to award an interim injunction (see Chapter 10): this probably remains a power that only the courts can exercise.

impose time limits by which submissions must be made.

- To award compound interest.
- To award and assess the costs of the arbitration. This includes the power (which the parties may overrule) to order that the recoverable costs of an arbitration shall be limited to a specified amount. Thus, the parties could incur whatever costs they wished but could not recover more than the limited amount if they won. Costs will usually "follow the event", as in litigation,[7] but the arbitrator will have the power to vary this rule where he considers that it would be inappropriate.

The arbitrator must apply the substantive law agreed, expressly or by inference, by the parties or, failing any such agreement, the system of law determined by the conflict of law rules he considers applicable. In appropriate circumstances if the parties agree, an arbitrator has the power to make an award in accordance with "other considerations". This means that the arbitrator may determine the case in accordance with the principles of "equity and fairness" and not in accordance with the strict letter of the law, as is common in some other, especially civil law, jurisdictions. In such cases, however, there is no right of appeal to the courts.

Some of these powers give to arbitrators the ability to make awards that the courts cannot. The power to award compound interest, for example, is not one that is available to courts except in very rare circumstances. This is important, because the inability of the courts to award compound interest in the majority of straightforward commercial cases is anachronistic and represents a serious weakness since it prevents the courts from compensating commercial clients for the real losses they have suffered.

Equally, the courts must almost invariably determine a case at an oral hearing: those occasions when they may dispose of a matter by affidavit evidence are rare[8] and, even then, a hearing must anyway take place when oral submissions are made by counsel or solicitors. An arbitrator now has the ability to decide (unless the parties otherwise agree) that there shall be no hearing, if he considers that that is an appropriate way of achieving the overriding statutory objectives that he must fulfil.

Mandatory and non-mandatory provisions

The Act draws a basic distinction between provisions that are mandatory and provisions that are non-mandatory. As it is the guiding theme of the Act that the parties should be free to adopt whatever procedures they wish, it follows that constraints should be kept to a minimum. Thus, many of the provisions are made subject to the right of the parties to agree otherwise, but there are some provisions that will apply whether or not the parties agree.

7. See Chapter 24.
8. See Chapter 26 on Originating Summons procedure.

Examples of mandatory provisions are those involving:

- Stay of legal (i.e. court) proceedings. In order to give effect to an arbitration agreement, the parties have an automatic right, irrespective of any agreement to the contrary, to apply to court to stay any legal proceedings commenced in breach of the arbitration agreement. In this case, there is a mandatory duty on the court to grant a stay unless it is satisfied that the arbitration agreement is null and void, inoperative or incapable of being performed. (The old rule that made separate provision for non-domestic arbitrations is repeated in the Act, but this provision has not been introduced—see below.)
  A stay can be ordered irrespective of the fact that a condition precedent to the arbitration (such as a conciliation procedure) would need to be invoked before the arbitration agreement became applicable. That procedure must still be followed, but the application for a stay may be made before it is begun.
- The power of the court to extend agreed time limits.
- The application of statutes of limitation.
- The power of the courts to remove an arbitrator.
- The immunity of the arbitrator.
- The general duty of the tribunal to act fairly and impartially.
- The general duties of the parties.
- The enforcement of the arbitral award.
- The right of the court to hear applications in respect of the jurisdiction of the tribunal.

Apart from the mandatory provisions (only some of which are set out above) the Act provides that all other provisions are non-mandatory, in respect of which the parties may make their own arrangements, and in default the arbitrator may impose his own rules provided that they are consistent with the principles laid down by the Act.

F. THE ROLE OF THE COURT IN ARBITRATION

The old system involved what were often said to be too many possibilities for delay by tactical applications to court, particularly by lengthy appeals from the award. Now the involvement of the courts is generally kept to a minimum and is intended to be supportive of the process rather than to offer a parallel alternative or opportunities for delay and obstruction.

The following are some of the most important powers given to the court to assist the arbitral process:

- To enforce any pre-emptive order of the arbitral tribunal.

- To issue subpoenas compelling the attendance of witnesses at the arbitration hearing.
- To grant interim injunctions in aid of the arbitration (for example, *Mareva* and *Anton Piller* orders[9]).
- To extend the time for a party to begin an arbitration.
- To enforce an award[10].
- To hear and determine applications as to the jurisdiction of the arbitrator.
- To hear appeals as to the arbitrator's award.

Unless the parties otherwise agree, a party may appeal to the court on a question of law arising out of the award. An appeal may only be made with the consent of the parties or leave of the court. Leave will only be given if the court is satisfied:

(a) that the determination of the question will substantially affect the rights of one or more of the parties;
(b) that the question was one which the tribunal was asked to determine;
(c) that, on the basis of the findings of fact in the award:
    (i) the decision of the tribunal on the question is obviously wrong, or
    (ii) the question is one of general public importance and the decision of the tribunal is at least open to serious doubt, and that, despite the agreement of the parties to resolve the matter by arbitration, it is just and proper in all the circumstances for the court to determine the question.

The parties may if they wish exclude the right of appeal. Under the old regime a distinction was drawn in such cases between domestic and non-domestic arbitrations. In the case of the former the right of appeal could only be excluded if the exclusion agreement was entered into after the start of the arbitration, whilst in the case of the latter an exclusion agreement could be entered into before that time (see below). That distinction is currently no longer in effect.

G. MISCELLANEOUS MATTERS

The immunity of arbitrators

The Act introduces the concept of the immunity of arbitrators, and it is mandatorily provided that an arbitrator shall not be liable for anything done or omitted in the discharge of his functions as arbitrator unless the act or omission is shown to have been done in bad faith.

9. See Chapters 10 and 11 respectively.
10. See Chapter 29.

Privacy and confidentiality

As will be seen below (see section H), the privacy and confidentiality of the arbitral process are regarded as key advantages. However, the Act controversially does not make any provision in this respect, relying instead on the old common law rules. It was apparently thought by the draftsman that the old rules were too complicated to codify. Nevertheless, it is expressly provided that nothing in the Act shall be construed as excluding the operation of any rule of law as is consistent with its provisions. Accordingly, the old common law rules of privacy and confidentiality, insofar as they relate to arbitrations, still apply.

Domestic and non-domestic arbitrations

Before the Act, a distinction was drawn in two main respects between domestic and non-domestic arbitrations. The difference between the two was that the former involved arbitrations between parties domiciled in England and Wales or Northern Ireland; whereas non-domestic arbitrations involved one or more foreign parties. The distinction applied in the case of applications to the court to stay legal proceedings begun in breach of an arbitration agreement and in respect of the rights of the parties to an arbitration agreement to exclude the right to apply to the court for rulings on points of law. In this latter case, in a domestic arbitration, such an agreement could only be made after the arbitration had begun. The distinction is preserved in the Act in respect of both of the two points mentioned but, following public consultation, the relevant sections have not been introduced and are therefore not currently in force.

Time limits

Where the arbitration is required to be begun within a certain time, the court may now only extend that limit if the reasons for the failure to comply were outside the contemplation of the parties when they agreed the time limit, and where it would be just to extend it, or, alternatively, where the conduct of one party would make it unjust to enforce the time limit strictly.

Reasons

An arbitrator's award will now have to give reasons, unless the parties have otherwise agreed, or if the award itself is made by consent.

Separability

A non-mandatory provision of the Act is that an agreement to submit disputes to arbitration that is contained in a contract dealing with other issues ("the substantive agreement") is separate from the substantive agreement. The effect of this is that if for any reason the substantive agreement is (or is alleged to be) invalid, or no longer exists, the agreement to arbitrate will survive. Note that this provision applies in cases where the arbitration agreement is governed by the Act even if the *seat* is established elsewhere.

Removal of arbitrators

The courts retain their earlier power to remove an arbitrator, but the circumstances in which they may do so are more limited. The old expression "misconduct" has been abandoned.

H. THE ADVANTAGES AND DISADVANTAGES OF ARBITRATION

The advantages and disadvantages of arbitration may be summarised under the following headings:

Privacy

An arbitration takes place in private and the proceedings and the arbitrator's award are not open to the public. This makes it suitable for disputes that concern confidential commercial matters that the parties do not want to be ventilated in public.

Simplicity

In many cases—for example in disputes arising in the commodity markets—arbitrations may be dealt with purely "on paper", that is, by the submission of the essential contractual documents to the arbitrator who determines the dispute without hearing oral evidence or submissions. More complex cases can, of course, follow a different course if appropriate.

Enforcement

It is often thought to be easier to enforce abroad the award of an arbitrator than an order of the court. Court orders are enforceable abroad through a system of reciprocal international treaties. However, in a number of important cases (in particular in the United States and the United Kingdom) no treaty exists and accordingly enforcement of court orders can prove problematic.[11] Arbitral awards, however, are usually enforceable with greater freedom under the rules of the *New York Convention on the Recognition and Enforcement of Foreign Arbitral Awards of 1958*. This Convention is subscribed to by most sovereign states and facilitates the enforcement of arbitral awards abroad.

11. See Chapter 29.

Economy and speed

Arbitration offers opportunities for a legal dispute to be resolved quickly and cheaply. Under the new Act, these opportunities are likely to develop as arbitrators adopt procedures appropriate to the particular features of any given case rather than uniform procedures.

There are nevertheless a number of problems associated with arbitration which may still apply despite the new legislation and which must be taken into account in deciding whether to arbitrate and what procedures to adopt.

Thus:

The purported speed of arbitrations can often be illusory. Waiting for a fashionable arbitrator to become available is seldom less frustrating than waiting for a court hearing.

Privacy is of little comfort if the procedure is protracted.

The fees of the arbitrator and the cost of the arbitration facilities such as the hearing room and secretarial services must be paid for by the parties. The court is effectively free.

It is not possible to obtain Legal Aid for arbitrations. This may cause injustice by preventing an impecunious party from achieving the legal resolution of his dispute. (Under the old regime, a plaintiff could be allowed to disregard the arbitration agreement and sue in the courts with the benefit of Legal Aid, especially where it was said, for example, that his lack of funds was brought about by the conduct of his opponent that is said to be the subject of the dispute. Under the Act, this opportunity would appear to be lost, the court being obliged to grant a stay of court proceedings unless the conditions referred to in section E are satisfied. This is a consequence of the fact that the distinction between domestic and non-domestic arbitrations has not been brought into force.)

It is not possible to join into an arbitration a person who is not a party to an arbitration agreement, without his consent. Contrast this with court proceedings, when it is usually possible to join a party into litigation whether he agrees or not.

Specialisation

An arbitrator is an adjudicator chosen by the parties, rather than imposed by the court, and he may be selected because of his knowledge of and experience in commercial transactions of the sort in issue. It should be remembered, of course, that many judges also have considerable experience of the trade practices that are involved in most commercial litigation.

I. ARBITRATION, EXPERT'S VALUATION OR DETERMINATION, AND ALTERNATIVE DISPUTE RESOLUTION

The differences between arbitration and litigation have already been referred to. This section highlights the differences between arbitration and other methods of dispute resolution.

Expert's valuation or determination

Many commercial disputes are resolved by this means. It applies where parties to a contract instruct another party to adjudicate on their dispute, and is widely used in specialist fields of commercial practice, such as rent reviews, commodity disputes, claims for damages for breach of warranty and valuations necessary in share sale agreements.

The process may involve different procedures at the parties' option but most typically involves submissions in writing by the parties followed by adjudication or valuation in writing of the expert by a certificate.

The process is intended to be quick, inexpensive and held in private. The process is different from arbitration in that the courts normally have no control, but although the expert is not generally amenable to the supervision of the courts, he may be sued for negligence in appropriate cases.

An expert's decision cannot be enforced in the same way as an arbitrator's award and it is necessary to take a separate action to enforce compliance.

A process similar to arbitration is *adjudication*, which is becoming common in the construction industry. Its purpose is to promote a quick and interim resolution to a pressing problem on the basis of brief submissions. Generally, the resolution is binding on the parties until the dispute is finally determined, in the absence of agreement, by litigation or arbitration.

Alternative dispute resolution ("ADR")

In Chapter 2 we described in outline the developments in the field of ADR, which is becoming an increasingly popular means of resolving disputes. The process of ADR is much less formal than either arbitration or litigation and almost entirely beyond the powers of the courts, which will only be involved if it is necessary to enforce any agreement that is thereby reached.

J. CONCLUSION

The Act is still at a very early stage of implementation and it is too soon to evaluate its effect on the future of arbitration in England. However, it is clear that it will bring about a fundamental reform in the nature of arbitrations in England, as regards domestic and also, possibly more importantly, international arbitrations that will be heard in England. It will be interesting to see whether the reformed arbitration system will be used in preference to the system of litigation that may be introduced following Lord Woolf's proposals, which are outlined in Chapter 40.

CHAPTER 32

COMMERCIAL PROPERTY LITIGATION

Property litigation has numerous special procedures and problems. This chapter describes the main features of claims for rent, forfeiture, dilapidations, and security of tenure in commercial leases, and also the problem of who is liable to the landlord in respect of these matters.

A. NON-PAYMENT OF RENT

A landlord whose tenant has failed to pay the rent has a wide range of remedies:

- — An action for rent.
- — Distraint on goods at the premises.
- — Service of a notice on sub-tenants requiring payment of rent directly to the landlord.
- — Service of a statutory demand[1].
- — Obtaining recompense from a third party (original tenants, previous tenants or sureties of the current or former tenant).
- — Forfeiture of the lease for non-payment of rent[2].

In some situations, certain parties have rights against the landlord to disclaim onerous leases, to apply for a vesting order, and to obtain assistance from former tenants or their guarantors. Each of these situations is considered below.

(i) An action for rent

A common way of recovering debts due under leases is by starting legal proceedings.

Even if the amount due is not in dispute, legal proceedings are sometimes issued so that a court judgment can be obtained against the tenant, which could be enforced against his assets, for example a debt owed from a third

1. See Chapter 33.
2. Forfeiture upon other grounds is dealt with in section B below.

party. This method can also be used against anyone else who may be liable (see (v) below).

(ii) Distraint

Distraint (often referred to as "distress") is a process by which a landlord or his bailiff seizes goods on the premises, sells them and applies the proceeds of sale to discharge the rent arrears.

Distress can be a very swift and effective remedy for a landlord. If rent is not paid, a landlord can distrain the day after the rent was due.[3] The landlord can instruct a certificated bailiff, without any involvement of the court. Although the express purpose of distress is for the landlord to sell the goods seized to meet the rent arrears, the feared disruption to business and potential loss caused by the seizure of goods by the landlord can often result in prompt payment by the tenant of the arrears, provided that there are monies out of which payment can be made. It can force a tenant with cash flow difficulties to prioritise the landlord's debt.

It is often not possible to distrain for arrears of service charge.[4]

A bailiff will require a landlord to indemnify him from any claim by the tenant or a third party. The landlord will have to pay the bailiff's fee, and it should be borne in mind that if the goods are actually sold, the net proceeds of sale are usually only a fraction of the goods' true value.

Distress can be levied even if the tenant is in receivership. Where, however, bankruptcy proceedings or winding up proceedings have been commenced against the tenant, the right to keep the proceeds of sale of distrained goods is limited. There are further restrictions on levying distress if a company is in voluntary liquidation or if court proceedings have commenced to put the tenant into compulsory liquidation, or when the tenant company is in administration.

A landlord can seize goods owned by somebody other than the tenant. However, most third parties can serve a notice on the landlord making it clear that the goods do not belong to the tenant and requiring the landlord to return the goods seized.

The bailiff will usually take possession of the goods by drawing up an inventory of them. This imposes certain restrictions with regard to the goods. In particular, it formally warns the tenant that he must not move or otherwise deal with those goods. After a period of five days the landlord or bailiff may take the goods and sell them. The tenant has the right to extend this period to up to 15 days by service of a notice. The tenant must not interfere with those

3. Distress cannot be commenced after dusk or on a Sunday.
4. In practice it is only possible to do so in rare circumstances where:
—the lease specifically says that service charge can be recovered as rent; and
—the amount due has been agreed or otherwise ascertained.

goods during the intervening period or else he may commit a criminal offence and be liable to the landlord for treble their value.

If you are not the tenant, and you learn that a landlord has distrained upon your goods but has not yet sold them, then you may in certain circumstances be able to serve on the landlord a notice stating that the tenant has no interest in those goods. It is essential that such a notice is served as soon as possible. Until the landlord receives that notice he may sell the property and your only right would then be to sue the tenant for the value of the goods that have been seized and sold (and as the tenant may be insolvent this right may be worthless).

(iii) Sub-tenants: notice to pay rent and distress

It is possible for a landlord to levy distress on goods owned by a sub-tenant where a landlord's immediate tenant is in arrears with rent (subject to the sub-tenant's right to recover his goods, outlined above). More usually (because it is easier and less provocative), the landlord will serve a notice on the sub-tenant obliging the sub-tenant to pay all his future rent direct to the head landlord. The sub-tenant is then obliged to pay the head landlord his rent until the arrears are discharged in full.

(iv) Service of statutory demand

The service of a statutory demand is often an effective, and cheap, method of collecting undisputed debts. Its use is explained in greater detail elsewhere.[5] It can be used by a landlord where there is an undisputed amount of rent, service charge or insurance premium due from the tenant over £750. If the tenant does not pay a sum rightly demanded within three weeks, the landlord may issue court proceedings to bankrupt the tenant (if an individual) or put it into compulsory liquidation (if a company). This method can also be used against any third parties who may be liable (see (v) below).

(v) Who (apart from the current tenant) is liable under the lease?

Privity of estate

Under the law of *privity of estate*, the *current tenant* will always be liable to pay the current rent, service charge and other sums due under the lease, as will any guarantor of the current tenant.

5. See Chapter 33.

Privity of contract

In addition, the following will be liable as a matter of agreement or contract law (sometimes called "liability in privity of contract"):

- the original tenant under the lease; and
- a previous assignee who has agreed with the landlord, as is usual, on taking on the lease to observe the tenant's obligations under it; and
- a guarantor of a former tenant;

but only when both of the following conditions are met:

- in the case of rent, service charge and other fixed sums payable under the lease, they are notified in writing (in prescribed form) of the amount outstanding within six months of its becoming due[6]; and
- *either* the lease was granted before 1 January 1996[7] *or* the claim is against the immediately preceding tenant (that is, the tenant who assigned the lease to the current tenant) and the preceding tenant agreed to guarantee the current tenant's obligations as a result of a requirement for him to do so under the lease. (This requirement is known as an "authorised guarantee agreement".)[8]

It follows that if the current tenant is late in paying any sum under the lease, the landlord should protect his legal position by sending the required notice to at least one other person who might be liable within the six-month time limit.[9]

(vi) Forfeiture for non-payment of rent

It is possible for the landlord to forfeit the lease for non-payment of rent. This major topic is dealt with in section B.

(vii) Liquidation/disclaimer

A company which goes into liquidation may avoid (or "disclaim") contracts (including leases) which are a burden. If a lease has no commercial value, a liquidator will often disclaim it. The insolvent company's obligations under the lease will then cease. Instead, the landlord may prove (usually as an

6. This is an additional requirement, following a change in the law on 1 January 1996. It applies to all leases, whenever granted.
7. Or granted as a result of an agreement entered into before 1 January 1996.
8. This represents the law following changes introduced on 1 January 1996.
9. The notice must inform the person liable:
   (a) that the charge is now due;
   (b) of the amount the landlord intends to recover from him with (if payable) interest (the basis of calculating interest must also be specified);
   (c) if it is possible that the liability will be increased (for example, because of an outstanding rent review), that that is the case.

unsecured creditor) in the liquidation for his expected loss of future rents.[10]

Even though the disclaimer ends the obligations of the current tenant in liquidation, the original tenant and any other previous assignees, and any guarantors or sureties, remain liable for the remainder of the term of the lease if they were liable prior to the disclaimer.

(viii) The right to apply for a "vesting order"

Anybody who remains liable under the lease following disclaimer has a right to apply to the court for a "vesting order". This order grants the applicant a new lease directly, usually on the same terms as, and for the unexpired duration of, the disclaimed lease. Although the applicant is liable under the terms of the new lease, he will at least have the benefit of the property and would be able to use it himself or (subject to obtaining the landlord's consent) assign it to somebody solvent who would be able to pay the rent or underlet it.

A vesting order can only be made within three months of the applicant becoming aware that there has been a disclaimer. It is, therefore, essential to act quickly.

Example

A buys an existing lease (granted before 1 January 1996) from the original tenant ("OT"). When the landlord, L, gives OT consent to assign the lease to A, he (as is usual) requires A to agree to pay the rent for the rest of the term of the lease. Some years later, A assigns the lease to T. T subsequently goes into liquidation and T's liquidator disclaims the lease. The legal position is as follows: T no longer has to pay the rent from the date of the disclaimer onwards. However, L can claim the rent from both OT and A for the rest of the term of the lease. If L claims the rent from OT, OT can require A to reimburse him. A's only remedies are to prove in the liquidation of T for his outlay to OT or L and to apply to the court for a vesting order within three months of learning of the disclaimer.

(ix) Assistance for former tenants or their guarantors

A former tenant or guarantor who is obliged to pay rent or service charge because the current tenant has failed to pay will usually have the right to claim that money from the current tenant or (usually) from the person to whom he had assigned the lease (if not the current tenant).

Additionally, a former tenant or his guarantor who has paid the current tenant's rent or service charge as a result of a notice served on him by the landlord may require the landlord to grant him an overriding lease, that is, a lease on exactly the same terms as the current lease (plus three days), that comes between the landlord's interest and the lease of the current tenant. This enables the person actually paying the rent to have the commercial benefit of the premises. Initially, the overriding lease would not confer the right to occupy the premises, but merely to obtain the rent from the current tenant. The advantage to him is that the overriding lease puts him in the position of a landlord vis-à-vis the current tenant, enabling him to distrain for rent or to forfeit the current tenant's lease for non-payment of rent, if desired. Unless

10. See Chapter 33 for further details of how to prove in the liquidation.

the arrears were paid off, this would allow the former tenant to use the premises. Thus, although the former tenant may have to continue to pay the rent, he can at least occupy the premises himself, or sub-let them.

B. FORFEITURE

Virtually all properly drawn leases and tenancy agreements include a forfeiture clause (sometimes called a "proviso for re-entry"), entitling the landlord to end the lease if any rent is, say, more than 14 or 21 days in arrear or if any other covenant in the lease has been broken by the tenant. The effect of forfeiture is to end the lease prematurely. The landlord re-enters the property and (subject to the right of those affected to apply for relief from forfeiture, described below) any sub-tenancies or mortgages of the lease fall away. The landlord can regain possession (if necessary through court proceedings). Similarly, the tenant is released from all future obligations to pay the rent, service charge and other sums under the lease, and to perform the other covenants in the lease.

Forfeiture from a landlord's point of view

Forfeiture can be an effective way of recovering sums in arrear under the lease or remedying a breach of covenant where the lease has a commercial value. This is particularly so in a time of rising rents. However, because forfeiture relieves tenants and others liable from their obligation to pay all future rent, it is not in the landlord's interest to forfeit a lease where he wishes to maintain the existing rental stream. As an alternative to forfeiture the landlord should consider commencing legal proceedings instead to recover any loss he has suffered.

Restrictions on forfeiture

Irrespective of how the lease is drafted, the law imposes certain restrictions on forfeiture. These are:

- The concept of "waiver".
- Section 146 of the Law of Property Act 1925 in non-rent cases.
- Relief from forfeiture.

Waiver

It is possible for a landlord, even inadvertently, to waive his right to forfeit in respect of certain breaches in the lease. If, once he or his agent has learnt of the breach, the landlord does anything which shows that he regards the lease to be continuing (if, for example, he or his agent accepts rent or sends out a demand for rent falling due after the breach took place or levies distress) he will be treated as having chosen to keep the lease continuing and will have waived his right to forfeit the lease for that particular breach.

Section 146 of the Law of Property Act 1925: non-rent cases

Irrespective of what the lease provides, the landlord cannot forfeit a lease, *other than for non-payment of rent* (or sums such as service charges which are defined as rent), without first serving a "Section 146 Notice". The notice must specify the particular breach of the covenant in the lease that the landlord complains of; what the tenant must do to remedy the breach (if it can be remedied); and, if the landlord requires compensation for the breach, how much compensation is required. The landlord must then allow the tenant a reasonable time to remedy the breach complained of.[11] Only then may the landlord forfeit the lease.

Methods of forfeiture

Forfeiture can be effected by one of two methods. In the case of business premises where nobody who is opposed to forfeiture is present on the premises at the time of forfeiture, the landlord can forfeit simply by physically re-entering the property. This is usually done by changing the locks. Alternatively, and for non-business premises, the landlord can forfeit the lease by initiating court proceedings.

Relief from forfeiture

A tenant whose lease has been forfeited has a right to ask the court to reinstate his lease (called "relief from forfeiture"). The effect of the tenant being granted relief is that it is as if the forfeiture never occurred.

Where the lease has been forfeited for non-payment of rent the tenant will usually be able to obtain relief subject to the court's requirement that he pays all rent arrears and the landlord's costs, provided he applies to the court within six months of the date of forfeiture.

Where the lease has been forfeited for other breaches of covenant, the tenant also has a right to apply for relief. Normally the court will grant relief from forfeiture provided that the tenant rectifies the breach where possible. The tenant will also usually have to pay the landlord's costs of the proceedings.

Sub-tenants and mortgagees

Forfeiture automatically ends any sub-tenancies and mortgages of the lease. For this reason, a sub-tenant also has a right to apply for relief from forfeiture.

11. Even when the breach is irremediable the landlord must still give the tenant time to consider his legal position. 14 days should be sufficient.

If successful, the sub-tenant will usually be granted a fresh lease direct from the landlord on the same terms as the forfeited headlease, except that the term of the new lease will be no longer than the remaining term of the original sub-lease. If the headlease was forfeited for non-payment of rent, the sub-tenant may have to pay all the arrears of rent due on the headlease in order to obtain relief. Similarly, a mortgagee whose leasehold security has been forfeited will have a right to apply for relief from forfeiture and would usually be granted a fresh lease direct to him as a substituted form of security.

C. DILAPIDATIONS AND REPAIRING OBLIGATIONS

A lease of part of a building will commonly require the tenant to maintain the interior and the landlord to maintain the exterior and structure of the building, with the tenant paying for this through the service charge. Leases of an entire building often require the tenant to keep all of the building in repair and to decorate it periodically. However, if a tenant fails to repair, the landlord's remedies against the tenant may well be limited.

In all cases if a landlord sues a tenant for his failure to repair, the landlord can only recover from the tenant the lower of:

— the cost of the repair; and
— the reduction in the value of the landlord's interest in the property as a result of the tenant's failure to repair. (This will usually be less, and sometimes considerably less.)

Example
The premises are in a poor state of repair at the end of the lease. To restore them to the state they should have been in, had the tenant complied with his repairing obligations, would cost £15,000. The landlord has found a new tenant, who is willing to take the premises on normal market terms, but requires a contribution of £10,000 towards the fitting-out works to take account of the poor state of repair of the premises. The tenant's liability to the landlord for damages for breach of its repairing obligations would, therefore, be £10,000.

Different rules apply, depending on when during the lease the landlord makes a dilapidations claim.

(i) During the lease

Except where there are fewer than three years of the lease to run, the landlord cannot sue the tenant for his failure to repair without first serving a notice on the tenant specifying the breaches of the tenant's repairing obligations of which he complains and giving certain other information. Immediate legal advice should be taken, because the tenant can within 28 days serve a counter-notice on the landlord the effect of which is severely to restrict the landlord's right to sue the tenant for such breaches.

(ii) At the end of the lease

It is usual, just before or just after the end of the lease, for the landlord to instruct his surveyor to prepare a "schedule of dilapidations", detailing exactly what the tenant has failed to repair or redecorate and specifying what must be done to put the property back into the correct state of repair required under the lease. This may include removing fixtures installed by the tenant or his predecessor or undoing past alterations to the property.

The following points should be borne in mind:

— The landlord may intend at the end of the lease to demolish the premises or make structural alterations of the kind which would make the repairs the tenant is obliged to do valueless. In such a case, the landlord is barred from making a dilapidations claim against the tenant.

— If it is clear that repair work does need to be done, it may be cheaper for the tenant to engage his own workmen, or find his own contractors to do the work before the lease expires. The tenant has no right to do the work after the lease has expired. This may cost less than the amount the landlord claims it would cost him to do the repairs himself. This approach has two additional cost advantages to the tenant:

    If the landlord does the work he will be entitled to claim the professional fees incurred in tendering and supervising the work.

    If the landlord has to delay reletting the premises because he must do the repair work first, he might be able to claim his lost rental income from the outgoing tenant.

The surveyor will charge the landlord a fee for preparing the schedule of dilapidations as will the lawyer for his role. The landlord will usually attempt to recover these fees from the tenant but he is in fact only able to do so if the lease specifically says he can.

D. SECURITY OF TENURE: COMMERCIAL LEASES[12]

Many business tenants will have a right under the Landlord and Tenant Act 1954 to remain in their premises after their lease expires. The statute sets out a procedure which enables most business tenants to apply to the court for a new tenancy. The landlord has only a limited number of grounds on which he

12. Security of tenure provisions apply to some other types of lease as well, but these are not within the scope of this Guide.

may legitimately object to the court ordering the grant of a new tenancy.[13]

> *The law gives these rights to tenants who occupy the premises in their tenancy for the purposes of their business or profession. There are a number of exceptions.*[14] *The law automatically continues the tenancy beyond the date it would otherwise expire until either the landlord or tenant serves a notice in a prescribed form terminating the tenancy. Once such a notice is served the tenant will be able to apply to the court for a new tenancy, but only if the correct procedure is followed, the correct counter-notices served and the time limits strictly adhered to. If notices are received, legal advice should be sought at once as delay can deprive either party of his statutory rights.*
>
> *If the tenant does not wish to stay in the property when the term of his lease expires, he must either vacate the premises before the term expires or write to the landlord at least three months before the date on which the term of the lease ends saying that he does not wish the tenancy to be continued. If the tenant fails to do either of these, the tenancy (and the tenant's obligation to pay rent and service charge) will continue and the tenant will only be able to determine this obligation on giving the landlord three months' notice, such notice to expire on a quarter day.*[15]

E. ADJUDICATION METHODS

Disputes under leases may be determined by litigation, arbitration or by expert's valuation. For an account of arbitration and expert's valuation, see Chapter 31.

13. In broad terms, they are:
    (a) serious failure by the tenant, in breach of the lease, to repair the premises;
    (b) persistent delay in paying rent;
    (c) substantial breaches of other terms in the lease by the tenant;
    (d) the landlord has offered the tenant suitable alternative accommodation;
    (e) the tenancy was created by sub-letting part only of the property comprised in a superior tenancy of which the landlord is the immediate landlord, and the landlord can get substantially more income by letting the entire property as a whole and he intends to do so;
    (f) the landlord requires the property back because he intends to demolish or do substantial construction work on it; or
    (g) the landlord wishes to use the premises for his own business or to live in, having held his interest for at least five years.

If the landlord succeeds in opposing the tenant's application on grounds (e), (f) or (g) alone, he must pay the tenant a set amount of compensation.

14. These include:
    (i) genuine "licences" which do not confer a right to exclusive occupation;
    (ii) tenancies excluded from the Landlord and Tenant Act 1954 by a court-sanctioned agreement;
    (iii) certain fixed-term tenancies lasting six months or less.
15. The quarter days are 25 March, 24 June, 29 September and 25 December.

CHAPTER 33

INSOLVENCY PROCEEDINGS

This chapter describes the system available for the collection of undisputed debts from debtors who are refusing or claiming to be unable to pay. It is concerned primarily with debts owed by companies, but also draws attention to the principal differences between that procedure and the similar procedure for the recovery of debts from individuals. It is beyond the scope of this chapter to comment in any detail on insolvency procedures other than compulsory winding up and bankruptcy proceedings, but a brief description of the nature and uses of such other proceedings is given at the end of the chapter.

A. INTRODUCTION

Insolvency proceedings are not a substitute for conventional litigation. They should only be used for the collection of debts where there is no real dispute that the debt exists.

> *Any attempt to use insolvency proceedings to pressurise the debtor into paying an amount which it can reasonably argue it does not owe is an abuse of the process of the court, which may have serious consequences for the creditor.*

B. GROUNDS FOR ISSUE OF PETITION

Insolvency proceedings against companies (with which this chapter is primarily concerned) are commenced by the issue of a *winding up petition*, by which the creditor asks the court to wind up the debtor company (that is, *put it into liquidation*).

By far the most common ground for winding up petitions is that the debtor is *unable to pay its debts*. A company is deemed to be unable to pay its debts if, among other things:

— A *statutory demand* for the debt has been served on the company and the company has not paid within 21 days of service.

— It is proved to the court's satisfaction that the company is *unable to pay its debts as they fall due.*

Where the debtor is an individual, the proceedings are commenced by a bankruptcy petition, which must always be preceded by a statutory demand.

(i) Statutory demands

A statutory demand is a formal legal document, which must be in a prescribed form and which is usually prepared by a lawyer. It must set out full particulars of the debt and explain to the debtor the consequences of failure to pay within the 21 days allowed. A statutory demand may only be used for a debt which exceeds £750.

A statutory demand should be served by leaving it at the debtor company's registered office. It should not be sent by post.

(ii) Inability to pay debts as they fall due

If the court finds that a debtor has not paid or given appropriate security for an undisputed debt exceeding £750, it will be satisfied that the debtor company is unable to pay its debts as they fall due.

This is so even if the debtor company can establish that its assets vastly exceed its liabilities and that it could easily pay the debt if it wanted to.

C. THE ISSUE, SERVICE AND ADVERTISEMENT OF A PETITION

A winding up petition, upon issue, is allocated a hearing date by the court, which will usually be six to eight weeks from the date of issue.

The petition must usually be served on the debtor company by leaving it at its registered office.

The petition must be advertised in *The London Gazette* not earlier than seven business days after service of the petition on the company (to give the debtor company time to pay) and not later than seven business days before the hearing date (to give other creditors who may read the advertisement time to decide whether to attend the hearing and support or oppose the petition).

There are no corresponding provisions for advertisement of bankruptcy petitions in the case of individual debtors.

The consequences for the debtor company of the issue and advertisement of the petition are severe:

— If a winding up order is eventually made, all dispositions of the debtor company's property from the date the petition was issued (*not* from the date of the order) will be void, unless the court otherwise orders.

- Because of this, anyone who sees the advertisement (or otherwise hears about the petition) is unlikely to be prepared to do business with the debtor company until it is known whether a winding up order will be made.
- All clearing banks check *The London Gazette* daily. If an advertisement of a winding up petition against one of their customers appears, they will immediately freeze all of that customer's bank accounts. This will leave the debtor company unable to pay its employees, suppliers or anyone else, which may have serious consequences for the debtor company's business.
- Even if the debtor company is prepared to pay the debt, the petition cannot be withdrawn once it has been advertised.

D. THE HEARING OF A PETITION

It is relatively rare for a petition to be opposed on the allocated hearing date. This is because, to avoid the adverse consequences of advertisement of the petition, the debtor company will usually have:

- paid the debt or agreed to pay by instalments prior to advertisement (if it can afford to do so and the debt is not disputed); or
- persuaded the creditor that the petition cannot succeed (because there is a dispute about the existence of the debt) and that the petition should therefore be withdrawn prior to advertisement; or
- if the debt is disputed and the creditor will not agree to withdraw the petition, obtained an injunction to stop the creditor advertising or otherwise proceeding with the petition and/or an order dismissing the petition (see further, below).

If the debtor company has not paid or given appropriate security for the debt or taken action to oppose the petition, a winding up order will usually be made on the first hearing date. If the debtor company or other creditors attend on the first hearing to oppose the petition, the hearing will be adjourned to a later date when the court has time to hear argument.

E. THE CONSEQUENCES OF A WINDING UP ORDER

If a winding up order is made, the debtor company goes into compulsory liquidation and control of the debtor company and its assets passes to the liquidator (who, in the first instance, usually is a government appointed officer known as the Official Receiver). The liquidator will then realise the debtor company's assets (that is, sell them or otherwise convert them into cash) and distribute the proceeds to the debtor company's creditors.

The effect of winding up orders on creditors generally (with the exception of certain classes of secured and preferential creditors) is that they all rank equally for a dividend payable from the debtor company's assets, once realised. Unsecured creditors' dividends are calculated *pro rata* in accordance with the value attributed to their debts.

F. DISPUTED DEBTS

If the debtor company disputes the debt, it may apply for an injunction to restrain the creditor from issuing, advertising or otherwise proceeding with a petition and, where a petition has been issued, for an order striking out the petition.

> *In the case of individual debtors, where the debtor wishes to dispute the debt, he does so by applying to have the statutory demand set aside. A bankruptcy petition cannot then be presented until the application has been heard.*

If the debtor company can establish that the debt is disputed in good faith and on substantial grounds, an injunction will usually be granted and any petition which has been issued will be struck out as an abuse of the process of the court.

The law and procedure relating to injunction applications is dealt with elsewhere in this Guide.[1] Applications for injunctions can be very expensive and, if the debtor company succeeds in its application, the creditor will be ordered to pay the debtor company's costs.

— Because the use of insolvency proceedings in cases of disputed debts represents an abuse of the process of the court, the court will often order the petitioning creditor to pay the debtor company's costs on *the indemnity basis*. The effect of this is explained in more detail in Chapter 24, but the important point to note is that an indemnity costs order obliges the paying party to pay virtually all of the costs incurred by the receiving party.

It should be remembered that debts may be disputed not only on the ground that the debt itself has not fallen due, but also on the ground that the debtor company has a cross-claim against the creditor which equals or exceeds the amount of the debt. This is called a "set-off".

1. See Chapter 10.

Example
An investment adviser contracts to provide advice and services to a company for a fee. The advice and services are provided and an invoice is rendered. There is no dispute that the fee is payable under the terms of the contract. The company, however, alleges that the advice given was negligent and that as a result it has suffered loss which exceeds the amount of the fee. If the company's cross-claim is based on reasonable grounds, the debt in respect of the fee will be disputed and any petition based on it struck out.

The same consequences follow even if the petitioning creditor knew nothing about the dispute at the time the petition was issued. It is for this reason that using the insolvency route for recovery of debts has been described by the court as "a high risk strategy". If there is an indication that the debt may be disputed, the proper way to proceed is to issue a writ and, where appropriate, seek summary judgment.[2]

The petitioning creditor does not obtain priority over other creditors, save in respect of the costs of the petition, which are paid out of assets realised in the liquidation.

As stated above, where the debtor is an individual, the bankruptcy petition must be preceded by a statutory demand. If the debt demanded is disputed, the proper procedure for challenging the debt is to apply to have the statutory demand set aside.

G. TACTICAL CONSIDERATIONS

The first question to ask when considering how to recover a debt is whether the debt is disputed. If it is, insolvency proceedings are inappropriate and a conventional writ should be issued.

If there is no dispute about the existence of the debt, the insolvency route is an available option. An obvious example would be an unpaid invoice. It will not, however, always be the preferred option. Selecting the best option will depend upon the circumstances of the case and in particular the perceived financial circumstances of the debtor.

If the reason for non-payment of the debt is that the debtor is having cash flow difficulties and is paying only those debts which it cannot avoid, insolvency proceedings will often be the best route. Presentation of the petition will exert the maximum possible pressure on the debtor company to pay.

If, on the other hand, the debtor company has no available cash with which to pay the debt, but does have substantial non-cash assets, serious consideration should be given to conventional litigation as an alternative. Summary judgment[2] can be obtained swiftly in cases where there is no dispute and the resulting judgment debt can then be enforced against the debtor's non-cash

2. See Chapter 12.

assets in the normal way.[3] A judgment creditor who completes the enforcement of a judgment debt by seizure and sale of, or obtaining security over, the debtor's assets will be able to keep all of the proceeds of sale of those assets. He will not have to share them equally with the company's other creditors as would be the case on winding up.

If the creditor has concerns about dissipation of the debtor's assets, insolvency proceedings may be the correct route. In this instance, the creditor may ask the court to appoint a provisional liquidator (who will immediately take control of the debtor company's assets), which can be done at any time after issue of the petition. Furthermore, a liquidator, once appointed, has wide investigative powers which would not be available in ordinary litigation.

The creditor should note, however, that the purpose of a liquidation is to realise the debtor's unsecured assets for the collective benefit of all unsecured creditors, and that, save as to certain costs, a creditor who starts a winding up will not obtain any better *pro rata* return than any other unsecured creditor. Further, it is quite common for there to be nothing left in a liquidation for distribution to ordinary unsecured creditors because of the priority afforded to secured and preferential creditors.

H. OTHER INSOLVENCY PROCEEDINGS

There follows a brief description of the nature and uses of insolvency procedures other than compulsory winding up and bankruptcy proceedings.

Some of these procedures are intended to protect a debtor from the enforcement of the claims of creditors on an individual, rather than collective, basis, or to enable a reorganisation plan to be produced and implemented. They may well result in the temporary or permanent suspension of conventional debt collection procedures so that claims can be dealt with collectively.

Company voluntary arrangement ("CVA")

A CVA is a relatively informal procedure with only minimal court involvement. A proposal is put by the company's directors[4] to its creditors which, if approved by 75 per cent in value of the unsecured creditors and by a simple majority of the shareholders, becomes binding between the company and its creditors and is then implemented under the supervision of an insolvency practitioner. Court approval is not required. The rights of secured creditors to enforce security are not affected without their agreement.

3. See Chapter 29.
4. Or by its administrator (see below), or liquidator.

Members' voluntary liquidation ("MVL")

An MVL is the liquidation of a solvent company at the instance of its shareholders. The liquidator realises the company's assets, pays off all the creditors and distributes the surplus to the company's members.

Creditors' voluntary liquidation ("CVL")

A CVL is the equivalent of an MVL where the company is insolvent. Although a CVL is started by the company's directors and members, the appointment of the liquidator must be approved by the company's creditors who, as they will not be paid in full by reason of the company's insolvency, exercise some control over the conduct of the liquidation.

Administrative receivership

An administrative receivership is a procedure which may only be instituted by banks or other creditors of the company who have security over the whole (or substantially the whole) of the company's undertaking and assets, which security consists of or includes a floating charge (that is, "secured creditors"). The secured creditor chooses and appoints the administrative receiver, whose primary duty is to realise the company's assets for the benefit of the secured creditor. Administrative receivership is often accompanied by or followed by a liquidation.

Administration

Administration is begun by order of the court, usually, although not necessarily, made on the application of the company. The most common grounds for making an administration order are that an administration is likely to lead to the survival of the company as a going concern or to a more advantageous realisation of the company's assets than would a liquidation. Once an administration order has been made, the company is largely protected from the measures that creditors might otherwise have been able to take whilst the administrator seeks to achieve the objective of the administration. The administrator's proposals require the approval of a majority by value of the company's unsecured creditors but do not normally require court sanction.

Individual voluntary arrangement ("IVA")

An IVA is a procedure applicable to private individuals that is similar to a CVA for companies. The principal difference is that, unlike a CVA, the court will grant an interim order before the proposal is put to the individual's creditors, the effect of which is to protect the individual from those creditors until he has had the opportunity to put the proposal to them for approval.

CHAPTER 34

EMPLOYMENT LITIGATION

Disputes between employer and employee have become increasingly frequent, and often reflect fundamental changes in the way society approaches these problems. Here are described the main features of the traditional common-law disputes, and also the modern statutory laws. A chart on page 251 summarises the procedures involved in employment litigation.

A. INTRODUCTION

Under English law, employment rights fall into two distinct categories, namely *contractual* and *statutory*.

Whilst there is considerable overlap between these two categories they are regarded as separate and this is reflected in the manner in which employment litigation is conducted.

— *Contractual* claims are generally dealt with in the High Court or county court, as with any other civil litigation.
— *Statutory* claims are dealt with by the Industrial Tribunal.

B. CONTRACTUAL CLAIMS

Wrongful dismissal

This is a claim by an employee for breach of a contract of employment and is usually made either by writ in the High Court or by Summons in the county court. Certain of such claims may now also be made in the Industrial Tribunal.

The claim is usually for damages, and will generally be appropriate where an employee is complaining that he or she has been dismissed without being given the full notice period specified in the employment contract. As a result, the employee will be claiming a monetary sum equivalent to the salary and benefits which would have been earned over the notice period if it had been allowed to run in the usual way.

Wrongful dismissal claims are governed by the general rules of procedure set out in other sections of this Guide. Those of particular importance in such claims include:

- Obtaining summary judgment with damages to be assessed.[1]
- Considering summary judgment if the contract provides for a fixed sum to be paid in the event of an early termination of employment.
- The production of experts' reports to assess the level of loss suffered by the employee. Often expert evidence[2] will be given to assist the court in establishing whether the employee has acted reasonably in attempting to reduce the loss by seeking and obtaining alternative employment (generally referred to as "mitigation of loss").
- Payments into court.[3]
- Interim payments.[4]

Employment covenants and confidential information

An employer may have to seek to enforce these covenants in the contract of employment.

The covenants would be, for example, such provisions as seek to prevent the employee from:

- Soliciting or dealing with the employer's customers within a specified period after termination of employment.
- Soliciting or enticing away the employer's existing employees, for example where the employee is part of a team.
- Competing with the employer's business, again within a certain specified period and possibly within a limited geographical area.
- Disclosing the employer's confidential information/trade secrets either during employment or after termination of such employment.

While the initial claim would be for damages the employer may wish to seek other remedies such as an *injunction*:

- To prevent breach of a covenant in a contract of employment.
- To enforce a provision in the contract of employment so that the employment contract is continued but the employee is required to stay away from the business premises or not to have any contact with the employer's other employees or customers (known as "garden leave").
- To prevent the breach of covenants relating to confidential information.

In addition, the following orders may be appropriate:

1. See Chapter 12.
2. See Chapter 20.
3. See Chapter 21.
4. See Chapter 15.

— A *delivery up* order in relation to documents or other property belonging to the employer.
— An *Anton Piller* order.[5]

The principles applicable in these circumstances are those which relate to interlocutory injunctions generally.[6]

The general rule for enforcement of such covenants is that any attempt to restrain an individual from earning his living is void on grounds of public policy. The employer will therefore have to establish that the restrictions in the covenants are reasonably necessary to protect his legitimate business interests. An employer should also note that if he, as the employer, has terminated the employment by breaching the contract, then the covenants will fall away and he will not be able to enforce them.

C. CLAIMS IN THE INDUSTRIAL TRIBUNALS

Background

Industrial Tribunals were created by statute in 1964. Over the years their jurisdiction has increased rapidly, and is still growing. The procedure of these tribunals is governed by statutory regulations. In accordance with the general philosophy of their introduction, the principle is that their approach should be less formal and that they should be more accessible than the High Court or the county court.

The tribunal generally comprises three members:

— a chairman who is a qualified lawyer with at least seven years' experience; and
— a representative from a trade union or a consulting organisation for employees; and
— a representative from one of the employer federations.

It is important to note that decisions of the tribunal are made on a majority basis, so that the two "lay members" can overrule the chairman.

Jurisdiction

The principal statutory claims which can be heard by a tribunal are:

— Unfair dismissal.
— Application for a redundancy payment.
— Disputes over written particulars of employment.

5. See Chapter 11.
6. See Chapter 10.

- — Maternity issues.
- — Claims under the Wages Act 1986, now consolidated in the Employment Rights Act 1996.
- — Discrimination/equal opportunities claims under the Equal Pay Act 1970, the Sex Discrimination Act 1975, the Race Relations Act 1976 and the Disability Discrimination Act 1995.

An important point to note is that since July 1994 the tribunals have also had jurisdiction over contractual claims and employer's counterclaims, subject to the maximum claim in any such action being £25,000 (although claims in relation to the employee covenants described in section B above and claims for personal injuries are specifically excluded from the tribunals' jurisdiction).

- — Tribunals also have jurisdiction under Article 119 of the Treaty of Rome (Equal Pay) and also on claims made under European Directives against state authorities.

Procedure

A person wishing to bring a claim ("the applicant") commences proceedings by filing an originating application to the Central Office of the Industrial Tribunals in Bury St Edmunds, Suffolk which is then despatched to the relevant Regional Industrial Tribunal.

This originating application will be treated as presented when it is received by the Central Office rather than when it is sent to it. This is important to note as each of the various claims over which the tribunal has jurisdiction (other than European law) has specific statutory time limits within which such a claim is to be made.

Time limits

All applications are to be presented within a certain time limit, generally prescribed in the relevant statute under which the claim is brought. For example, an unfair dismissal claim must be made within three months from the date on which the contract of employment terminated. The tribunal has jurisdiction to hear late applications at its discretion.

Notice of appearance

If the employer ("the respondent") wishes to defend an application a written notice of appearance must be completed and returned within 21 days of receiving a copy of the originating application. This sets out the employer's grounds of defence.

This can be done on a prescribed form (IT3) (which is available from the tribunal), or again by providing the relevant details in writing.

Employers should exercise care as regards the grounds on which to resist the application as, if a particular ground is omitted at this stage and the employer subsequently wishes to rely on such a ground, the applicant may successfully resist an application to amend the notice of appearance or apply for an adjournment, possibly at the employer's expense.

However, the tribunal is generally fair and lenient with regard to applications to amend both originating applications and notices of appearance.

Pre-hearing review

This is in the nature of a preliminary hearing, to deal with cases where either party has no reasonable prospect of success. A pre-hearing review can be ordered by the tribunal itself or on the application of either party. Generally speaking, the employer will be requesting the tribunal to hold a pre-hearing review on the basis that the applicant has no case, or a very weak one.

If a pre-hearing review is ordered, both parties to the proceedings may submit written representations and/or appear to present oral arguments, but no evidence is presented.

The tribunal will consider the application and representations. If it agrees that a particular party has no reasonable prospect of success, it may make an order against that party requiring him to deposit a sum not exceeding £150 as a condition of being allowed to continue with the proceedings.

A tribunal must have regard to the party's means in fixing the sum payable. If a deposit is ordered it must be paid within 21 days. Failure to do so will result in the particular party's case being struck out.

The effect of the pre-hearing review is that if, after a warning is issued and the deposit is paid, the party to whom the warning was given fails in establishing his claim, the deposit is forfeited and in addition the tribunal can make an order for costs against that party (see the section on costs, below).

Interlocutory matters

Where prior to the full hearing of any case either party wishes:

- to apply for further particulars of the grounds on which his opponent relies or of any facts or statements relevant to his opponent's case; or
- to ask for disclosure of certain documents; or
- to ask for a person to attend as a witness and produce any relevant documents

that party may apply in writing for such an order to a tribunal chairman.

The chairman will generally make such an order but allow the other party a reasonable period in which to object.

Failure to comply with the order could result in the party's case being struck out or preclude him from relying on those documents or that particular ground of defence.

Discrimination questionnaires

A separate procedure applies in discrimination cases where an applicant can serve a statutory questionnaire under the Sex Discrimination Act, the Race Relations Act or the Disability Discrimination Act. This is in addition to the need to lodge a Notice of Appearance. Whilst the employer is under no obligation to reply to such a questionnaire, the tribunal may draw inferences from a refusal or failure to reply. It is, therefore, generally advisable where possible to respond to such questionnaires as openly and freely as possible.

Evidence

The rules of discovery applicable in the High Court and county court are not strictly applied in the tribunal so that there is no overriding duty on the parties to disclose all the relevant documentation in their possession, custody or power. As a result, documentation for tribunal hearings tends to be less cumbersome than in general civil litigation.

If possible, it is advisable for the parties to agree a bundle of documents for the hearing.

As a rule, the tribunal will wish to hear oral evidence from all relevant witnesses. In recent years it has become common practice for parties to exchange signed witness statements prior to the hearing which will form the basis of the evidence to be given by that witness. A witness can then be cross-examined by the other party.

If it is not possible to call a witness, for example if he is out of the country or unavailable owing to illness, evidence may be given by means of a written signed statement. Such statement should be sent to the tribunal and the other party at least seven days before the hearing and it will then be admissible as a written representation. However, it is up to the tribunal to decide, bearing in mind that the witness is not available for cross-examination, how much weight can be given to this evidence.

Legal representation

The original intention of tribunals was to make the procedure as informal as possible so that both employer and employee could make their own representations to the tribunal. However, the complexity of employment law including the influence of European law has meant that, in the main, parties employ legal representatives.

Legal Aid is not available for the applicant in the tribunal. However, advice leading up to the hearing can be obtained under the "Green Form Scheme" which is a form of legal aid covering preliminary advice. Advice can also be obtained from Citizens' Advice Bureaux and, in addition, an organisation called the Free Representation Unit can provide advocacy for applicants at the tribunal.

Costs

As a general rule a successful party in a tribunal will not be awarded costs, other than in situations where a warning has already been given as a result of the pre-hearing review (see above).

Costs will only be awarded against a party if in the opinion of the tribunal that party has acted frivolously, vexatiously, abusively, disruptively or otherwise unreasonably in bringing or conducting the proceedings.

Settlement

As soon as proceedings have been issued the *Advisory Conciliation and Arbitration Service* ("ACAS") will become involved and will attempt to promote a settlement between the parties. If such a settlement can be reached it will be recorded on an official form (COT3) which will have the effect of suspending the proceedings.

The other means of settlement is via a compromise agreement, which requires the applicant to have taken independent legal advice and complied with certain other conditions which are set out in the employment protection legislation. A compromise agreement can be made even before proceedings have been issued.

Remedies

The remedies available will depend on the particular jurisdiction covering the case.

Generally, however, in unfair dismissal cases the tribunal can either make a monetary order for compensation or can order re-instatement or re-engagement of the employee. The latter remedies are awarded only in very rare circumstances.

In unfair dismissal cases, the tribunal makes two awards:

- a *basic* award—calculated on a specific formula which takes into account the employee's age, length of service and gross weekly wage up to a maximum of £210 per week; and
- a *compensatory* award—to represent the employee's actual loss up to a maximum of £11,300. There is no limit to compensation claims in discrimination cases.

An order for payment of money made by the tribunal is enforceable as if it were a judgment of the county court, but must first be registered with the county court.

Interest is payable on any compensation ordered by a tribunal which has not been paid within 42 days of the issue of the written decision. This is payable at the rate fixed from time to time by statute. The current rate is eight per cent.

Recoupment

Where an employee has received unemployment benefit or income support between the date of termination of employment and the date of the compensatory award the employer is entitled to withhold any such amount from payment to the employee until the Department of Social Security has indicated the amount it wishes to recoup from the award.

The recoupment system applies only to an award by the tribunal and not to any payment agreed by the parties. This is an incentive for the employee to settle any action without recourse to the tribunal.

Appeals

An appeal from a decision in the tribunal is heard by the Employment Appeal Tribunal with a right of appeal to the Court of Appeal and then to the House of Lords. (It is possible for a reference to be made to the European Court of Justice on a relevant point of law at any stage.)

An appeal from a tribunal decision can only be brought on a point of law and must be lodged within 42 days of the date on which the decision is sent to the party making the appeal.

Legal Aid is available to employees for such appeals.

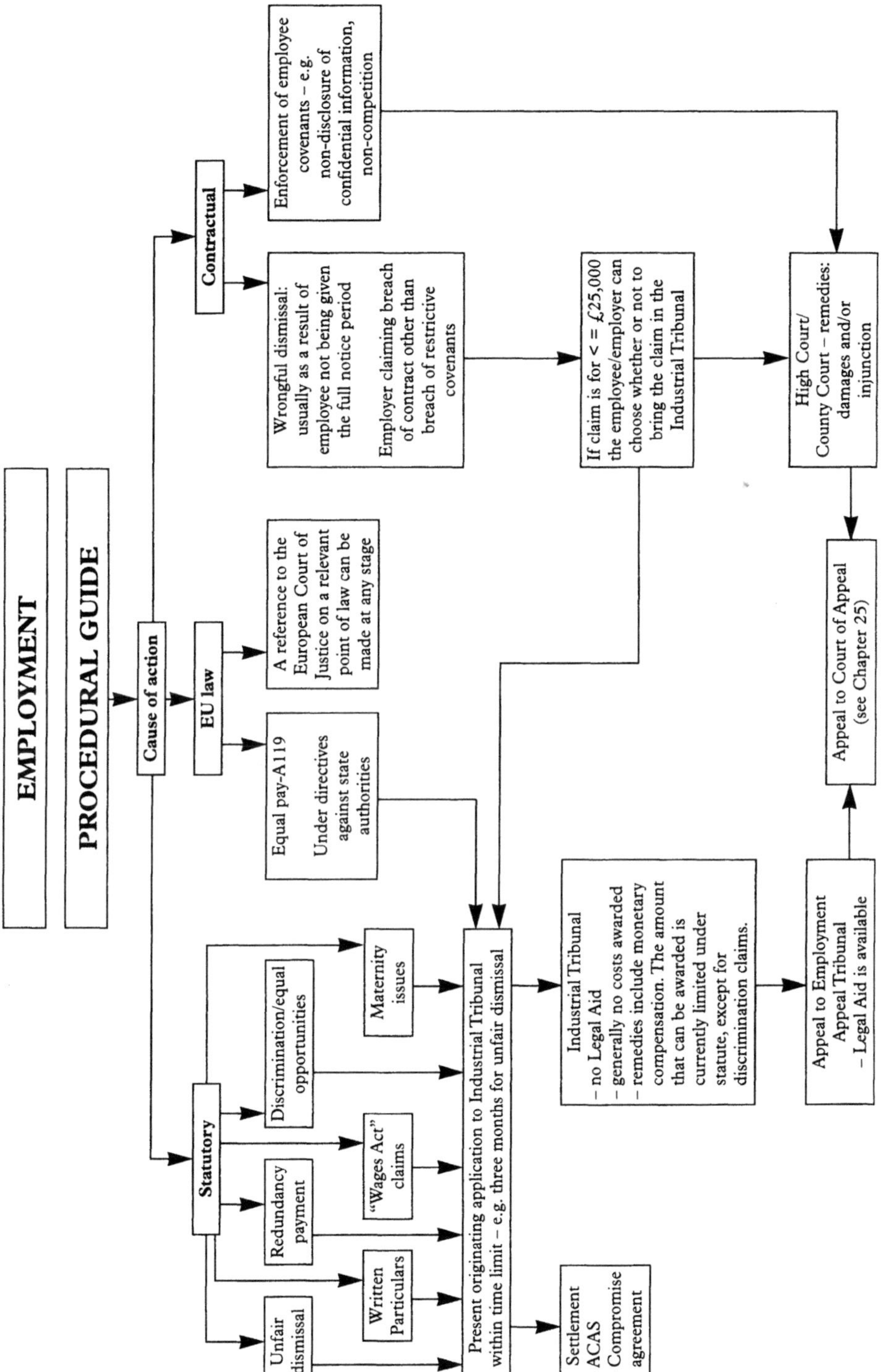
EMPLOYMENT
PROCEDURAL GUIDE
Cause of action
Statutory
EU law
Contractual
Unfair dismissal
Written Particulars
Redundancy payment
"Wages Act" claims
Discrimination/equal opportunities
Maternity issues
Equal pay-A119
Under directives against state authorities
A reference to the European Court of Justice on a relevant point of law can be made at any stage
Wrongful dismissal: usually as a result of employee not being given the full notice period
Employer claiming breach of contract other than breach of restrictive covenants
Enforcement of employee covenants – e.g. non-disclosure of confidential information, non-competition
Present originating application to Industrial Tribunal within time limit – e.g. three months for unfair dismissal
Settlement
– ACAS
– Compromise agreement
Industrial Tribunal
– no Legal Aid
– generally no costs awarded
– remedies include monetary compensation. The amount that can be awarded is currently limited under statute, except for discrimination claims.
If claim is for < = £25,000 the employee/employer can choose whether or not to bring the claim in the Industrial Tribunal
High Court/
County Court – remedies: damages and/or injunction
Appeal to Employment Appeal Tribunal
– Legal Aid is available
Appeal to Court of Appeal (see Chapter 25)

CHAPTER 35

JUDICIAL REVIEW

This chapter summarises the rules and procedures by which decisions of public bodies may be challenged in the courts. A chart on page 260 sets out the main steps involved in such cases.

A. INTRODUCTION

In the post-war years the expansion of the areas in which public bodies, either directly or through subordinates, have come to exercise influence on the lives of companies and individuals in the private sector has led to a corresponding development in the ways in which the courts will review and possibly overrule their decisions.

This is an extremely important constitutional development in which both the judiciary and the lawyers have played a prominent role. It has recently become somewhat controversial, as the courts are alleged by the executive to be trespassing into politics.

This field is very complex and only a summary is presented, which is dealt with under the following headings:

(1) The orders: what the court may do.
(2) Who may apply, and against whom orders will be made.
(3) What has to be proved.
(4) The procedure involved.

B. THE AVAILABLE ORDERS

Judicial review is concerned with reviewing the decision-making process itself rather than the merits of the decision. The basis of the jurisdiction is that the High Court[1] can make bodies that are subject to judicial review do their legal duty or stop them from doing things that they have no power to do.

In reviewing a particular decision of a public body, or the failure to perform

1. Note that the county courts do not have jurisdiction in this area.

a public function, the court's principal purpose is to ensure that the applicant is given fair treatment by the authority to which he has been subjected.

> *The court cannot substitute its own decision for that of the body itself. It will either quash (annul) a decision that has been made or restrain (prevent) the body from acting as it had intended to act. It will ultimately be for that body to go through the process again, albeit possibly on the basis of directions from the court as to how it should go about reaching its new decision.*

The court in a judicial review case may make one or more of three main orders, namely *certiorari*, *prohibition* and *mandamus*.

- *Certiorari* is used to quash decisions that have been made in the past.
- *Prohibition* is used to restrain any wrongful activity from starting or continuing.
- *Mandamus* is a pre-emptive order requiring the body to perform a public duty.

The orders are discretionary and will not be made, for example, where there is undue delay or where the applicant's own conduct is unmeritorious or where he has acquiesced in the decision or where other available procedures have not been exhausted.

Declarations, damages and injunctions

The court has power when making one of these orders to grant injunctions and declarations, for example as to the matters that should properly be taken into account by the body when re-examining its decision.

In addition, the court has power to order damages ancillary to one of the main orders.

C. THE PARTIES TO THE PROCEEDINGS

The parties are called the "applicant" and the "respondent". Certain rules must be satisfied before someone has the necessary status to be an applicant or to be a body whose decisions are subject to judicial review.

The applicant

The applicant must have a "*sufficient interest*" in the matter to which the application relates. It is necessary to show that the applicant is affected by the decision complained of. These requirements are known as the "*rules of standing*" and provide the gateway giving access for private individuals to challenge the decisions of public bodies. The applicant, who is almost always a *private* person, must show why he has the status to challenge the decision, which must always be that of a public body. In practice, the procedure (at least at the stage of the application for leave—see section E, below) often seems to involve the court working backwards from its view on the merits: if it decides that the merits of the application are good, then the applicant's standing may not be impeached. A stricter view may be taken at the main hearing, however.

The respondent

There are two main types of body whose decisions may be subject to judicial review:

— statutory bodies; and
— some non-statutory bodies established to perform public duties.

The process applies to all bodies performing statutory duties or public functions of a quasi-judicial or an administrative nature. Many applications for judicial review are against statutory bodies but there is an increasingly large number of situations where bodies which do not derive their powers from statute have been made subject to judicial review. The test seems to be that such a body will be subject to judicial review if:

(i) there is an important *public* or *governmental* element involved—as, for example, where the body performs regulatory functions; and
(ii) the source of its power derives *otherwise than from the consent* (e.g. by contract) of those over whom it exercises its power.

Examples of bodies which the courts have recognised to be susceptible to judicial review include: Ministers of State, Departments of State, Local Authorities, Licensing Justices, Immigration Officers, the Gaming Board, the Milk Marketing Board, Prison Boards of Visitors, LAUTRO, IMRO, the SIB, the Civil Servants Service Appeal Board, the Takeover and Mergers Panel, the Independent Television Commission and the Inns of Court. It will always in any case be necessary to examine the function or consequence of the decision as well as the source of the powers of the body concerned.

D. THE RULES OF JUDICIAL REVIEW

There are three principal grounds upon which administrative actions are subject to control by judicial review:

— *Illegality.*
— *Irrationality.*
— *Procedural impropriety.*

Illegality

This involves an excessive use of public power—that is, that the decision went beyond what the body was lawfully empowered to do. This is the so-called *ultra vires* doctrine.

Irrationality

There are two main bases to this rule: *irrelevance* and *unreasonableness.*

— Although it may not be possible to identify anything specifically "*ultra vires*" in a decision, it may yet be possible to challenge the reasoning that lies behind it. This is the so-called "Wednesbury unreasonableness" principle,[2] and is as follows:

> "The court is entitled to investigate the action of [the public body] with a view to seeing whether it has taken into account matters which it ought not to take into account, or conversely, has refused to take into account matters which it ought to take into account."

— Once that answer is resolved in favour of the body (that is, that it did not offend the "relevance" rule), it may still be possible to show that whilst the body may have kept to the issues it ought to have considered, it nevertheless came to a conclusion that no body properly considering the problem and acting reasonably could have reached.

Procedural impropriety

Traditionally known as "the rules of natural justice", the two rules of *audi alteram partem* (the right to be heard) and *nemo judex in causa sua* (the rule against bias) now come under the more fashionable heading of "procedural impropriety" which import duties of impartiality and fairness. This area has developed considerably and now includes matters such as the circumstances when there is a duty to give reasons for a decision.

The right to be heard

The essential parts of this rule are:

— the right to be given advance knowledge of the opposing case; and
— the right to answer charges.

2. So-named after the local authority involved in an historic post-war court judgment.

The rule against bias

There are three principal examples:

- Where a case is pre-judged before evidence or argument is heard.
- Where the decision-maker is biased against the applicant.
- Where the decision-maker has private dealings with an interested person.

In addition, it may be possible under this heading to show that a person was encouraged by an authority's conduct to act in a certain way, which would make it unfair for that body to hold against him if he does so act. This is the so-called rule of *legitimate expectation.*

Grounds for refusal of relief

There are circumstances where, even when the applicant can make out a case for judicial review, he will be refused relief. These are generally where the applicant has delayed in bringing his claim.

The rules on delay are severe and applied strictly. An application must be made in every case within three months from the date when the grounds for the application first arose unless the court considers that there is good reason for extending the period within which the application shall be made.

> *The fact that the application has been made within the three-month period does not mean that it has been made promptly and will be allowed. The three-month period is an outer limit and the applicant still has to show that he has brought his case as quickly as was reasonably possible.*

E. PROCEDURE

Proceedings for judicial review are organised by the Crown Office, a part of the High Court. The procedure is in two stages. First, an application is made for leave to apply, which is made either "on paper" (when the judge considers the case alone on the basis of what the claimant says in his written application) or at an oral hearing. If unsuccessful, the application for leave may be renewed either by oral hearing before the judge if the refusal was at the paper stage, or before the Court of Appeal by way of re-hearing following an oral hearing in the court below.[3] If leave is granted, the main application for judicial review goes before a judge for a full *inter partes* hearing on affidavit evidence. There is a right to renew the application (if unsuccessful) to the Court of Appeal and

3. It is possible to apply to the Court of Appeal direct following a paper refusal.

there can be a final appeal to the House of Lords (except against the refusal of initial leave).

— A renewal of a hearing differs from an appeal in that it involves a complete re-hearing, and the court is not concerned with the original judgment.

The application for leave

Application for leave to seek judicial review is made by filing at the Crown Office a request for judicial review supported by an affidavit verifying the facts relied on.

The determination of the application for leave is usually fairly brief. The court must be satisfied that the applicant has an arguable case, a sufficient interest to bring it and has not been guilty of undue delay. What is essentially involved is a "quick perusal" of the available material to see if it discloses a serious case and is not frivolous.

The respondent will not usually attend on the leave stage, but in a complex case the court may invite the respondent to make representations.

Steps following the grant of leave

Within 14 days of leave being granted the applicant must enter for hearing a Notice of Motion with the Crown Office.

The applicant must also serve on the respondent and all those directly affected a copy of the motion and the affidavit in support of the application. The respondent and other parties directly affected may serve evidence in reply.

— A respondent may in exceptional circumstances apply to the court to set aside the order granting leave. This is very rarely done.

Interlocutory procedure

Judicial review procedure is not strictly speaking adversarial (although in practice it may be) and therefore the usual interlocutory procedures, whilst to some extent technically provided for, are in practice difficult to utilise. This may be one of the principal difficulties standing in the applicant's way.

— Under the rules there are express provisions for discovery and inspection of documents, and cross-examination of witnesses, but these are difficult to exercise in practice and the courts tend to lean against them.

The hearing

At the hearing, argument is made by the lawyers for both sides on the basis of the evidence submitted by affidavit and whatever documents are or may have become available. There is a limited and rarely invoked power for the oral cross-examination of witnesses. Parties who have not been served but who have a proper interest in the case will probably be heard, but will not usually be awarded costs.

Costs will usually "follow the event".[4]

Appeals

Appeal lies from the High Court to the Court of Appeal but only with leave either of the High Court or the Court of Appeal. The time limit is 28 days from the date of the judgment. A further appeal lies to the House of Lords on a point of law of general public importance provided that either the Court of Appeal or the House of Lords gives leave. No appeal to the House of Lords is possible against a decision to refuse leave to apply at the outset.

4. See Chapter 24.

JUDICIAL REVIEW

PROCEDURAL GUIDE

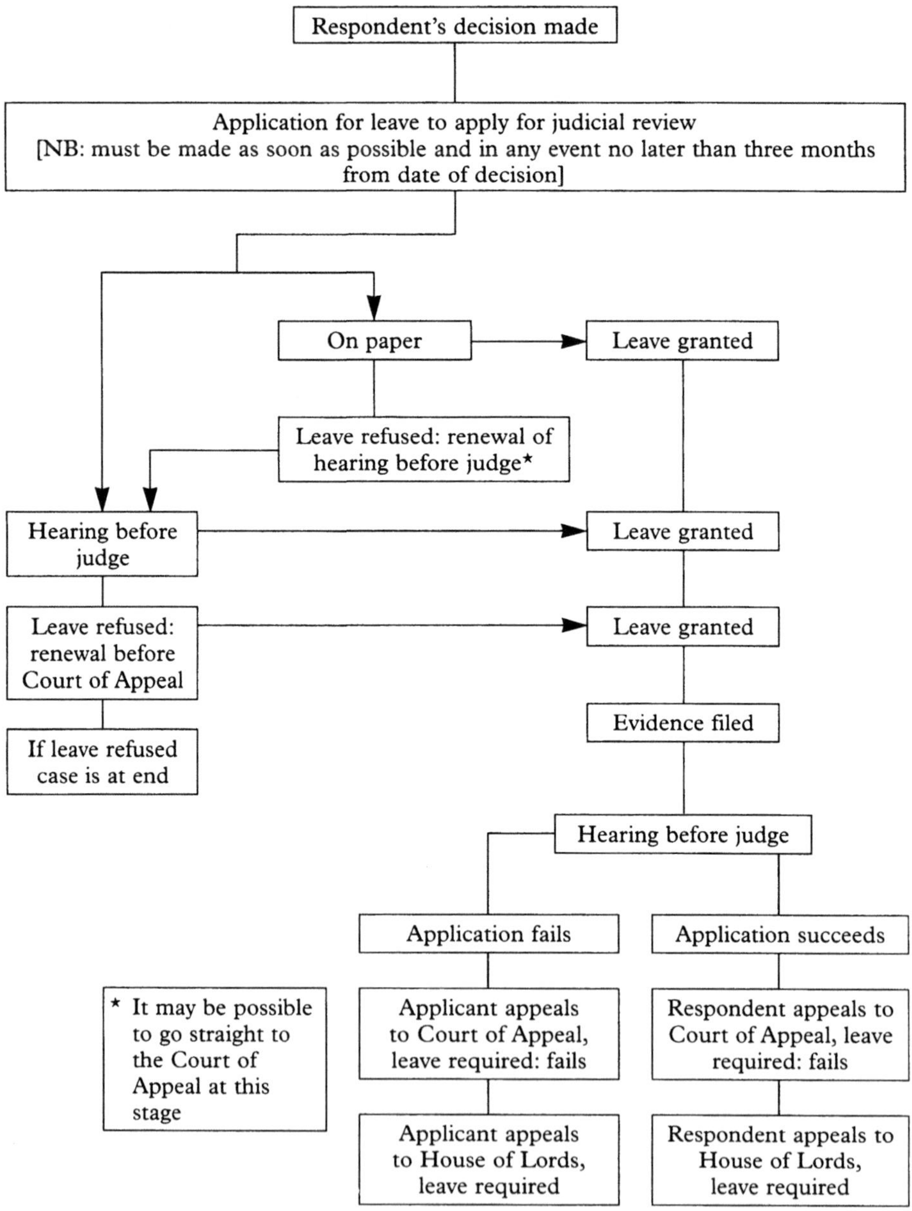

CHAPTER 36

LITIGATION INVOLVING BANKS

This chapter considers a variety of problems that can arise when banks become involved in litigation.

A. INTRODUCTION

It is outside the scope of this Guide to attempt to give an account of general banking law and practice. However, although it is generally true that there are no special litigation rules or procedures for the determination of banking disputes, because of the importance of banks and banking facilities in commercial and everyday life banks are frequently involved in litigation and they are sometimes subject to special rules of practice or procedure. This chapter describes some of the situations that may arise in cases concerning banks and the rules to which they will in those cases be subject.

B. INJUNCTIONS

A general account of the procedures for obtaining an injunction is contained in Chapter 10. Banks are most typically concerned with the following types of injunction:

— Injunctions to restrain the performance of banking obligations.
— *Mareva* injunctions[1].
— Injunctions in aid of tracing claims.

Injunctions to restrain the performance of banking obligations

Very stringent rules are imposed by the courts in respect of claims to restrain a bank from performing obligations owed to third parties. Such claims most typically arise in connection with applications by plaintiffs in respect of letters of credit, performance bonds and bank guarantees.

1. See Chapter 11.

The courts regard a bank's obligation to honour its undertakings as central to the stability of financial life and will not except in very exceptional cases entertain an application by a customer to restrain his bank from performing an obligation to a third party undertaken at his request.

The approach of the courts is:

- To treat the banking obligation (for example, the obligation created by a letter of credit) as separate from the commercial transaction to which it relates. The courts look only to the issue of validity of the banking obligation and not to the substance of the underlying transactions between the parties (for example, the issue of delivery of goods or the provision of services).
- To consider whether there is a substantial argument that the performance bond or other instrument is invalid. If it is not, then in general no injunction will be granted, even though restraints may subsequently be put on the recipient of the proceeds themselves.
- Only to grant such an injunction where it is proved (and not just by the uncorroborated evidence of the customer) that the bank knows that the third party beneficiary has demanded payment fraudulently.

Even in those rare cases where such proof can be given, the customer must still satisfy the other requirements for the granting of an injunction, as outlined in Chapter 10. In particular, it must be shown that there is a serious issue to be tried on the question of fraud and that the *balance of convenience* lies in favour of the customer. In practice, this will only very rarely be possible. This is because the damage to the bank's reputation if it dishonours a contractual obligation to a third party will be extremely difficult to quantify and probably could not anyway be remedied by an award of damages; whereas if no injunction is granted and the bank makes payment under the instrument and at trial it can be shown to have known that the beneficiary's claim was fraudulent, the bank would be liable to make restitution to the customer, who would not therefore have sustained irreparable loss.

Mareva injunctions

It is extremely rare for a *Mareva* injunction to be made *against* a bank, for reasons of public policy and the consequential need to ensure public confidence in the banking system, and to prevent the risk of a run on a bank. For those reasons, any application for a *Mareva* injunction against a bank is likely to be heard in chambers.

Although a *Mareva* injunction is made against a defendant (who is almost never a bank), invariably such an order will involve at least one bank because it will affect a defendant's bank accounts, here or abroad. For that reason, there has arisen a complex series of rules developed by the courts to cover the position of banks when their customers are subject to a *Mareva* injunction.

The basic rules in relation to *Mareva* injunctions are set out in Chapter 11. In this section, attention is drawn to some of the most typical problems that affect banks in such cases.

—*Worldwide* Marevas

Special problems of enforceability often arise in respect of worldwide *Marevas*, which often involve assets held in banks which have offices both in and outside the jurisdiction of the court issuing the injunction. This is particularly so where the bank is based overseas and is subject to the jurisdiction of the English courts only because it has a branch office in England and where the injunction falls to be complied with abroad.

In cases where the bank has no presence in England the court will stipulate that the order shall not affect any persons outside the jurisdiction of the English courts until it shall be declared enforceable or be enforced by a foreign court (and then it shall affect them only to the extent of such declaration or enforcement) unless they are:

"(a) the person to whom this order is addressed or an officer of or an agent appointed by a power of attorney of such a person or (b) persons who are subject to the jurisdiction of this court and (i) have been given written notice of this order at their residence or place of business within the jurisdiction, and (ii) are able to prevent acts or omissions outside the jurisdiction of this court which assist in the breach of the terms of this order."

However, this so-called "*Babanaft* proviso"[2] would not exempt a foreign bank with branches in England and overseas because it would be likely to be subject to limb (b). In such cases, it might be unjust for the bank to be subject to the order as, for example, it is possible that the courts of its place of incorporation or where compliance with the terms of the order will take place may later find the bank to have been in breach of its obligations to the defendant, its customer. To accommodate this problem, a practice has begun for the English courts to apply the following further protection, namely:

"Nothing in this order shall, in respect of assets located outside England and Wales (and in particular [specify if necessary the foreign country concerned]), prevent [the bank] or its subsidiaries from complying with:

(i) what it reasonably believes to be its obligations, contractual or otherwise, under the laws and obligations of the country or state in which those assets are situated or are under the proper law of the account in question;
(ii) any orders of the courts of that country or state."

—*Problems of compliance*

(a) Identifying the defendant's bank account

Ideally, the plaintiff should identify the specific accounts to which he wishes the *Mareva* injunction to apply. If, as is often the case, it is not possible to do so, a bank which is served with a *Mareva* injunction that applies to all the

2. So-named after the case in which the principle was first laid down.

defendant's accounts held with it may at the plaintiff's cost, and should, as a matter of good practice, conduct a full search throughout its system. It would be sensible first to verify with the plaintiff or his solicitor whether that is what they wish.

Alternatively, the bank may obtain an order against the defendant requiring him to disclose details of all his accounts for the purposes of compliance. In practice, there is little real opportunity for a bank to do this and accordingly it will almost always need to conduct a thorough search to comply fully with the terms of the order.

If the plaintiff specifically requests the bank to carry out a search of some or all of its branches, he must agree in advance to meet the bank's costs of doing so. (A bank will usually be entitled to its costs of complying with a *Mareva* in any event.)

(b) Joint and nominee accounts

Mareva injunctions can be specified to apply to a joint account or an account in the name of someone other than the defendant. In such cases, the order must specify that it so applies and must be served on the other account holder. Because of the possibility of injustice, such orders will only rarely be made, and then only where it appears to the court that there is good reason for supposing the assets in the account belong solely to the defendant and not the nominee or other joint account holder.

(c) Financial limits to Mareva *injunctions*

Once a *Mareva* injunction is served upon a bank it has an obligation to freeze the assets held in the defendant's accounts. Because the defendant's accounts may have a credit balance in excess of the protection to which the plaintiff may reasonably be entitled, *Mareva* injunctions almost invariably impose a financial limit up to which the order shall apply. Sums in excess of that limit are beyond the scope of the order.

(d) Currency problems

If the order is made in terms of a currency different from that in which the funds in a given account are held, the bank should consider conversion of the funds standing to the credit of the account at the prevailing buying rate, sufficient to comply with the financial limits contained in the order. It is prudent in such a case for the bank to seek the court's prior approval before doing so.

(e) Non-cash assets

Difficult considerations may arise in the case of assets other than cash such as letters of credit, performance bonds or bank guarantees.

The benefit of such instruments would generally be subject to a *Mareva* injunction but a court (in recognition of the need to maintain public confidence in the banking system) would not prevent a bank from honouring its undertaking to comply with such obligations. The defendant would remain liable by the terms of the order in respect of any credit he himself received thereunder, or of the proceeds of them.

(f) Documents of title

The policy of the courts is that such orders do not apply in respect of documents of title such as share certificates and title deeds held as custodian, unless the order specifically refers to them, which it rarely will. This avoids the bank being required to form its own view of the value of such assets.

(g) Past transactions on the defendant's account

The general obligation of a bank to freeze the defendant's account up to any limit specifically named in the order also prevents it from honouring cheques drawn on the account by the defendant customer before the order was made (unless the order specifically permits this).

This restraint does not apply where the defendant has before the date of the order used a cheque guarantee card or credit card, in which case the bank has an obligation to the payee to remit the funds to him. Such transactions after the date of the order are subject to freezing in the usual way. Because of this, banks will generally cancel cheque guarantee and credit cards as soon as they have notice of this order.

(h) Disposals in the ordinary and proper course of business

Orders which permit disposals of assets by the defendant in the ordinary and proper course of business can give rise to particular problems for banks. How can the bank determine whether cheques drawn on the defendant's account relate to the ordinary course of his business? The best practice is for the bank to monitor activities on the account and, if in doubt as to the size or frequency of withdrawals, to seek guidance from the court.

(i) Costs of compliance

The problems which banks sometimes encounter in complying with the order can give rise to significant expense if they take legal advice or make applications to the court. Provided, however, that such expenses are reasonably incurred, they will be recoverable by the bank from the plaintiff under the undertaking to pay third party costs given by the plaintiff as a condition of being granted the order.

(j) Rights of set-off

Mareva injunctions should typically contain a provision preserving a right of set-off that a bank may have in respect of any facility which it gave to the defendant before it was notified of the injunction. If the order omits such a provision it would be unsafe for a bank to exercise a right of set-off without first applying to court for relief.

Injunctions in aid of tracing claims

A tracing claim provides a mechanism which enables a plaintiff to trace assets which he claims are his own into the hands of someone else who has no right to them, or into the hands of a third person (such as a bank) who is holding them for the wrongdoer. Such claims often involve assets held in overseas accounts. The English courts have a wide and often exercised discretionary power to grant injunctions in such cases.

C. THE COMPULSORY DISCLOSURE OF INFORMATION

In a number of important respects litigation may involve procedures whereby a bank's duty of confidentiality to its customers may give way to an overriding duty to the court or to some third person to disclose confidential information. These duties have increased over the years and some of the most important are explained in this section.

Disclosure in *Norwich Pharmacal* cases

The English courts have a limited and discretionary power to order a bank to disclose information that may be confidential to its customer in accordance with the rule of discovery (outlined in Chapter 18, section K) known as the "*Norwich Pharmacal*" rule and which is applicable to cases where a stranger to a dispute has, without fault, facilitated or become mixed up in the wrong-doing of some other person. In practice, these so-called *Norwich Pharmacal* orders can be very far-reaching and may extend to correspondence and internal memoranda relating to a bank and to cheques drawn on it. Because of this and of the problems of confidentiality, *Norwich Pharmacal* orders are only rarely made and usually only in cases of urgency.

Disclosure in aid of tracing claims[3] ("*Bankers Trust*" cases)

Just as the courts have a discretionary power to grant an injunction in aid of a tracing claim to freeze the assets held in a bank account, so also may they

3. See section B, above.

order a bank to disclose not only details and statements of the account but also the identity of the account holders, so as to assist the plaintiff in discovering where his money is. This is similar to the *Norwich Pharmacal* principle. The power is cautiously exercised and the court will only make such an order where the plaintiff demonstrates a real prospect that the information sought may lead to the location or preservation of assets to which he is making a claim.

Further, it is normally necessary for the plaintiff to describe with precision the documents and information sought.

The court will assess the balance of convenience between the parties. The plaintiff clearly has an interest in obtaining the information and documents sought but equally the bank has obligations of confidence to its customers. In view of this, the court will usually only make such orders in exceptional circumstances. In addition to satisfying the court on these issues, the plaintiff must show that there is a good case that the property he is tracing is his. He must also give an undertaking to the bank to pay damages for any loss that it might thereafter prove it has sustained.

In cases involving foreign banks or foreign branches of English banks provisions similar to the *Babanaft* proviso are adopted to offer suitable protection against the possibility of liability for breach of confidentiality in overseas jurisdictions.

The bank has a right to be paid on the indemnity basis[4] its costs and expenses of complying with a *Bankers Trust* order. The documents and information obtained may only be used for the purposes of the tracing claim, and for no other.

A *Bankers Trust* order should only be sought in urgent cases. Where there is no urgency, the proper procedure is to seek an order under the Bankers' Books Evidence Act 1879 (see below).

Such an order is often sought at the same time as a *Mareva* injunction. The main defendant should be the wrongdoer, but banks against which orders are sought should be joined into the action as defendants. Compliance is by an affidavit deposing what property of the plaintiff the bank has or had and where it went to.

Bankers' Books Evidence Act 1879

A bank's documents may be compelled to be brought before the courts in civil proceedings by the general power of subpoena, but there also exist special powers under the Bankers' Books Evidence Act 1879 and related legislation to bring bankers' books to court and to prove certain matters in relation to bank accounts, the object of which is, in a general sense, to make it easier for litigants to prove facts without the need unduly to involve representatives of banks in the process.

4. See Chapter 24.

The legislation covers two separate situations. First, it enables statements in bankers' books to be proved without direct oral evidence from bank staff; and, secondly, it enables bankers' books to be produced for inspection. The statutory definition of "bankers' books" includes all account books, ledgers and documents containing records of transactions whether manual or printed or in microfilm or electronic or computerised form, but is in practice construed restrictively by the courts so as to exclude, for example, cheques and paying-in slips received by the bank.

— *Proof of statements in bankers' books*
  Subject to certain conditions, a statement in bankers' books is *prima facie* evidence of the truth of the statement and of the fact that the statement has been made. This rule avoids the need for officers of a bank being called to prove the fact that a statement has been recorded, and the truth of that statement.

— *Compulsory inspection of documents*
  The courts have power to order that any party to legal proceedings may on application to court inspect the books of a banker and take copies of any entry. The power is discretionary and is exercised only if the applicant can make out a proper case. It is normally confined to the accounts of a party to the litigation, and will only be extended to cover accounts of non-parties if it can be shown that the account is in reality that of one of the parties to the litigation.

  Such orders will almost never be made in respect of accounts involving overseas transactions held outside the jurisdiction with foreign banks. Equally, the English courts will normally oppose the enforcement in their jurisdiction of orders of foreign courts giving access to the contents of bankers' books.

Disclosure in foreign proceedings

In Chapter 6 an outline was given of how the English courts will respond to a request by a foreign court for assistance in collecting evidence for proceedings pending before it. In cases concerning a request for evidence in respect of banking information that is confidential to customers, the English courts will exercise a balance between the need to assist the foreign court and the need to maintain banking confidences.

Insolvency Act 1986 disclosure

The court has power under section 236 of the Insolvency Act 1986 to require parties who are in a position to assist the office holder of a company that is in administrative receivership, liquidation or administration,[5] to appear before the court to answer such questions concerning the affairs of the company before his appointment as may reasonably be put and to which the office holder reasonably needs answers to enable him to carry out his functions. A bank suspected of having information concerning the company may under this procedure be required to produce documents to the office holder by answering oral questions or by making an affidavit. In such cases, the bank has very few rights to oppose the production of documents or information, the claim to customer confidentiality or, indeed, the possibility of prejudice to the bank, having generally little or no weight.

Disclosure to the Commissioners of Inland Revenue

It is outside the scope of this Guide to comment upon specialist fields such as Inland Revenue practice. It should nevertheless be noted that in the case of the Commissioners of Inland Revenue the courts assess the claim to access to documents held by banks in respect of the affairs of taxpayers who may be or have been customers generally by reference to tests less strict than those applicable in the case of claims to discovery between parties to civil proceedings, especially insofar as concerns the specificity of the description of the document sought. Again, claims to customer confidentiality carry little or no weight.

Disclosure in compliance with criminal law obligations

Note also that there exist serious burdens of compliance with criminal law statutes, most notably the Drug Trafficking Act 1994 and the Police and Criminal Evidence Act 1984. It is beyond the scope of this Guide to comment upon them in detail.

D. GARNISHEE ORDERS[6]

One of the most frequently employed methods of enforcing orders made against parties to litigation is the attachment of debts by a garnishee order. This type of order applies most often to bank accounts as, where a customer's account is in credit, the bank is indebted to the customer to the extent of credit balances which are, as a matter of law, debts due from the banks to their customers.

A garnishee order is made in two stages. First, the judgment creditor applies

5. See Chapter 33. Note also that similar procedures are available in cases of personal bankruptcy. Section 235 of the Insolvency Act contains further provisions enabling an office holder to obtain information from a range of parties who include former advisers to the company, and could apply to banks.

6. See also Chapter 29 on the enforcement of court orders and arbitral awards generally.

to court for an order *nisi* that is served on the *garnishee* which is a third party (such as a bank) who owes a debt to the judgment debtor. The order *nisi* has immediate effect but the garnishee may apply to the court to vary or discharge the order by showing good cause. If he does not do so or, if he does, but fails, the second stage is reached and the order becomes *absolute*. The effect of a garnishee order is to require the garnishee to pay to the judgment creditor or into court funds that the garnishee owes to the judgment debtor, so that the judgment debtor cannot defeat the judgment creditor's remedy.

In the case of banks, the following points should be noted:

— A bank served with a garnishee order *nisi* must freeze the account attached and notify its customer. If the order is made *absolute*, the monies that are so attached must be paid to the judgment creditor or into court.
— The garnishee order must be limited to the amount of the judgment debt and cannot be for a greater sum. This leaves any surplus in the account free from the order.
— The order must specify the account to be attached and should be served on the head office of the bank and, from prudence, on the branch where the account is maintained.
— A garnishee order only requires the garnishee to pay the judgment creditor the amounts it owes to the judgment debtor. It does not of itself create a relationship of debtor/creditor between the garnishee and the judgment creditor. The rights secured by a garnishee order generally rank behind prior charge over the judgment debtor's property held in the account.
— Monies paid into an account attached by a garnishee order after it is served are not subject to the attachment; but once a bank is served with a garnishee order it is good practice to close the account attached and open a new account and notify its customer. Monies received later by the bank for its customer's account should be credited to the new account, to which subsequent drawings should be debited. This new account will be outside the scope of the garnishee order.
— In the case of deposit accounts special problems used to arise because the bank's obligation to pay its customer is frequently conditional on the performance of a routine step such as the making of a demand or the production of account books. Those difficulties now no longer stand in the way of an attachment of monies standing to the credit of deposit accounts and may by statute be disregarded in the majority of cases.
— The English courts probably have a discretionary jurisdiction to attach monies standing to the credit of overseas accounts of banks which are subject to the jurisdiction of the English courts. It is likely however that the discretion would be exercised sparingly and would be influenced by the possible exposure to its customer that the bank may face in the

country where the funds are held if the fact of the order of the English court will not be a defence to an action by the customer in that country for breach of some obligation owed to it there by the bank.

— Although a judgment may be given by an English court in a foreign currency, a garnishee order may only be made in sterling. Foreign currency debts must therefore be converted into sterling at the date the garnishee order is made.
— Where the account is denominated in a foreign currency, the bank should immediately after service of the order *nisi* attach the foreign currency equivalent of the sterling amount of the garnishee order, convert it into sterling as soon as reasonably practicable, and inform the court of the amount of foreign currency attached and of the rate of exchange used on conversion.
— Special difficulties arise in respect of accounts held in the name of trustees and nominees. A garnishee order may be made in respect of such accounts, but only sparingly.
— Equally, a garnishee order may be made in respect of a joint account, but only where the underlying debt is owed by the joint account holders. Note however that a judgment against a partnership may be enforced by a garnishee order against the private accounts of the partners individually.
— A bank may wish to assert that monies it owes to the judgment debtor and which are held to the credit of his account with the bank should be reduced, for the purposes of compliance, by sums which the judgment debtor owes to the bank. In such cases, the following rules may apply:
  (i) No reduction may be allowed where the bank's entitlement does not exist at the time when the garnishee order is served upon it.
  (ii) Where the judgment debtor owes money to the bank at the time of service, then the order *nisi* will not be made *absolute* if the two debts are capable of being *set-off* in law. Contrast this with a claim by the bank against the judgment debtor that can only be characterised as a *counterclaim*, when no such relief will be given and the order will be made *absolute*.[7]
— In the case of a debtor company against which an order for compulsory winding up is made, an order *nisi* will not be made *absolute*. Similar provisions apply in bankruptcy.

7. See Chapter 9, section B for a further account of the difference between set-offs and counterclaims.

CHAPTER 37

INSURANCE LITIGATION

This chapter deals with disputes arising where there is in existence a contract of insurance.

A. INTRODUCTION

There are no special rules applicable to the way in which litigation in insurance matters is conducted. The principles which apply are the same as those which apply to the resolution of disputes generally. There are, however, a number of features of the law of insurance which are unique to it. This means that the types of issues which arise in an insurance dispute may not commonly be met elsewhere; and so the tactics which are adopted in insurance litigation may differ from those which apply in other commercial disputes. In particular, insurance litigation is often multi-party; that is, there may be a large number of plaintiffs and a large number of defendants in any given case. This is because, in the commercial sphere, insurance policies are often entered into for the benefit of a number of insureds and the amounts of the insurance are often very large. It is common, therefore, for a contract of insurance to have, as parties to it, a large number of insureds and a large number of insurers.[1]

Insurance law is highly sophisticated in nature. Contracts of insurance are construed by reference to rules which have been developed by the courts in the insurance sphere, and the rights and obligations of the parties to a contract of insurance are to be analysed accordingly. For example, the obligations of parties entering into a contract of insurance may be more onerous than those affecting parties entering into a commercial contract. And an insurer who makes payment to an insured in respect of a loss is entitled to seek compensation for the loss from third parties who may have been liable to the insured in relation to such loss.[2]

Such special features give rise to issues in insurance litigation which may not be present in litigation in the general commercial context.

1. See Chapter 30 for a further account of representative and group actions.
2. This is the right of subrogation, which is dealt with below.

B. PARTIES TO AN INSURANCE DISPUTE

Disputes arising out of insurance policies typically occur when the event or events insured against have taken place and the liability of the insurer to pay out the amount of the insurance has apparently arisen. Most commonly, therefore, the plaintiff in an insurance dispute will be the party which, in common language, took out the insurance; that is, the insured. The defendant will typically be the person or company which has agreed to pay out the insured sum on the happening of the event insured against; that is, the insurer.

Often there will be in existence contracts of reinsurance. These are contracts whereby the insurer has insured with reinsurers its own potential liability to make payment under the original contract of insurance. In such cases, the insurer becomes the insured, insofar as concerns its contract of reinsurance.

The above demonstrates why insurance litigation may raise procedural complications which are not features of more straightforward commercial disputes. We deal subsequently with the procedural ways in which these complications can be accommodated and the ways in which the court can assist their resolution.

Subrogation

After payment of a loss under an insurance policy, the insurer has conferred on it two rights. It receives the benefit of the rights and remedies which the insured had against third parties which, if satisfied, would extinguish or reduce the loss. It also has the right to claim from the insured any benefit it receives from third parties to compensate the insured for the loss in respect of which the insurer has given indemnity. Both these rights arise as a result of the doctrine of subrogation.

The first right may involve the insurer in suing the third party in the name of the insured and the insured must, in accordance with the insurance contract, assist the insurer to do so. The second right may involve the insurer in suing the insured to recover the benefit received.

The effect of the doctrine of subrogation is that the insured cannot recover more than it has lost. Enforcement of the first right gives the insurer the power to recoup from third parties some or all of that loss. Enforcement of the second right ensures that the insured can only recover its loss and no more.

C. THE STRUCTURE OF AN INSURANCE DISPUTE

The claim

Most often, the insured will make the claim. Commonly, it will be for the recovery of the insured sum, based on the premise that the risk insured against has occurred and the insured has suffered loss. Sometimes it will be for a declaration as to the rights of the insured under the relevant insurance policy. On some occasions, the claim will be brought by the insurer. Generally, the insurer will be seeking a ruling from the court that it has no liability to the insured under the insurance policy. The grounds on which such a claim may be made will reflect the grounds on which the insurer would have relied in order to defend the claim of the insured, if the insured had commenced the proceedings.

Defences

Lack of insurable interest

A person wishing to take out insurance must have an insurable interest in the subject matter of the insurance. Sometimes the insurable interest is an essential ingredient in the nature of the particular contract of insurance. Sometimes statute provides that it is a condition of the validity of the insurance policy. If the insured does not have the insurable interest required, the policy is unenforceable by the insured. This means that the insurer will be able to pay out on the insurance if it wishes but, if it does not, the insured will be unable to compel it to do so. If the insurable interest is required by statute, then its absence will make the contract of insurance illegal and it will be void. In this case, if there is litigation, the court will refuse to enforce the contract, even if the insurer does not oppose its enforcement.

It is not possible to give a comprehensive definition of what will or will not be an insurable interest. This will require an analysis of the contract in question and, if appropriate, the relevant statutes.

Illegality

If a contract of any kind is illegal in its inception or in its performance the court will not allow it to be enforced. Insurance business is regulated by statute which requires an insurer to have complied with the requirements of statute in order to be authorised to enter into contracts of insurance. Where an insurer is unauthorised an insured can, nevertheless, enforce the policy or can treat it as invalid. The insurer, however, cannot rely on its lack of authorisation as a ground for avoiding liability under the policy.

Void or voidable

Sometimes the contract of insurance may be void or voidable. This can happen because there has been a mistake; that is, the parties have misunderstood the nature of their contract with each other.[3] Sometimes there may have been a

3. The law of mistake in insurance is similar to the law of mistake in contract. It is technical and beyond the scope of this Guide.

misrepresentation: that is, the insurer or insured may have said something which is untrue, whether deliberately or accidentally. In this case the party which has been misled can elect not to be bound by the contract.

Non-disclosure

Sometimes there will be non-disclosure. Unlike commercial contracts, a party to a contract of insurance must disclose to the other party all material facts: that is, all facts that a prudent insurer would wish to know when assessing whether to assume the risk or what premium to charge. Parties to an insurance contract have a legal duty of utmost good faith in their dealings with each other.[4]

Non-compliance

Sometimes there will be non-compliance with or breach of a term of the contract. In such cases, the innocent party may refuse to be bound by the contract.

Each of the above defences is based, essentially, on the fault of one of the parties. Sometimes claims may be brought or defended on grounds which do not require fault. Often, they will arise as a result of uncertainty over the true meaning of the contract of insurance. In such cases, the court will be asked to decide what the contract of insurance means and the conduct or behaviour of the parties to it may be of no relevance. Sometimes the court may be asked to rectify the contract; that is, to conclude that the contract, as written, does not properly reflect the intention of the parties to it and to rewrite the contract so that it does reflect that intention. Sometimes, the defence will combine questions as to the behaviour of the parties and as to the true meaning of the insurance policy in the light of that behaviour.

D. HOW THE COURT DEALS WITH INSURANCE DISPUTES

The Commercial Court

Where commercial actions are begun in the Queen's Bench Division of the High Court, they may be entered on a list of cases for trial in the Commercial Court.[5] The definition of commercial action includes a case which relates to insurance.[6]

The judges who sit in the Commercial Court are described as commercial judges. They will be highly experienced, both as barristers and, subsequently,

4. A contract of insurance is a contract "*uberrimae fidei*".
5. See Chapter 27 for a description of the Commercial Court and its business.
6. "Commercial action" is defined in the Rules of the Supreme Court to include any cause arising out of the ordinary transactions of merchants and traders and, without prejudice to the generality of those words, any cause relating to the construction of a mercantile document, the export or import of merchandise, affreightment, insurance, banking, mercantile agency and mercantile usage.

as judges, in dealing with commercial disputes. The Commercial Court has its own practice guide, which is designed to ensure that disputes before it are disposed of expeditiously and efficiently.

Judges in the Commercial Court are anxious to streamline the cases which come before them. Ways in which this can be achieved are by cases being consolidated or tried together. Consolidation occurs where there are separate cases which the judge orders should be combined into one case. Trial together occurs where there are several cases which are tried at the same time as each other or sequentially, but at the same court hearing.

Lead cases

Sometimes, one or more insureds may have several claims for loss which they make against one or more insurers in the same action. The grounds of defence may differ from claim to claim. Some claims may be susceptible to all of the grounds of defence, whereas others may be susceptible to one only or to some, but not all, of them. It may be possible to select one claim in which all the issues arise, so that the disposal of that claim will, in effect, dispose of all the others. In such cases, the court will be astute to select that claim as a lead case and order that it be tried alone, in the knowledge that the decision in that claim will be determinative of all the others.

E. THE LLOYD'S LITIGATION

In the late 1980s and early 1990s, a huge volume of claims arose as a result of the way in which business at Lloyd's had been transacted in the 1970s and 1980s. It is beyond the scope of this Guide to give details of the reasons why the litigation arose. The courts were faced with a magnitude of claims which, in the absence of active case management by the courts, it would have been impossible to try. The majority of the cases were pending in the Commercial Court and the judge in charge of the Commercial List embarked on active case management, making regular statements about the progress and management of the Lloyd's litigation. Among the features of that active case management were:

- The division of the litigation into six classes of case.
- The identification of and decisions on a number of preliminary issues by the court, which would resolve issues common to one or more categories of case. The Court of Appeal and the House of Lords actively expedited appeals in those matters.
- The selection by the court from cases in a particular category of lead cases for trial as to liability and general principles relating to the calculation of damages, in the hope that those decisions would give broad guidance for other cases in the same category.

— Active case management techniques, such as the use of sample Names[7] and limitations on formal discovery.
— The establishment of a liaison committee to facilitate distribution of information to parties involved in the Lloyd's litigation and their legal advisers.

Although the Lloyd's litigation has substantially been concluded, the court continues to develop the active case management techniques. This more interventionist approach is gaining popularity and is reflected in the reforms foreshadowed by the Woolf report.[8]

F. THE DEEP POCKET DEFENDANT

Insurance litigation is, typically, an arena where one party, the insured, may be impecunious, whereas the other party, the insurer, may have substantial financial backing. Because of the English rule that an unsuccessful litigant must pay the costs of a successful litigant the financial consequences for an impecunious insured which loses its case are likely to be far more severe than those for a financially sound insured which loses its case. The risk to the unsuccessful insured greatly outweighs the risk to the unsuccessful insurer. This can be a major disincentive to an insured in bringing what may be a meritorious and justifiable claim against an insurer. It is common for insurers to take advantage of their comparative financial strength and to force an insured, through the use of the tactical manoeuvres which the English litigation system allows, to settle its claim at what may be an unfairly low figure or even to abandon it altogether. The English procedure does not properly cater for this imbalance of financial strength. The inequality which it can bring about, while it may occur in all types of litigation, is especially prevalent in the insurance sphere.

This inequality may be ameliorated by the resolution of disputes through means other than the English litigation system.

G. ALTERNATIVE DISPUTE RESOLUTION

The idea of alternative dispute resolution, whereby parties to litigation have their dispute resolved through methods other than trial by judges, is also gaining in popularity. Insurance litigation may be particularly amenable to alternative dispute resolution techniques, especially where there are multiple parties to any claim. It is often very difficult for any of the parties of its own volition to generate settlement talks, whereas the intervention of a disinterested

7. Insurers at Lloyd's are known as "Names".
8. See Chapter 40.

third party can often enable such talks to take place in a constructive and non-confrontational way. Insurance disputes often involve foreign, as well as domestic, parties. Insurance and reinsurance companies typically are foreign. Although, by the very nature of their business, they are likely to be sophisticated and well versed in litigation, it is sometimes difficult to reconcile the views and perceptions of individuals and corporations who are used to different legal systems and legal rules. The intervention of one or more mediators, who may be able to engage in a species of subtle diplomacy, explaining and understanding different points of view, can often help to resolve the difficulties which these differing legal backgrounds may generate.

CHAPTER 38

CONTEMPT OF COURT

This chapter describes how the courts enforce compliance with their orders, and try to prevent the issues before them from being prejudged or prejudiced.

A. INTRODUCTION

The purpose of the law of contempt of court is to prevent or punish conduct that interferes with the administration of justice. This area of the law operates in the interests of all who take part in court proceedings, whether as parties, witnesses, judges or lawyers. However, the law of contempt also imposes restraints upon many persons, particularly on the Press, whose freedom to report on cases is restricted by the law in this area. In many cases, the courts will balance the need to safeguard the proper administration of justice with the interests of permitting freedom of speech.

Example
X and Y are defendants in a major criminal fraud trial. Shortly before the trial starts, a newspaper publishes an interview with Z, who will be one of the witnesses in the trial. Z asserts or implies that X and Y are guilty of the offence with which they are charged. The editor and publishers of the newspaper are liable to face contempt proceedings.

B. CRIMINAL AND CIVIL CONTEMPT

Contempt of court is either *civil* or *criminal.*

An example of *civil contempt* is a failure to obey an order of the court.

Example
P, the manufacturer of a well-known brand of toy, obtains an injunction against D to prevent him from selling imitation toys in the UK. D ignores the injunction and continues to sell the toys. D may be subject to proceedings for civil contempt.

Examples of *criminal contempt* include conduct which is calculated (that is, likely) to interfere with the due administration of justice or to bring the courts into disrepute. This can take various forms, including committing contempt in the face of the court (such as insulting the judge in his presence), publishing matter prejudicial to a fair trial (such as the example given in the introduction to this chapter, or, for example, publishing a story that presumes the guilt of a defendant who protests his innocence), scandalising the court (for example, a newspaper publishing an article to the effect that "X" will not get a fair trial because a particular judge is presiding), and numerous other acts interfering with the course of justice. The categories of contempt are not closed.

C. UNINTENTIONAL CONTEMPT

It used to be the case that if the requisite prejudicial conduct was committed, the offender faced contempt proceedings, regardless of whether he intended to commit contempt. Following a reform of the law by statute, contempt regardless of intent is now limited to publications which create a "substantial risk" to the course of justice and where the relevant proceedings will be seriously impeded or prejudiced. Moreover, if a publisher can prove that he took all reasonable care and he did not know that proceedings were "active" (which term is explained in section F, below), he has a defence to the charge of contempt. This defence will not be available, of course, where a person has intentionally committed contempt.

D. THE PENALTIES FOR CONTEMPT

Contempt is regarded as a serious matter by the courts, and may be punished by a substantial fine (unlimited in the higher courts), or imprisonment for a fixed term (up to two years), or both. The court may also take security for good behaviour. When the offence is committed by a company, although the company itself for obvious reasons cannot be imprisoned, depending on the circumstances its officers may be punished and the company's assets may be seized.

In considering the appropriate punishment, the court may allow a party to purge his contempt by apologising to the court. It may also suspend the operation of the order committing the offender to prison. It is also possible to appeal against an order for contempt. The appeal is made to the Court of Appeal.[1]

E. ENFORCEMENT

The jurisdiction of the court in contempt proceedings arises out of its inherent jurisdiction to enforce its own orders. Nevertheless, in civil contempt it will generally be one of the parties which applies to the court to enforce an order made in its favour. In criminal contempt, the responsibility for the instigation

1. See Chapter 25.

and control of contempt proceedings rests with the Crown (through the offices of the Attorney-General). It is possible for a civil contempt to be waived by the parties so that an order is not enforced, but this is not possible for a criminal contempt.

The power of the court to punish for contempt is exercised by an order of committal. Since committal is such a grave matter, a detailed procedure has to be carefully followed in obtaining a committal order. The order of committal is enforced by the tipstaff, an officer of the court, who is empowered to seize the offender and imprison him.

F. SOME PARTICULAR ASPECTS OF CONTEMPT OF COURT

The *sub judice* rule

It is often said, in the media or by persons who are involved with proceedings, that a particular matter is "*sub judice*". It is not always understood what this rule means, when it applies and what its effect is.

The phrase "*sub judice*" means, literally, "under consideration by the court". The law prohibits the publication of matter which will prejudice the conduct or outcome of proceedings where the proceedings are "active". In civil proceedings in the High Court, a case is not "active" until it has been set down for trial.[2] In criminal proceedings, a case is not "active" until an individual has been arrested.

Example

A newspaper plans to publish a series of articles investigating a matter of legitimate public concern, such as the fraudulent manipulation of an insurance company. After the publication of the first article, the fraudster issues a "gagging writ" in defamation proceedings designed to prevent publicity. However, the effect of issuing the writ does not of itself make the proceedings *sub judice*, and the newspaper is not in contempt by continuing to publish the articles (although may be liable in defamation).

However, care must be exercised, since the *sub judice* rule also applies to certain of the interlocutory stages of litigation (such as the application for an interim injunction) and to appeals, so the "active" period may arise both before an action has been set down for trial and after the trial has taken place, when an appeal has been lodged.

As stated earlier, it is a defence to contempt under the *sub judice* rule if a publisher can prove that, having taken all reasonable care, he did not know that the proceedings in question were active.

Care should be taken in talking to or otherwise communicating with the press or the media about a case in which you are involved. Whilst it is quite permissible, for example, to inform the press that you have commenced proceedings against X, or that you will be vigorously defending an action brought against you by Y,

2. See Chapter 22.

you should avoid discussing the particular facts or detailed merits of the case. Apart from the possible implications of such conduct in contempt proceedings, any written material may also need to be disclosed under the rules of discovery.[3]

Proceedings in open court

The general rule is that judicial proceedings must be conducted in open court, and that a fair and accurate report of such proceedings will not give rise to liability in contempt.

In some cases the court does not sit in public. The court will sit in private generally when it is hearing a matter of particular confidentiality: this may be a matter of commercial confidence, such as a patent action, or a matter of personal confidence, such as a family law case.

As well as regulating the conduct of its own proceedings, the court is also entitled to regulate the reporting of those proceedings. The court has powers to order that the reporting of proceedings, or part of the proceedings, be postponed, where it appears to be necessary for avoiding a substantial risk of prejudice to the administration of justice in those proceedings. Restrictions of this sort are most likely to be imposed where the court is concerned about whether a particular defendant is likely to obtain a fair trial, if no restrictions are imposed. When restrictions have been imposed, it will be a contempt of court to breach them.

Conduct of witnesses

If you fail to attend court or to produce documents without justification and in disobedience of a subpoena,[4] you will be in contempt of court.

If you are a witness, and in the course of giving your evidence during trial you discuss the case with someone else, you may be in contempt of court. It is likely that you will be reminded by the court and by the lawyers, before you give your evidence, that you must not discuss the case while you are giving evidence. When you have completed giving your evidence and have been released by the court, you are free to discuss the case with whom you wish.

The courts regard the protection of witnesses as vital to the administration of justice. The threatening of a witness, or any attempt to bribe or influence him, is likely to amount to a contempt of court as well as being a criminal offence.

3. See Chapter 18.
4. See Chapter 19.

CHAPTER 39

THE EUROPEAN COURT OF JUSTICE

This chapter outlines the relationship between the English courts and the European Court of Justice in Luxembourg.

A. INTRODUCTION

This Guide is intended to give an introductory account of the rules and procedures of English litigation and arbitration. It is not intended to deal with the specialist and complex subject of European laws and procedures. However, as the English courts are often faced with questions of European Community law it may be helpful to give a brief description of how the two systems are related.

When a question of European Community law comes before an English court, the court has a choice.[1] It may either decide the question itself (according to European Community law); or it may refer the question to the European Court of Justice, sitting in Luxembourg, for a preliminary but binding ruling. The English court will apply that ruling to the case before it and give judgment accordingly. In this way, the policy that European Community law should be applied uniformly is promoted.

B. REFERENCE BY THE ENGLISH COURT

The English court may of its own volition or on the application of any party order that a question before it be referred to the European Court of Justice. An order may be made by a judge, in the High Court or the county court or the Court of Appeal, or the House of Lords, but not by a master or a district judge. An order may in theory be made at any stage of the proceedings, but it is more usual for it to be made at the trial when the facts have been found. It must, however, be made before final judgment has been given.

Although the parties often draft the terms of the reference themselves it must be approved by the court and it is directed to the European Court of Justice by the Senior Master, or by the appropriate official in the county court.

1. Except in the mandatory circumstances referred to in section C, below.

The proceedings before the English court will then be stayed pending the determination of the reference.

The reference must seek direction on a point of general principle, rather than guidance on the application of the principle to the facts of any particular case. When the ruling is received from the European Court of Justice, the English court will lift the stay of proceedings and give judgment on the facts in accordance with the ruling.

C. MATTERS THAT MAY BE REFERRED

A reference to the European Court may be made under various European Community Treaties, for example under Article 177 of the Treaty establishing the European Community. The matters that may be subject to the rulings are:

- The interpretation of the relevant Treaty.
- The validity and interpretation of acts of the institution of the European Community.
- The interpretation of the statutes of the bodies established by an act of the Council, where their statutes so provide.

References may be *mandatory* or *discretionary.*

Mandatory references

Where any question that may be referred to the European Court is raised in a court from whose rulings there is no appeal, the reference to the European Court is mandatory. This most typically applies in the case of the House of Lords.

In such a case, the court must still be satisfied that there does, indeed, exist a question in need of a reference: this itself may pose a difficulty if there is doubt as to the effect of an earlier line of authority from the European Court.

Discretionary references

In other circumstances, courts have a discretion to request the European Court to give a ruling on any matter necessary for it to give judgment. This may be of the court's own volition or on the application of one of the parties. The question of whether a reference is necessary has been interpreted by the English courts as denoting a requirement that the question referred must be very largely determinative of the issues in the action. If the English Court thinks the point is clear, no reference should be made. The discretion to make a reference is affected by a variety of matters, including the delay entailed by, and the likely increase in the costs of the litigation occasioned by, the reference; the difficulty and importance of the issue raised; and whether issues of European Community policy are involved.

D. PROCEEDINGS IN THE EUROPEAN COURT OF JUSTICE

The European Court determines the issue before it at an oral hearing when the parties may make submissions based on written representations lodged previously. The Court has power to make orders for discovery of documents. Following an adjournment, the Advocate-General gives an opinion and the Court makes its ruling. This is binding on the English court which must nevertheless still apply it to the specific facts of the case before it.

The costs of the reference are in the discretion of the English court, not the European Court. If a Member State or the European Commission is involved in the reference there will be no order for the costs of their involvement.

CHAPTER 40

THE FUTURE OF LITIGATION IN ENGLAND

This chapter outlines the movement towards the reform of the litigation process in England and identifies the most important principles and rules that are embodied in the current proposals recommended by Lord Woolf, and generally endorsed by the Lord Chancellor, Lord Irvine of Lairg, Q.C.

A. THE MOVEMENT TOWARDS REFORM

As has been seen,[1] for a long time the present system of litigation was subject to increasingly vocal opposition, similar in kind to the criticisms directed towards the process of arbitration before the reforms that were introduced by the Arbitration Act 1996.

There were a number of central points of attack.

Perhaps the most important of these was the cost of litigation. It was plainly indefensible that straightforward claims involving comparatively small amounts of money by or against private individuals should be subject to the same procedures as major litigation between multi-national corporations, and that in such cases the legal costs could often be disproportionate to the sums in issue. Frequently, parties did not start litigation at all because of the costs involved.

It was also said that the time spent in litigation was unconscionably long. Why should it take years for a case to reach trial?

Another major cause of concern was the monopoly over the courts' time claimed by rich corporations who were able to browbeat less wealthy parties by a combination of money, legal representation and the ability to waste time by tactical manoeuvres.

The court system was thought to assist these tendencies. The split between the High Court and the county court procedures; the different procedures within the divisions of the High Court and of the specialist courts which formed part of those divisions; the large number of different procedures for different types of case; and the ability of the parties to dictate the pace of the case and to determine the issues that were put before the court—all were thought by some to lead to a system that had long lost its vitality and ability to respond to the needs of the parties, and to do justice.

1. See Chapter 1.

There was also thought to be fault in the administration of the courts themselves: that there was no one with overall control of the administration of civil justice and, whilst some judges in some courts exercised a degree of supervision over the course taken by cases before them, in general the judges took a non-interventionist role, allowing the parties to litigate almost at will.

In all of this, the clients' interests had been thought to have assumed a secondary importance.

This mounting public and professional concern led to a series of inquiries into the state of litigation in England which culminated, in 1994, in the appointment by the Lord Chancellor's Department of Lord Woolf, now the Master of the Rolls, to head a review to enquire into the current system.

In June 1995 Lord Woolf presented the first report of his findings. This led to a process of public and professional consultation that resulted in the publication, in July 1996, of his second and final report, which was accompanied by a preliminary set of draft rules of procedure. Lord Irvine instigated an independent review of those proposals and has largely endorsed them; and it seems that not all of them may be accepted or introduced at the same time. It is not at this stage possible to say when changes will be introduced, but it could be by 1999.

The recommendations of Lord Woolf have not, in any event, been unanimously welcomed, and there exists a significant body of professional opinion that is critical of parts of the proposals, and of the system of consultation that was followed. Despite this, it seems likely that at least a modified version of the proposals may be implemented.

If and when new rules are introduced we intend to publish a totally revised edition of this Guide in which we shall explain in detail the rules in their final form. Until then, the commentary in the next section may, we hope, suffice as an explanation of what at the time of writing are only proposals for a new regime.

The following section outlines the broad principles of the Woolf report, and sets out in summary the most important rules of procedure by which those principles may be implemented. The final section offers some tentative opinions on the extent to which they will achieve their set objectives.

B. THE PHILOSOPHICAL OBJECTIVES OF THE WOOLF REPORT

In his second report, Lord Woolf states that if his recommendations are implemented "the landscape of civil litigation will be fundamentally different from what it is now".

How is this to be achieved?

In much the same way as the Arbitration Act 1996 breaks new ground in identifying and explaining the basic principles of the legislation, so also does the Woolf report set out clearly the overriding objectives and philosophy that the new system will be designed to achieve. The overriding scheme of the new regime is to impose upon the courts and the parties who appear before them an obligation to deal with cases justly. This denotes principles of "equity, economy, proportionality and expedition". These principles are to be realised in the context of a modified adversarial system in which parties will retain a degree of control over the litigation but in which the courts will play a more interventionist role than before. The result may be a system that retains the best features of the adversarial common-law tradition whilst leaning towards some of those of the civil law jurisdictions.

It is key to the new philosophy that the parties should co-operate in the achievement of these aims. Although the retention of the adversarial system will mean that the parties each will have a case to prove or disprove by the production of evidence in court for determination by a judge who will adjudicate on what is put before him, the parties will be expected in future to adopt a sensible approach designed to ensure that justice is done in each case and that time-wasting and opportunistic tactics are not pursued.

The courts, equally, will have a much greater say in the way in which cases are conducted, and, by the mechanism of case conferences, will keep a closer day-to-day involvement in the course of the preparations.

The main features of the new system will be that:

- Litigation should be undertaken only as a last resort after other means of dispute resolution have been attempted. The courts should promote alternative dispute resolution, and there will be possible penalties for those parties who embark on litigation having refused reasonable offers of settlement.
- Although it will maintain the traditional adversarial approach to litigation, the process will be less adversarial than before. This will be encouraged by pre-litigation protocols on disclosure and the courts will be encouraged throughout the process to consider other means of dispute resolution.
- Expert witnesses will be expected to recognise their primary duty to the court, and be less partisan than before.
- The rules of court will be simplified, so that there will be one set of rules for all courts; one method only of beginning litigation of any description; and pleadings will be less technical and tactical in content. There will be a rationalised and uniform system of appeals.
- The process of discovery of documents will be stripped of its excesses and be deprived of its potential as a weapon of oppression by more powerful litigants.
- The courts will assume more responsibility for the fixing of trial dates so that cases will reach court sooner than before and be subject to more strictly enforced interlocutory timetables.
- The costs of litigation will be proportionate to what is in issue and subject to stricter controls. The balance of advantage in favour of rich

parties will be diminished by simplified procedures and tighter and more efficient timetables for preparations, and sanctions in costs for abuse.

— The system will be managed by a more efficient and centrally organised judiciary under the supervision of a new law officer, the Head of Civil Justice.

C. THE DRAFT RULES OF PROCEDURE AND RECOMMENDATIONS FOR THE FUTURE

The basic structure

The general philosophical objectives that underlie the Woolf report are to find their realisation through the rules of procedure which have so far been devised in draft. In this section are explained the main features of the current draft rules.

The most obvious characteristics of the draft rules are their lucidity and brevity, and the absence of distracting detail. This is a welcome change from the present rules which are cluttered with explanatory notes which are constantly amended and updated.

Under the new system all cases, in whichever court they may be presented, will in the future fall into one of the following three categories:

— Small claims.
— Fast track claims.
— Multi-track claims.

The dichotomy between the High Court and the county court will remain, as will the separate divisions within the High Court. However, with only relatively minor exceptions, for example with regard to intellectual property cases, the procedures for each court will be the same for each type of case.

There will be different procedures for each of these three types of case, but the procedures will be the same in every court for each type of case. Any particular requirements in any given case may be catered for by the court and the parties in the course of the pre-hearing conferences that are provided for under the draft rules.

Each case will be begun by the presentation of a *claim*, which will be a uniform and simplified document beginning the legal process, and applicable regardless of the remedy sought or what is in issue. Provision is made for giving judgment in cases that are undefended or where the claimant plainly has no realistic chance of success. Where the case is defended, the first thing for the court to do is to allocate it to one of the three categories. Whilst the court will have a general discretion to follow whatever course is appropriate in any given case, the rules described later will normally apply.

The underlying elements of all the rules, in respect of all types of case will be:

- The encouragement of settlements.
- The use of ADR.
- The identification at an early stage by the court of the main issues that should go to trial.
- The disposal at an early stage of weak and hopeless cases.
- The control of costs.
- The greater involvement and awareness of clients in the litigation process.
- The setting and enforcement of strict timetables for preparatory work and trial.

Small claims

Small claims will be those involving sums of less than £3,000. They will be heard by arbitrators appointed by the court who will be district judges, circuit judges (judges of the county courts or the Crown Courts) or some other person, at the court's discretion. Strict timetables for the preparation for trial will be given, leading to an informal hearing in private at which the rules of evidence will not strictly apply; or, alternatively, to an assessment by the arbitrator without a hearing. There will be a limited power to award costs, which will usually relate to out-of-pocket expenses such as court fees. There will be provision for the parties to disputes involving more than £3,000 to have their disputes resolved as a small claim, in which case slightly different rules as to costs may apply if thought to be appropriate.

Fast track claims

Fast track claims will be for sums of £3,000 or more and less than £10,000 where the court will give directions for the preparation of the case and set a timetable for steps to be taken before trial. A date for the trial will be given at an early stage. The standard length of the hearing will be half a day. Disclosure of documents will be limited, as will the ability of the parties to call expert witnesses. There will be a regime of fixed costs which will limit the amount recoverable by the winning party from the losing party and (save where there is an agreement to the contrary) the amount payable by each party to his own lawyers.

Multi-track claims

Multi-track claims will be for sums of £10,000 or more. This category will apply to all types of case not included in the other categories and will include a very wide variety of cases, ranging from relatively small claims to multi-party claims involving huge sums of money. The court will hold case management conferences and a pre-trial review which will be attended by the lawyers and the lay clients when it will fix timetables for procedural preparations and the trial date. Because of the wide range of cases within this category, the court will apply a flexible approach to every case and do what is thought right in the circumstances.

The most important new rules

It is not possible to summarise all the new proposals. The most important rules that are likely to be introduced will be those that deal with:

- Disclosure of documents.
- Summary judgment.
- Expert witnesses.
- Costs.
- Settlement offers.
- The role of the court in the management of litigation and the application of effective sanctions for defaults.

These are the rules that are intended to curtail the excessive costs of litigation and prevent abuses occasioned by any inequality of financial resources of the parties. Each is considered in turn.

Disclosure of documents

Lord Woolf identifies the process of discovery (or "disclosure" as it would then be called) as one of the root causes of delay and expense in the current system of litigation. As a result, he recommends that the procedure should be reformed by limiting the disclosure that parties must give. In fast track cases, the basic obligation will be limited to giving disclosure of documents upon which the party relies and those that may to a material extent be helpful to his opponent or harmful to himself. In multi-track cases the court may on application rule that additional discovery should be given of documents that explain the background "story" or which may lead to a train of enquiry that would enable a party to enhance his own case or harm his opponent's. This will only be ordered when necessary to do justice and where the benefit to be derived is in proportion to the expense and time involved in compliance and provided that the process does not impair a party's ability to continue with the litigation. In fast track cases such additional disclosure may be given but only exceptionally; and even in multi-track cases it seems that such orders will not freely be made. Small claims procedure will not be subject to these rules.

In the case of companies or firms disclosure must be of documents of which the company or firm is aware, through its officers or employees. A supervising officer would be required to be responsible for compliance with this rule.

An important innovation will be the right of parties to make application to the court *before proceedings have commenced* for disclosure by parties who are potential defendants. This rule is currently generally limited to medical negligence cases but would now have a much wider application.

The success of these rules will depend to a large extent on the trustworthiness of the parties. At present, one of the reasons why it is necessary for applications for further discovery to be made is that parties often do not make proper discovery unless forced to. It is not uncommon for a party not to produce all his documents until shortly before or even after the trial has started, and even then it frequently emerges that materials have been withheld. The new proposals rely on the parties being scrupulous to obey the rules. Experience shows that this may be optimistic and it may be a significant weakness in the proposals.

Summary judgment

A streamlined procedure for summary judgment will be introduced for cases where the plaintiff argues that there is no realistic prospect of the defendant winning; where there is a point of law which would determine the outcome of the trial; and where the defendant argues that the plaintiff's claim shows no cause of action. The procedure may be invoked by any party, or of the court's own volition.

The system would streamline the present diverse procedures for the resolution of these issues and, in particular, would require a plaintiff to show that the defendant has no realistic prospect of winning the whole or part of his case. Where necessary, oral evidence could be taken in addition to evidence on affidavit.

Expert witnesses

Lord Woolf considers that the usage of expert witnesses constitutes, together with the process of discovery, one of the two most serious abuses of the present system and he accordingly concentrates much attention on his recommendations for reform of the system regarding experts.

The present situation offers opportunities for tactical advantages to be taken over weaker opponents by the production of what may be superfluous experts' reports that are beyond the budget of an opponent. An industry of expert witnesses has developed that depends for its existence on being consulted on litigation matters. The costs of expert witnesses are frequently disproportionate to what is in issue or to the other costs of preparation. The witnesses themselves may not be impartial but only a part of the litigant's partisan armoury.

Under Lord Woolf's proposals, these abuses will stop. He makes a number of important recommendations:

- An expert witness will have an overriding duty to the court that will take precedence over his duty to his client. In this way complete impartiality will be encouraged.
- An expert witness may only testify with the permission of the court.
- An expert witness will only be called on if he can genuinely help the court. Thus, tactical evidence will be outlawed.

- The use of single experts should be encouraged to avoid the calling of an excessive number of witnesses. Where more than one witness is instructed they should co-operate with a view to producing a single report to the court.
- All experts' reports should be addressed to the court rather than to the party who commissioned them.
- All written and oral instructions to an expert witness should be produced with the report so as to prevent partisan or slanted instructions being given. Drafts of reports, if different from the final version, however, will not be disclosable.
- Optional training courses for experts should be encouraged to improve the quality of expert testimony, concentrating on the role of the expert within the legal system.

Costs

No comprehensive rules relating to costs have yet been drafted. However, one of the overriding objectives of the Woolf report is to contain costs, the escalation of which Lord Woolf regards as one of the main causes of the problems with the present system. The ability to force one's opponent into incurring costs that he cannot afford is one of the most obvious potential faults of the current system. The drive to reduce costs, therefore, lies at the heart of Lord Woolf's proposals.

Lord Woolf's principal recommendations in respect of costs operate at a number of different levels. Thus, some operate as general objectives of the new regime, which is intended to reduce the level of pre-trial activity and with it the incidence of costs. Further, the proposals aim to focus not just, as has been traditional, on who has "won" the litigation (with the consequence that he will be awarded all his costs) but also on his conduct in the course of winning, so that unreasonable behaviour will count against him. In addition, the scope of the steps that parties will have to take will be reduced and the court will be astute to narrow the issues in dispute to limit what has to be done in preparation for trial. Lastly, the court will impose more stringent costs penalties for non-compliance with its orders.

The following are the key features of Lord Woolf's recommendations:

- Strict limitations will apply to the costs recoverable in small and fast track claims.
- The way in which the case is handled should be proportionate to the issues involved.
- Disclosure of documents and expert evidence will be curtailed.
- Where a party has been responsible for a tactical application to court that has failed he should be required to pay the costs at once, rather than, as at present, being allowed to pay later when the order will be wrapped up in a final settlement and probably ignored.

— Indemnity costs should be payable at once by a party who fails to comply with directions.
— In multi-track cases the court should be informed at case management conferences and pre-trial reviews what costs have been incurred and what is estimated to be incurred in the future.
— Where one party wishes to follow a procedure (for example, the multi-track procedure) which is beyond the resources of the other and where the court agrees or where the case is regarded by the court of its own volition as sufficiently important, the court will have the power to allow that procedure to apply on condition that the additional costs will be paid for by the stronger party whatever the outcome.

Settlement offers

It is proposed that the present system regarding payments into court should be supplanted by a new procedure in which the making of offers "without prejudice save as to costs"[2] is given priority. Payments into court will remain a possibility, but they will have only a secondary importance. This will be the case even, it would seem, where there may be doubt as to whether the party making the offer has the funds to back it. Where a claimant who wins at trial has made an offer which is not accepted he may be entitled to much higher rates of interest on his award than otherwise. An offer to settle in this way may be made by either party to the dispute, and at any time before judgment has begun to be given.

Case management by the courts

One of the most important features of the new system will be the increased role of the courts in the management of litigation. Whilst this will apply throughout the system as a whole (that is, to all types of case), it will be in respect of cases in the multi-track that it will operate most fully. The key features of case management will be:

— The court will in all multi-track cases adopt a much greater degree of involvement in the progress of the case. Its role will differ according to the complexity of the claim, so that straightforward cases will be subject to a lesser degree of management than will complex, multi-party, actions.
— Management will principally be by a series of case management conferences leading to a pre-trial review shortly before the trial. These will be conducted by a procedural judge, who will usually be a master or district judge except in complex cases where a circuit or High Court judge will be nominated.
— The parties must co-operate in the process. This means not only that their lawyers must assist the court but also that the parties themselves

2. See Chapter 21.

must attend conferences and reviews so that they know what is happening and approve of what is being said and done in their name.

— In straightforward cases the court may give directions as soon as the case has been allocated to one of the three tracks. This may involve the court, if it regards the case as weak or hopeless, setting a trial date at once. In more complex cases there will usually be a case management conference held at once, provided that it would be cost-effective to do so.

— In some cases (for example, those that are currently the subject of Originating Summons procedure) the court may order that the case be decided without an oral hearing and without significant case management.

— The process will be assisted by the submission by the parties of completed questionnaires giving information about the state of preparations and the issues in the action and whether, for example, ADR has been attempted.

— The case management conference is intended to narrow the issues, and identify and contain the preparations. In particular, it should deal with the following types of issue:

(i) Specific disclosure of documents.
(ii) The main issues in the action.
(iii) Experts' reports.
(iv) The trial date.
(v) The costs already incurred and the likely costs in the future.
(vi) The possibility of ADR. Whilst ADR will not be mandatory, the court will be able later to impose penalties in costs if a party has unreasonably refused to attempt to resolve the case by this means.
(vii) Timetables for procedural steps. These will provide for matters such as disclosure of documents and the trial date. Some of these will be immovable, such as the case management conferences and pre-trial reviews and the trial date itself. Other deadlines may be varied either by the agreement of the parties or on application to the court. Where it is the parties who have agreed the variation the court must be informed so that new timetables may be set; and the court will have power to intervene and override the agreement if it thinks it necessary. Applications to vary a timetable must be made before a deadline has expired. If made too late, the court may allow the application, but only with a penalty.

— A streamlined procedure will apply in straightforward cases, in which emphasis will be laid on limiting disclosure, expert evidence and the length of trial.

— Once the preparations for trial have been made there will be a pre-trial review shortly before the trial. This will establish the issues for the trial and the order of events at trial.

Sanctions

In the past, parties to litigation have frequently been able to flout the rules of the court with relative impunity. Breaches of procedural orders are difficult to punish by the other party if the time involved in applying to court to compel compliance simply gives the person in breach more time in which to comply. Penalties in costs have not been a major deterrent because adverse costs orders are usually disregarded in a later settlement. The courts themselves have often been lenient to recalcitrant parties.

To overcome these problems, the new rules will apply more stringent sanctions for breaches. Their object will be to prevent abuse rather than to punish. Thus:

- The most usual sanction will be a penalty in costs. This may be enforced at once rather than at the end of the case.
- Where the fault is a failure to comply with an order of the court, for example in respect of disclosure or service of an expert's report, the sanction should be relevant to the breach. Thus, if a party has failed to serve an expert's report, he may be debarred from relying on expert evidence. In extreme cases, he may have his claim or defence struck out.
- The court may penalise conduct that, whilst not being a breach of a specific order, amounts to oppression.
- There will be only a limited right to apply to the court for relief against such penalties.
- Clients should always be made aware of penalties that have been imposed, so that where a client has inadvertently committed a breach through his lawyer's default he will hear of it.

The administration of the courts

In order to achieve the objectives of the new system an improved infrastructure will be introduced. This will involve greater organisation, technology and training for judges. It is in this area that many doubts have been raised. The new culture of court involvement will not be conjured up at once and is fundamentally against the grain of judicial tradition. Even if there is a new spirit abroad, it may take a considerable amount of manpower and money to make the system work.

D. WILL THE NEW SYSTEM WORK?

It is too early to offer any detailed comments upon the proposals for reform. Some commentators have been sceptical as to whether the courts will be able to develop the necessary manpower and expertise to operate properly the system of case management. The efficacy of the new system will depend to a very great degree on the willingness and the ability of the courts themselves to keep pace with the progress of cases, and essential to this is the question of whether the courts will be able to develop the manpower sufficient to service the very greatly increased role that the new proposals give to them.

Some critics have also questioned many of the detailed provisions, in particular the limitations to be imposed on discovery and expert witnesses. Whilst intended to improve the system, such innovations could be thought to impose impracticable and unrealistic restrictions, especially in large cases. Some commentators have also objected to what they regard as a lack of consultation in the process and do not consider that all the proposals should be introduced, at least without more public consideration.

Further, in the past, many of the problems of delay have seemed to stem from a lenient approach to the rules by the courts themselves, which have often sanctioned breaches and been prepared to overlook defaults. It could perhaps be said that it was not so much the rules that were at fault, but the extent to which the courts allowed them to be disobeyed.

The present system has found it difficult enough to cope with the volume of litigation. Too few judges are available to service the courts so that very often a deputy judge is appointed to try a case. The new regime will to some extent reduce the amount of court business by promoting out-of-court settlements and restricting the extent of pre-trial preparations; but this may be matched by a corresponding increase in the number of cases brought and the level of court involvement in interlocutory work. Concern has also been expressed at the speed with which the new system is being anticipated by the judiciary without there being any real training programmes introduced to assist in the acquisition of case management and related skills.

Finally, the rules themselves, whilst lucid and brief, will inevitably be developed when tested in operation and it may be expected that they in turn will be elaborated as have the old rules.

No one could sensibly dispute that litigation should be conducted fairly, expeditiously and as economically as possible and that in many ways the operation of the current system has shortcomings. It remains to be seen if any new system would offer a truly practical alternative. Could it be that, in future, more parties will consider arbitration as the most efficient system for achieving the resolution of their disputes according to a procedure to which they have agreed and which has been designed to meet their needs and aspirations?

GLOSSARY

Acknowledgment of Service	A form sent to the defendant with the writ in a High Court action, which the defendant should complete and send to the court to acknowledge receipt of the writ and state whether he intends to defend.
ADR	Alternative dispute resolution, that is, a consensual procedure for settling disputes with the assistance of a neutral party.
Affidavit	A sworn written statement of fact admissible for certain purposes as evidence.
***Anton Piller* order**	An order permitting the search of premises and seizure of specified items to preserve evidence.
Arbitration	A formal procedure for determination of disputes by an independent third party rather than the court.
Attachment of earnings order	A court order requiring the defendant's employer to deduct sums from his earnings and pay them to the plaintiff in satisfaction of a judgment debt.
Bailiff	A court-appointed or certified officer authorised to perform functions such as distraint and seizure.
Brief	A formal instruction given to counsel to appear at a hearing.
Brief fee	A fee payable to counsel (whether or not the hearing takes place) for accepting the brief.
Cause of action	The facts that give someone the right to bring an action.
Certiorari	An order made by the court in judicial review proceedings quashing a decision of an inferior tribunal or administrative body.
Chancery Division	One of the three divisions of the High Court, which deals with matters such as partnership, property, trust, company and patent disputes.

Charging order	An order giving a judgment creditor security for the judgment debt over specified assets (usually houses or other land and/or buildings or shares), owned by the judgment debtor.
Clerk of the Lists	A court official who determines when cases are to be tried.
Contempt of court	A breach of court orders or interference with or obstruction of the proper administration of justice.
Contribution proceedings	Proceedings between two or more persons who are liable to the same plaintiff for the same damage to determine, as between those persons, who should be responsible for what share of the damage.
Contributory negligence	Negligence on the part of the plaintiff which contributed to the loss suffered by reason partly of the defendant's negligence.
Costs	Costs incurred in the course of litigation or otherwise for the provision of legal services.
Counsel	A barrister.
Counterclaim	A cross-claim by the defendant against the plaintiff.
County court	The court which usually deals with actions of low value.
Court of Appeal	The court to which appeals are made from the judgments or orders of judges in the High Court and most decisions of county court judges.
Covenant	A promise contained in a deed to do or not to do an act.
Creditor	A party to whom money is owed.
Debtor	A party who owes money.
Default judgment	A judgment given to the plaintiff in High Court proceedings when the defendant fails to acknowledge service of the writ or to serve a Defence or, in the case of the county court, on the defendant's failure to serve a Defence.
Defence	A document forming part of the pleadings in which the defendant sets out his answer to the plaintiff's claim.
Directions	Instructions given by the court to litigants as to how the litigation should proceed following close of pleadings.
Discovery	The formal process for the pre-trial disclosure of relevant documents in the possession, custody or control of litigants.
Distraint	The process whereby goods are seized and sold in order to pay rent arrears (also known as "distress").

District judge — A junior judicial officer in the county court and the High Court outside London.

Enforcement — Methods employed to enforce compliance with court orders (including money judgments).

Equitable remedy — A remedy not available as of right, but only at the discretion of the court in order to achieve a "fair result".

***Ex parte* application** — An application at a hearing of which only the person making the application is present.

Expert's report — A written statement of the opinion of a proposed expert witness, which is served by the party wishing to rely on his evidence on all other parties prior to trial.

Expert witness — A witness who, owing to his specialist knowledge in a particular field, is allowed by the court to give evidence of matters of opinion in a field of expertise.

Family Division — One of the three divisions of the High Court, which usually deals with family matters.

Forfeiture — The repossession of leased property by a landlord following a breach by the tenant of one of the covenants in the lease.

Further and Better Particulars — A more detailed description of specified aspects of a pleading provided pursuant to a formal request made by an opponent.

Garnishee order — An order requiring a person to pay a debt to a third party rather than his creditor.

General List — The list of cases which have been set down for trial, but which have not been allocated a specific date for hearing.

Green Form Scheme — The scheme allowing persons satisfying a strict means test up to two hours' free legal advice (which is paid for from public funds).

Hearsay evidence — Evidence of matters not within the personal knowledge of the witness.

High Court — The court usually dealing with actions of high value or claims involving complex points of law or fact.

House of Lords — The last appellate court of England (apart from the European courts).

Indemnity basis — The basis for assessing costs payable by the losing party in litigation to the winning party where doubts as to the reasonableness of those costs are resolved in favour of the receiving party.

Injunction — A court order restraining someone from starting or continuing a course of wrongful conduct or compelling someone to take measures to remedy a wrong already committed.

Insolvency proceedings — Proceedings for the recovery of a debt which have the ultimate consequence (if the debt is not paid) of making an individual bankrupt or putting a company into liquidation.

Interim payment — Payment on account of the defendant's liability or likely liability to the plaintiff made by the defendant to the plaintiff pursuant to a pre-trial court order.

Interlocutory — Of or relating to the period between the issue of court proceedings and the trial.

***Inter partes* application** — An application at the hearing of which all parties relevant to the application attend and make representations to the court.

Judicial review — A review by the court of the decisions of inferior tribunals or administrative bodies.

Junior counsel — Any barrister who is not a leading counsel.

Jurisdiction — The power of a court to hear and decide the cases referred to it.

Land charge — An interest in land of a third party other than the land owner which, if duly protected by registration, will bind a purchaser of the land.

Leading counsel — A senior barrister who has been recognised by the Lord Chancellor's Department as specially skilled.

Legal Aid — Financial assistance given to parties from public funds to bring or defend claims.

Letter before action — A letter written by the plaintiff to the defendant setting out the bases of the plaintiff's claim and stating that proceedings will be commenced if the claim is not settled voluntarily.

Limitation period — The time period specified by statute within which a claim must be commenced (by issue of proceedings).

Liquidation — The process whereby a company is wound up.

Liquidator — A person appointed on the liquidation of a company to realise its assets for the benefit of its creditors.

Litigation — The process of determination of legal disputes by the courts.

Mandamus — An order made by the court in judicial review proceedings requiring an inferior tribunal or administrative body to perform a specified public duty.

***Mareva* injunction** — An injunction restraining a party from disposing of or otherwise dealing with its assets, or moving those assets abroad.

Master — A junior judicial officer who deals with certain interlocutory matters in a London High Court action.

Mediation — A form of ADR.

Ombudsman — An official appointed to oversee the operation of, and investigate complaints against, specified bodies.

Order absolute — A final order, usually following an order nisi.

Order nisi — An order made by which a specified outcome will occur at a later date unless cause is shown why that outcome should not occur.

Particulars of claim — The county court equivalent of the Statement of Claim in the High Court setting out the plaintiff's allegations against the defendant and the relief sought.

Payment into court — A sum paid into court by the defendant by way of offer of settlement to the plaintiff. It has important tactical and costs implications.

Petitioning creditor — A creditor who issues a bankruptcy or winding up petition.

Plaintiff — A person bringing a civil action.

Pleadings — The formal documents in which the parties set out their respective cases (Statement of Claim, Defence and Reply).

Privilege — The right to withhold specified categories of evidence on the ground of a recognised public interest in preserving certain types of confidentiality.

Prohibition — An order made by the court in judicial review proceedings restraining an inferior tribunal or administrative body from taking a wrongful step.

Queen's Bench Division — One of the three divisions of the High Court, which usually deals with tort and contract actions.

Queen's Counsel — Leading counsel.

Redundancy — The dismissal of an employee whose services are no longer required for reasons such as cessation or relocation of business or general cuts in employee numbers.

Refresher	A daily payment made to counsel for each of the second and subsequent days in which counsel appears in court.
Reply	A document forming part of the pleadings in which the plaintiff responds to the defendant's Defence.
Security for Costs	A sum of money paid into court by the plaintiff as security for the costs which the plaintiff will be liable to pay to the defendant if the plaintiff's claim fails.
Security of tenure	The statutory right of a tenant to remain in premises after his lease or tenancy agreement has expired.
Service	The delivery of a document to the party to whom it is addressed in accordance with formal rules of court.
Service charge	A sum payable to a landlord for provision of services to tenants.
Set-off	A defence to all or part of the plaintiff's claim arising from a monetary cross-claim which the defendant has against the plaintiff.
Setting down for trial	The formal step of having a case entered on the list of cases awaiting trial.
Specific performance	An equitable remedy by which the court orders a person to carry out his contractual obligations.
Standard basis	The basis for assessing costs payable by the losing party to the winning party where doubts as to the reasonableness of those costs are resolved in favour of the paying party.
Statement of Claim	A document forming part of the pleadings in High Court proceedings setting out the plaintiff's allegations against the defendant and the relief sought.
Statute	An Act of Parliament setting out legal rules which must be applied by the courts.
Statutory demand	A written demand in a prescribed form for payment of an outstanding debt, usually as a final formal step before commencing insolvency proceedings.
Strike out	The deletion of all or part of a pleading (usually the plaintiff's Statement of Claim) on the basis that it discloses no reasonable case in law or is frivolous and vexatious or otherwise an abuse of court process.
Sub judice	Under consideration by the court.
Subpoena	A court order requiring someone to appear in court to give evidence and sometimes to bring relevant documents with him.

Substantive law	The general system of law that creates rights and liabilities—for example, the law of contract, trusts and torts.
Summary judgment	A judgment obtained at an early interlocutory stage without a full trial, where the plaintiff can show that there is no reasonable defence to his claim.
Summons	A document applying for interlocutory relief in the High Court, or the county court equivalent of a writ in the High Court.
Taxation	The process whereby the court assesses the amount of costs recoverable by the winning party in litigation from the losing party.
Third party proceedings	A claim brought by a defendant against someone who is not already a party to an action seeking relief from the third party.
Ultra vires	An act or decision by a body or company which goes beyond the scope of its lawful powers.
Undertaking	A formal and binding contractual promise.
Unfair dismissal	The dismissal of an employee which is contrary to employment protection legislation (whether or not a wrongful dismissal).
Waiver	The giving up of a right in law.
Warned List	The list of cases which will shortly be called on for trial.
Winding up petition	A document issued to commence winding up proceedings against companies.
Without prejudice	Communications made in a genuine attempt to settle a dispute, which cannot be referred to in court if the case does not settle.
Witness statement	A written account of the evidence which a witness will give at trial.
Writ	A formal document prepared and presented by the plaintiff and issued by the court which sets the process of High Court litigation in motion.
Wrongful dismissal	The termination of employment in breach of contract.

INDEX

For Product Safety Concerns and Information please contact our EU representative GPSR@taylorandfrancis.com Taylor & Francis Verlag GmbH, Kaufingerstraße 24, 80331 München, Germany

Batch number: 10725800

Printed by Printforce, the Netherlands